HEROS DE L'ÂGE D'OR RÉUNI!

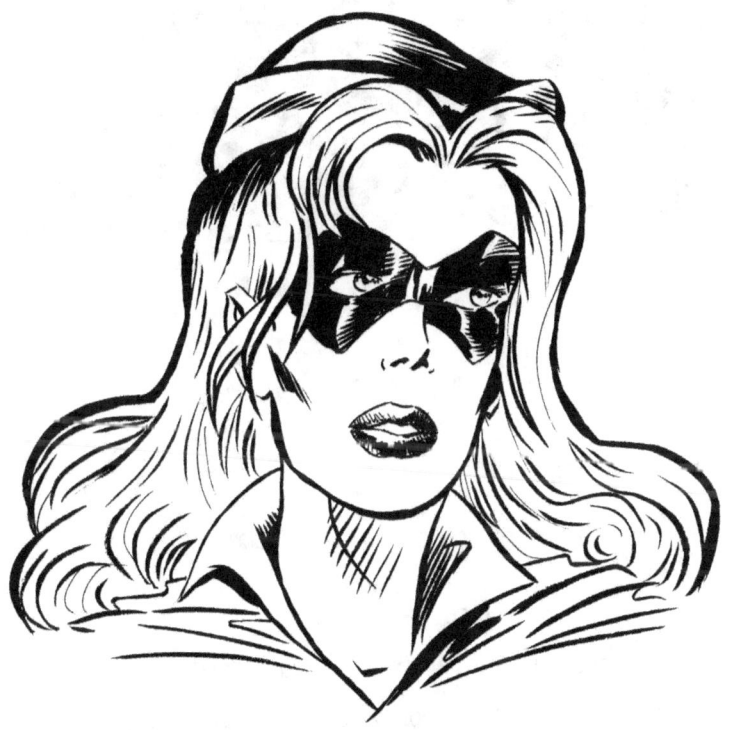

UNE COLLECTION DE PIN-UP DE CARACTÈRES DU DOMAINE PUBLIC

LIVRE DE POCHE!

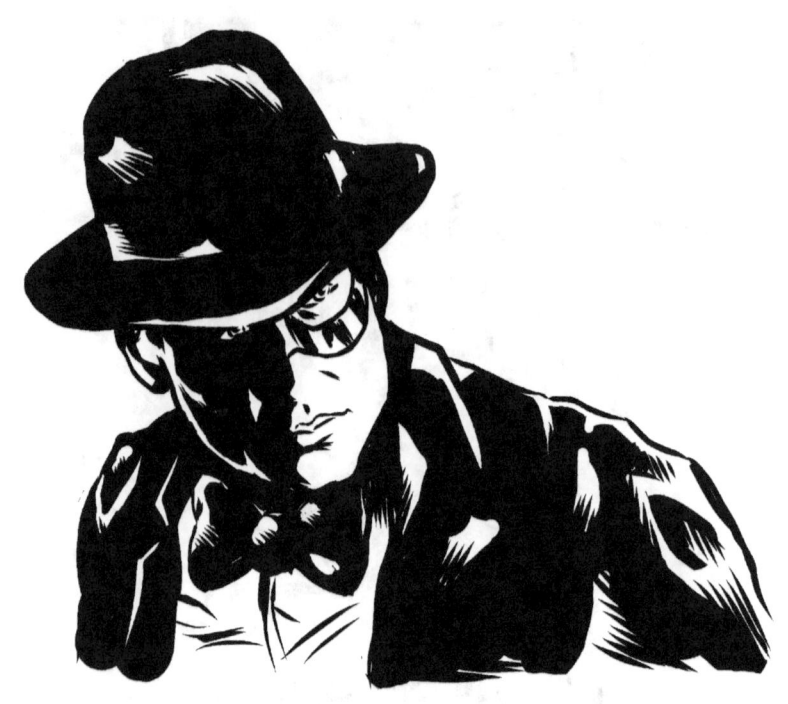

ILLUSTRATIONS:
A. G. CEGLIA , L. LIVI

HEROS DE L'ÂGE D'OR RÉUNI! – UNE COLLECTION DE PIN-UP DE CARACTÈRES DU DOMAINE PUBLIC
LIVRE DE POCHE!

LISTE DES CARACTÈRES

ALIAS THE DRAGON
(HARRY "A" CHESLER, SKYROCKET COMICS –ONE SHOT, 1944)

AMAZING-MAN
(CENTAUR PUBLICATIONS/COMIC CORPORATION OF AMERICA, AMAZING-MAN COMICS #5, SEPT. 1939)

AMAZONA THE MIGHTY WOMAN
(FICTION HOUSE, PLANET COMICS #3, MAR. 1940)

AMERICAN CRUSADER
(BETTER/NEDOR/STANDARD, THRILLING COMICS #19, AUG. 1941)

AMERICAN EAGLE
(BETTER/NEDOR/STANDARD, AMERICA'S BEST COMICS #2, SEPT. 1942)

ATOMIC THUNDERBOLT
(REGOR COMPANY, ATOMIC THUNDERBOLT #1, FEB. 1946)

BARRY KUDA & ALGIE
(HARRY "A" CHESLER, YANKEE COMICS #2, NOV. 1941)

BLACK ANGEL
(HILLMAN, AIR FIGHTERS COMICS #2, NOV. 1942)

BLACK BAT
(BETTER/NEDOR/STANDARD, BLACK BOOK DETECTIVE, JULY 1939)

BLACK CAT (LINDA TURNER)
(HARVEY, POCKET COMICS #1, AUG. 1941)

BLACK COBRA
(HARRY "A" CHESLER, DYNAMIC COMICS #1, OCT. 1941)

BLACK DWARF
(HARRY "A" CHESLER, SPOTLIGHT COMICS #1, NOV. 1944)

BLACK ORCHID & TIM
(CONSOLIDATED BOOK PUBLISHER, TOPS COMICS #N/A, 1944?)

BLACK SATAN
(HARRY "A" CHESLER, YANKEE COMICS #1, SEPT. 1941)

BLACK TERROR
(BETTER/NEDOR/STANDARD, EXCITING COMICS #9, MAY 1941)

BLACK TERROR'S VILLAINS
(BETTER/NEDOR/STANDARD; TORCH EXCITING COMICS #36, DEC. 1944; PUZZLER, AMERICA'S BEST COMICS #30, APR. 1949; BAROMETRI, EXCITING COMICS #22, OCT. 1942; KROLL MUL, THE BLACK TERROR #22, MAR. 1948; DR. GHOUL, THE BLACK TERROR #12, NOV. 1945)

BLACK VENUS
(HOLYOKE/AVIATION PRESS, CONTACT COMICS #1, JULY 1944)

BLACK WIDOW
(HOLYOKE/AVIATION PRESS, HOLYOKE, CAT-MAN COMICS #1, MAY 1941)

BLUE LADY
(CENTAUR PUBLICATIONS/COMIC CORPORATION OF AMERICA, AMAZING-MAN COMICS #24, OCT. 1941)

BRAD SPENCER WONDERMAN
(BETTER/NEDOR/STANDARD, COMPLETE BOOK OF COMICS AND FUNNIES #1, 1944)

CAPTAIN BATTLE & KANE
(HARRY "A" CHESLER, CAPTAIN BATTLE COMICS #3, WINTER 1942)

CAPTAIN FUTURE
(BETTER/NEDOR/STANDARD, STARTLING COMICS #1, JUNE 1940)

CAPTAIN GLORY
(HARRY "A" CHESLER, PUNCH COMICS #1, DEC. 1941)

CAROL PAIGE, BRAD SPENCER WONDERMAN'S GIRLFRIEND
(BETTER/NEDOR/STANDARD, COMPLETE BOOK OF COMICS AND FUNNIES #1, 1944)

CAVALIER
(BETTER/NEDOR/STANDARD, THRILLING COMICS #53, APR. 1946)

DOC STRANGE
(BETTER/NEDOR/STANDARD, THRILLING COMICS #1, FEB. 1940)

DR. FROST
(PRIZE, PRIZE COMICS #7, DEC. 1940)

DR. VAMPIRE
(HARRY "A" CHESLER, SKYROCKET COMICS #1, 1944)

DYNAMIC BOY
(HARRY "A" CHESLER, DYNAMIC COMICS #2, OCT. 1941)

DYNAMIC BOY, DYNAMIC MAN'S SIDEKICK
(HARRY "A" CHESLER, DYNAMIC COMICS #11, SEPT. 1944)

DYNAMIC MAN
(HARRY "A" CHESLER, DYNAMIC COMICS #1, OCT. 1941)

ECHO
(HARRY "A" CHESLER, YANKEE COMICS #1, SEPT. 1941)

ENCHANTED DAGGER
(HARRY "A" CHESLER, YANKEE COMICS #1, SEPT. 1941)

EAGLET, AMERICAN EAGLE'S SIDEKICK
(BETTER/NEDOR/STANDARD, AMERICA'S BEST COMICS #2, SEPT. 1942)

FANTOMAH
(FICTION HOUSE, JUNGLE COMICS #2, FEB. 1940)

FIGHTING YANK
(BETTER/NEDOR/STANDARD, STARTLING COMICS #10, SEPT. 1941)

FIREBRAND
(HARRY "A" CHESLER, YANKEE COMICS #1, SEPT. 1941)

FOUR COMRADES
(BETTER/NEDOR/STANDARD, STARTLING COMICS #16, AUG. 1942)

FRAN FRAZER
(MLJ, TOP-NOTCH COMICS #9, OCT. 1940)

GREEN LAMA
(PRIZE, PRIZE COMICS #7, DEC. 1940)

GREEN KNIGHT & LANCE
(HARRY "A" CHESLER, DYNAMIC COMICS #2, DEC. 1941)

GRIM REAPER
(BETTER/NEDOR/STANDARD, FIGHTING YANK #7, FEB. 1944)

HALE THE MAGICIAN
(HARRY "A" CHESLER, DYNAMIC COMICS #1, SEPT. 1941)

IRON SKULL
(CENTAUR PUBLICATIONS/COMIC CORPORATION OF AMERICA,
AMAZING-MAN COMICS #5, SEPT. 1939)

JILL TRENT
(BETTER/NEDOR/STANDARD, FIGHTING YANK #6, DEC. 1943)

JIMMY COLE, BOY SLEUTH
(BETTER/NEDOR/STANDARD, THRILLING COMICS #32, JAN. 1943)

JOHNNY REBEL
(HARRY "A" CHESLER, YANKEE COMICS #2, NOV. 1941)

JUDY OF THE JUNGLE
(BETTER/NEDOR/STANDARD, EXCITING COMICS #55, MAY 1947)

KAZA
(AJAX-FARRELL, FANTASTIC FEARS #8, JUL.-AUG. 1954)

KITTEN, CATMAN'S SIDEKICK
(HOLYOKE, CAT-MAN COMICS #5, DEC. 1941)

KITTY KELLY
(HARRY "A" CHESLER, PUNCH COMICS #1, DEC. 1941)

LADY LUCK [1]
(QUALITY, SMASH COMICS #42, APR. 1943)

LADY SATAN
(HARRY "A" CHESLER, DYNAMIC COMICS #2, DEC. 1941)

LADY SERPENT
(BETTER/NEDOR/STANDARD, THE BLACK TERROR #23, JUNE. 1948)

LADY TARNA
(BETTER/NEDOR/STANDARD, COMPLETE BOOK OF COMICS AND
FUNNIES #1, 1944)

LARRY NORTH
(BETTER/NEDOR/STANDARD, EXCITING COMICS V4 #1, JUNE 1941)

LIBERATOR
(BETTER/NEDOR/STANDARD, EXCITING COMICS #15, DEC. 1941)

MADAM SATAN [2]
(ARCHIE/MLJ, PEP COMICS #16, JUNE 1941)

MAJOR VICTORY
(HARRY "A" CHESLER, DYNAMIC COMICS #1, OCT. 1941)

MAN OF WAR
(CENTAUR PUBLICATIONS/COMIC CORPORATION OF AMERICA, LIBERTY
SCOUT COMICS #2, JUNE. 1941)

MASKED RIDER

1   LADY LUCK *MAY NOT BE PUBLIC DOMAIN*
2   MADAM SATAN *MAY NOT BE PUBLIC DOMAIN*

(BETTER/NEDOR/STANDARD, STARTLING COMICS #1, JUNE 1940)
MASTER KEY
(HARRY "A" CHESLER, SCOOP COMICS #1, NOV. 1941)

MEKANO & BILL FOSTER
(BETTER/NEDOR/STANDARD, WONDER COMICS #1, MAY 1944)

MR. E
(HARRY "A" CHESLER, PUNCH COMICS #1, DEC. 1941)

MIKE, DOC STRANGE'S SIDEKICK
(BETTER/NEDOR/STANDARD, THRILLING COMICS #24, 1942)

MISS MASQUE
(BETTER/NEDOR/STANDARD, EXCITING COMICS #51, SEPT. 1946)

MOTHER HUBBARD
(HARRY "A" CHESLER, SCOOP COMICS #1, NOV. 1941)

NELVANA OF THE NORTHERN LIGHTS [3]
(HILLBOROUGH, TRIUMPH-ADVENTURE-COMICS #1, AUG. 1941)

PHANTOM DETECTIVE
(BETTER/NEDOR/STANDARD, THRILLING COMICS #53, APR. 1946)

PYROMAN
(BETTER/NEDOR/STANDARD, AMERICA'S BEST COMICS #3, NOV. 1942)

QUEEN MERMA, BARRICUDA'S GIRLFRIEND
(HARRY "A" CHESLER, YANKEE COMICS #2, NOV. 1941)

RED ANN
(BETTER/NEDOR/STANDARD, THE BLACK TERROR #24, SEPT. 1948)

RED MASK
(BETTER/NEDOR/STANDARD, BEST COMICS #1, NOV. 1939)

ROBOROY, BRAD SPENCER WONDERMAN'S ASSISTANT
(BETTER/NEDOR/STANDARD, WONDER COMICS #19?, AUG. 1948)

3   NELVANA OF THE NORTHERN LIGHTS MAY NOT BE PUBLIC DOMAIN

ROCKET BOY
(HARRY "A" CHESLER, SCOOP COMICS #2, JAN. 1942)

ROCKETMAN & ROCKETGIRL
(HARRY "A" CHESLER, SCOOP COMICS #1, NOV. 1941)

SCARAB
(BETTER/NEDOR/STANDARD, STARTLING COMICS #34, JULY 1945)

SILVER KNIGHT
(BETTER/NEDOR/STANDARD, COMPLETE BOOK OF COMICS AND FUNNIES #1, 1944)

SPHINX
(BETTER/NEDOR/STANDARD, EXCITING COMICS #2, MAY 1940)

SPIDER WOMAN
(HARRY "A" CHESLER, MAJOR VICTORY COMICS #1, 1944)

SUB-ZERO MAN
(NOVELTY PRESS, BLUE BOLT V1 #1, JUNE 1940)

VEILED AVENGER
(HARRY "A" CHESLER, SPOTLIGHT COMICS #1, NOV. 1944)

WAR NURSE
(HARVEY, SPEED COMICS #13, MAY 1941)

WOMAN IN RED
(BETTER/NEDOR/STANDARD, THRILLING COMICS #2, MAR. 1940)

YANKEE DOODLE JONES & DANDY
(HARRY "A" CHESLER, YANKEE COMICS #1, SEPT. 1941)

YANKEE BOY
(HARRY "A" CHESLER, YANKEE COMICS #2, NOV. 1941)

YANKEE GIRL
(HARRY "A" CHESLER, DYNAMIC COMICS #23, 1947)

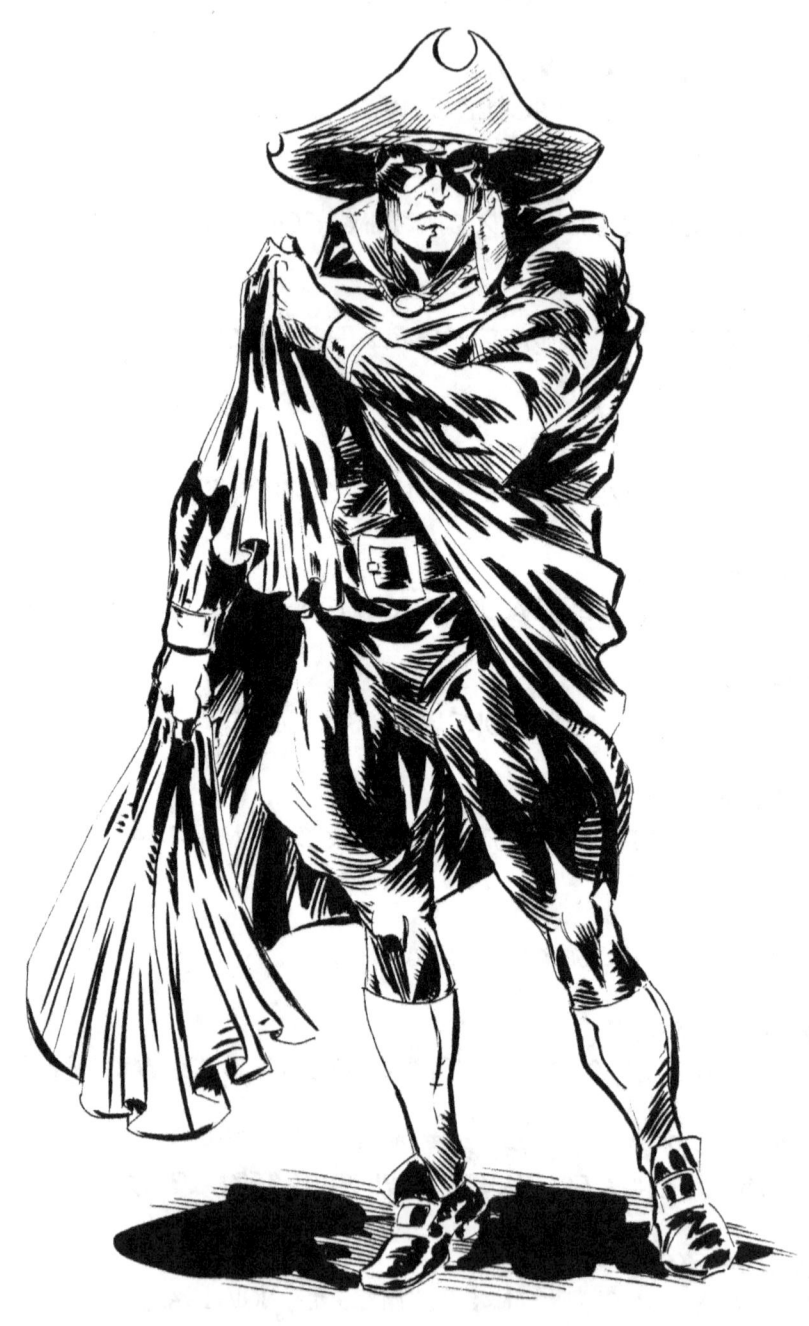

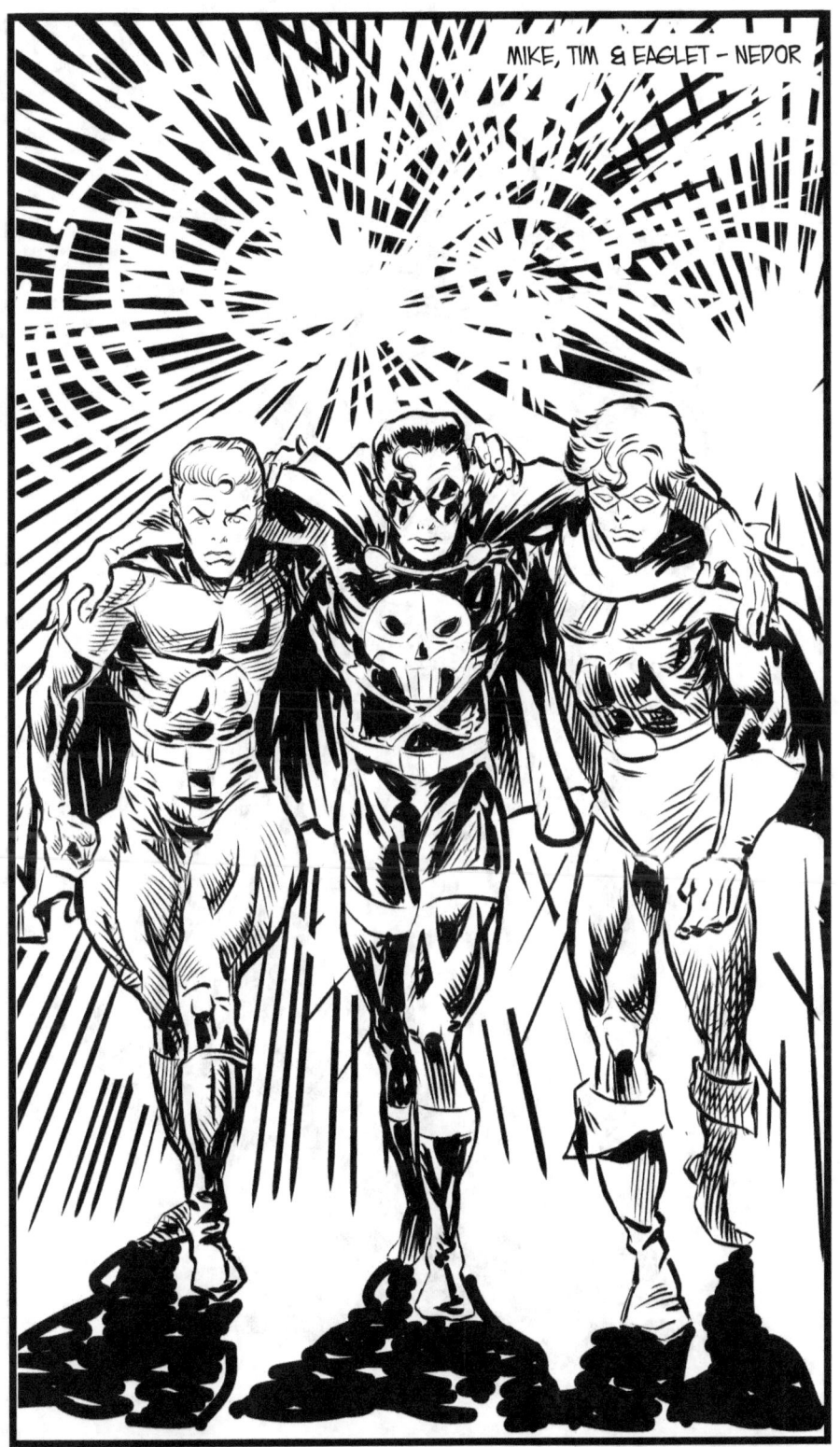

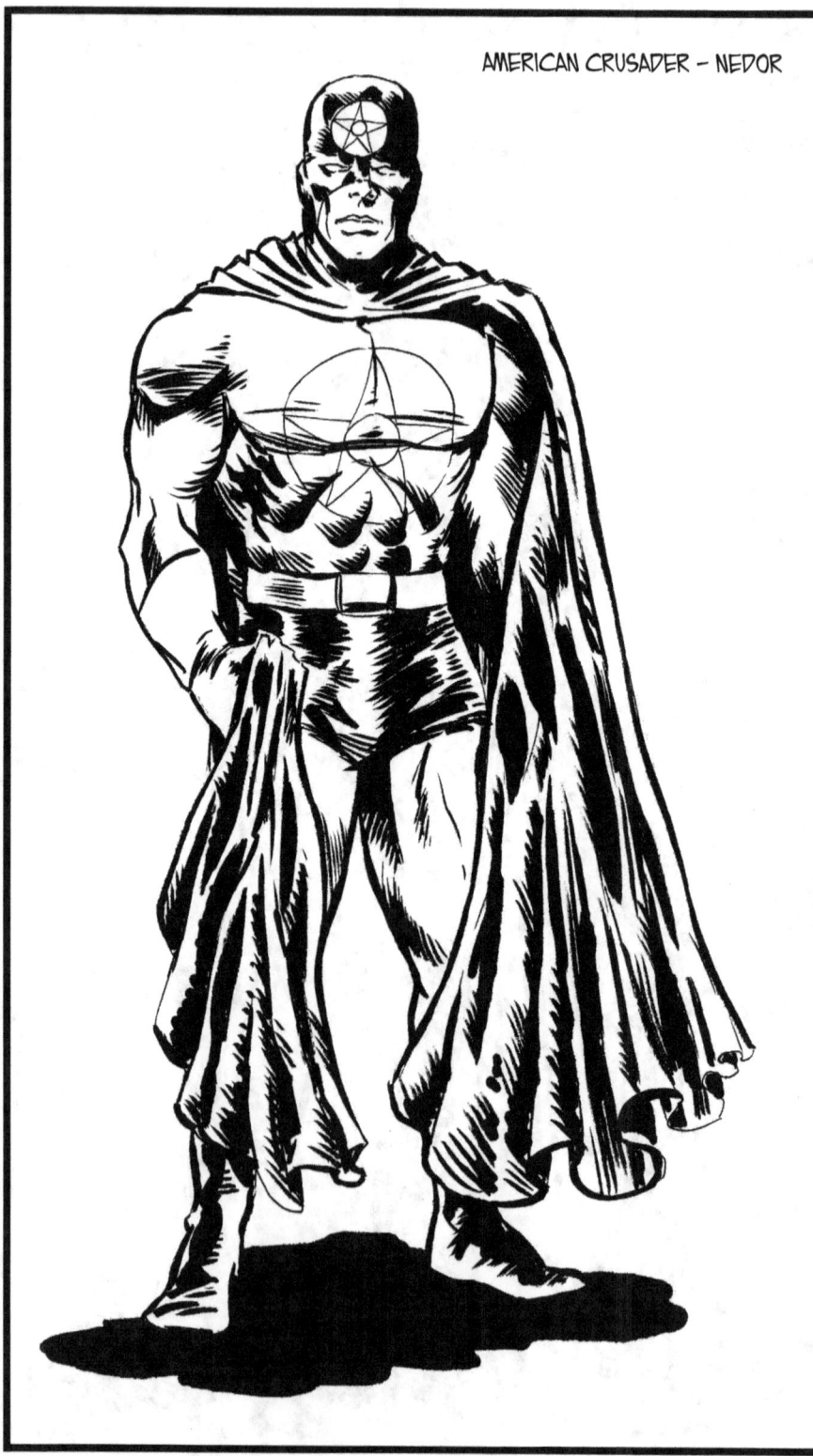

AMERICAN CRUSADER - NEDOR

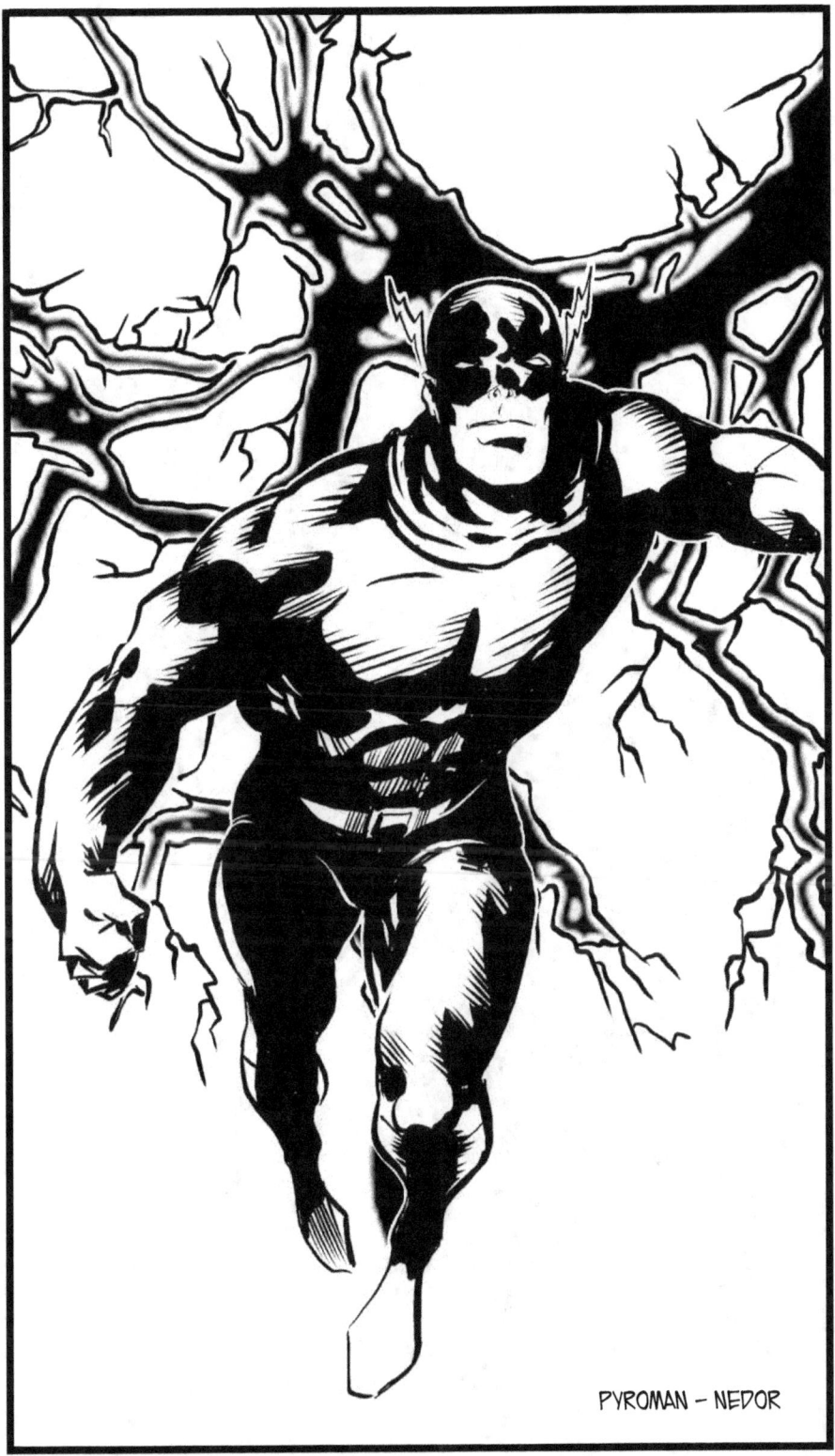

PYROMAN - NEDOR

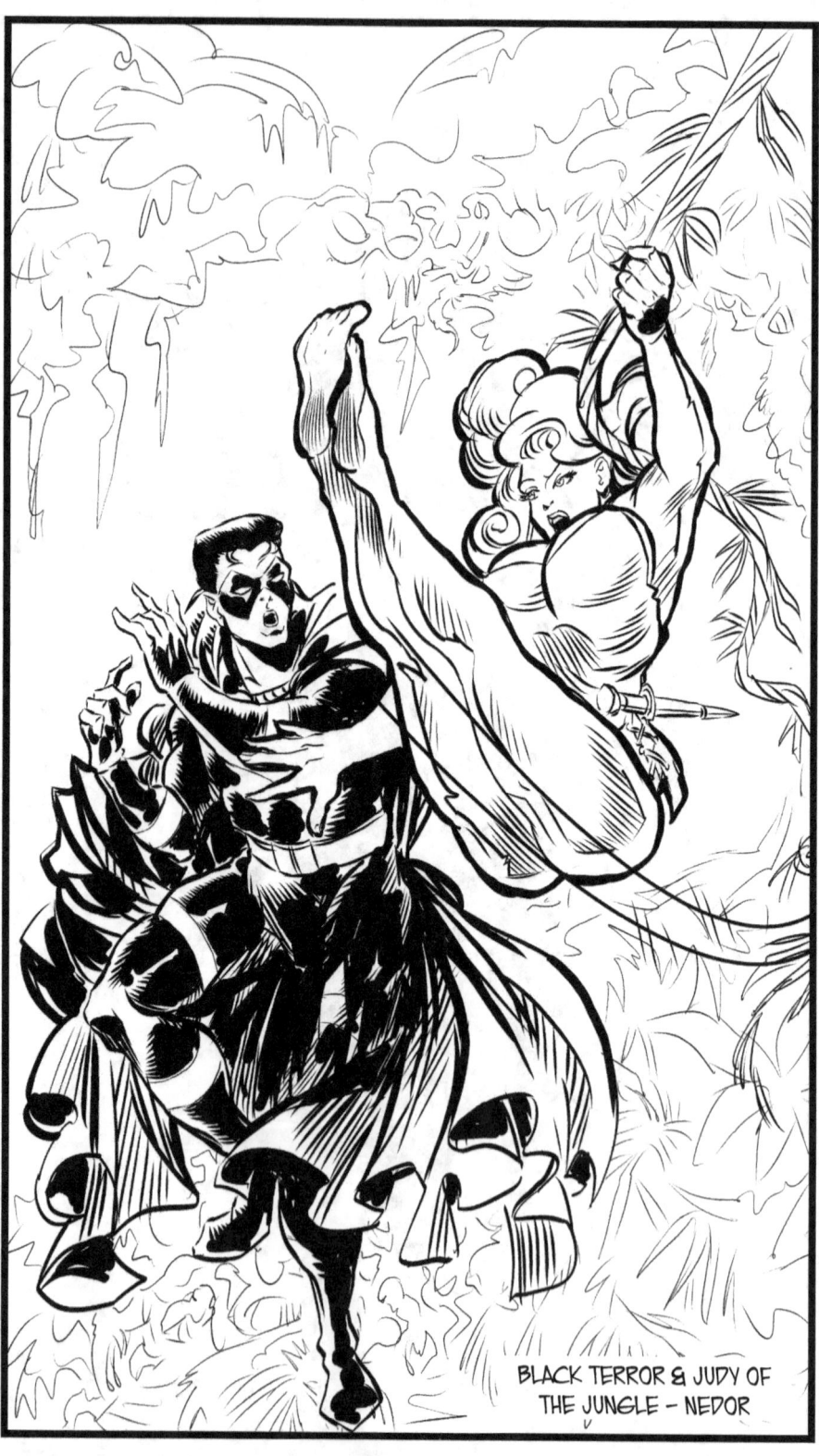

BLACK TERROR & JUDY OF
THE JUNGLE - NEDOR

FIGHTING YANK &
MISS MASQUE – NEDOR

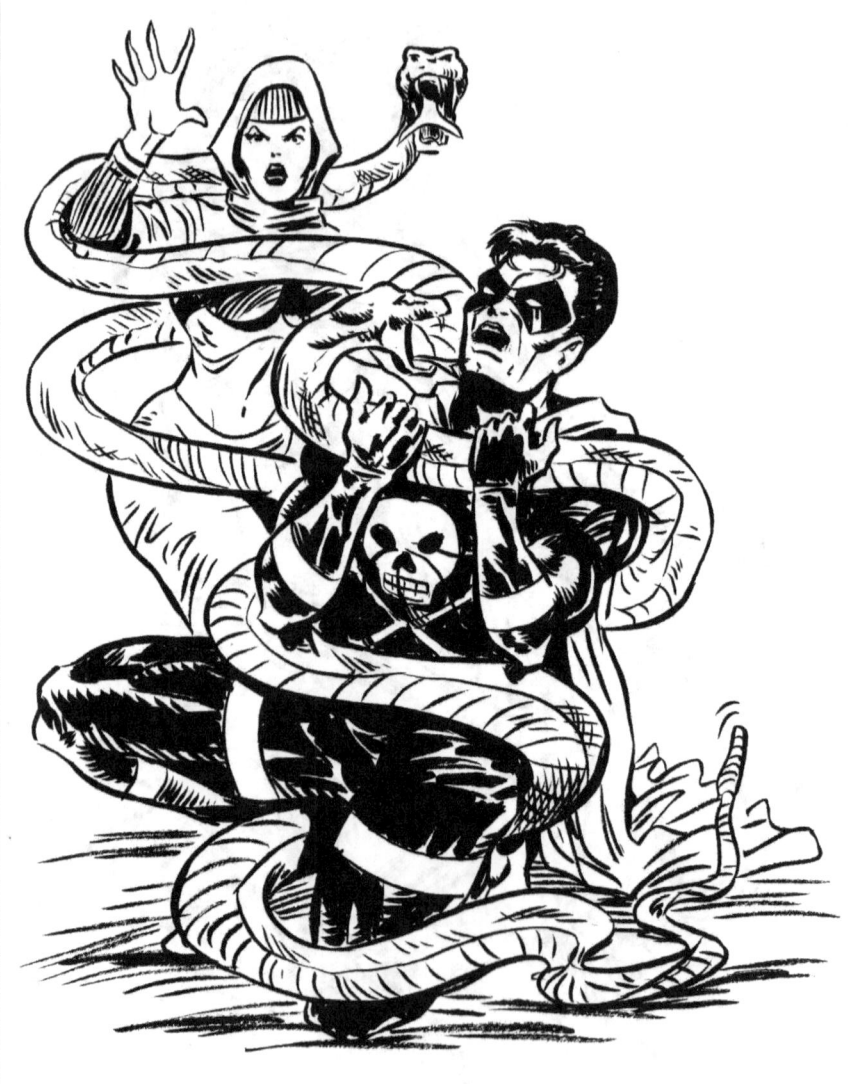

BLACK TERROR VS LADY SERPENT- NEDOR

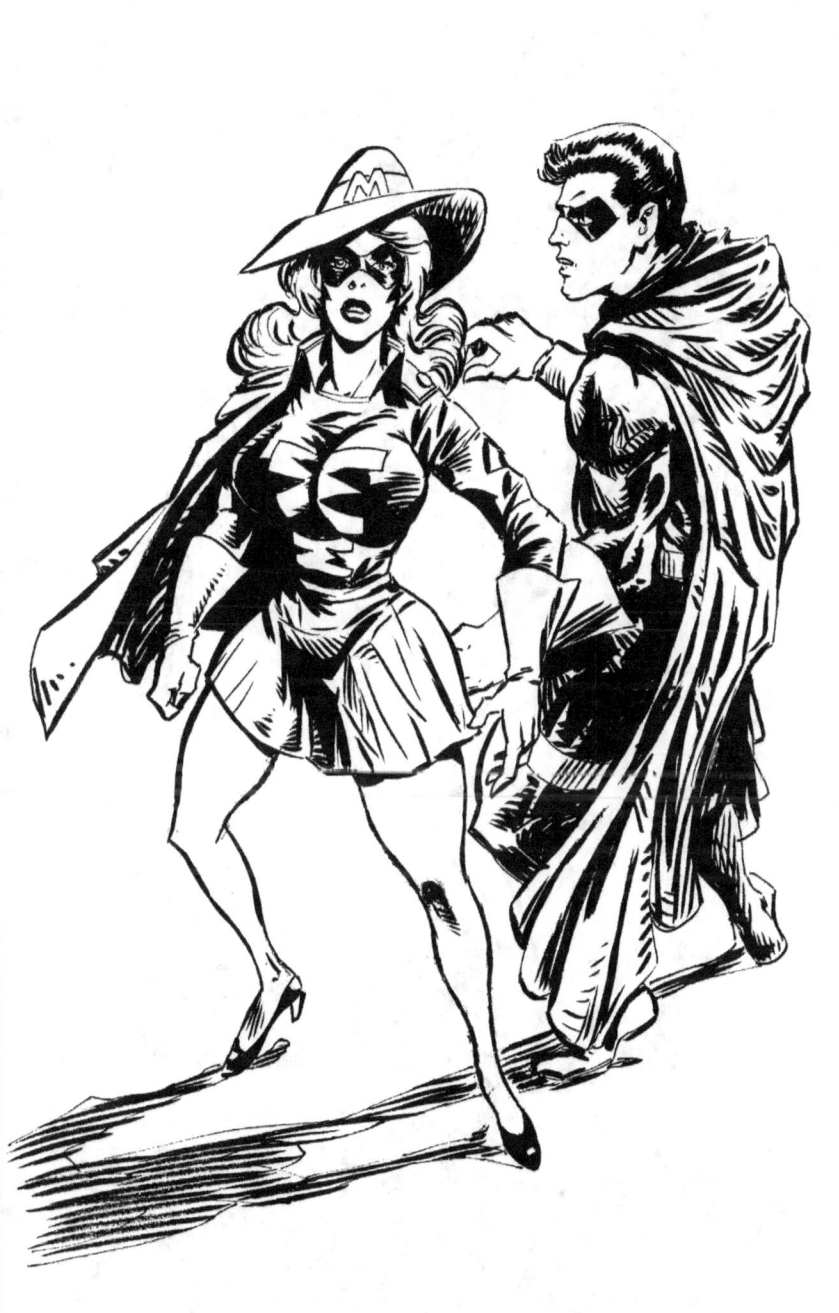

BLACK TERROR & MISS MASQUE – NEDOR

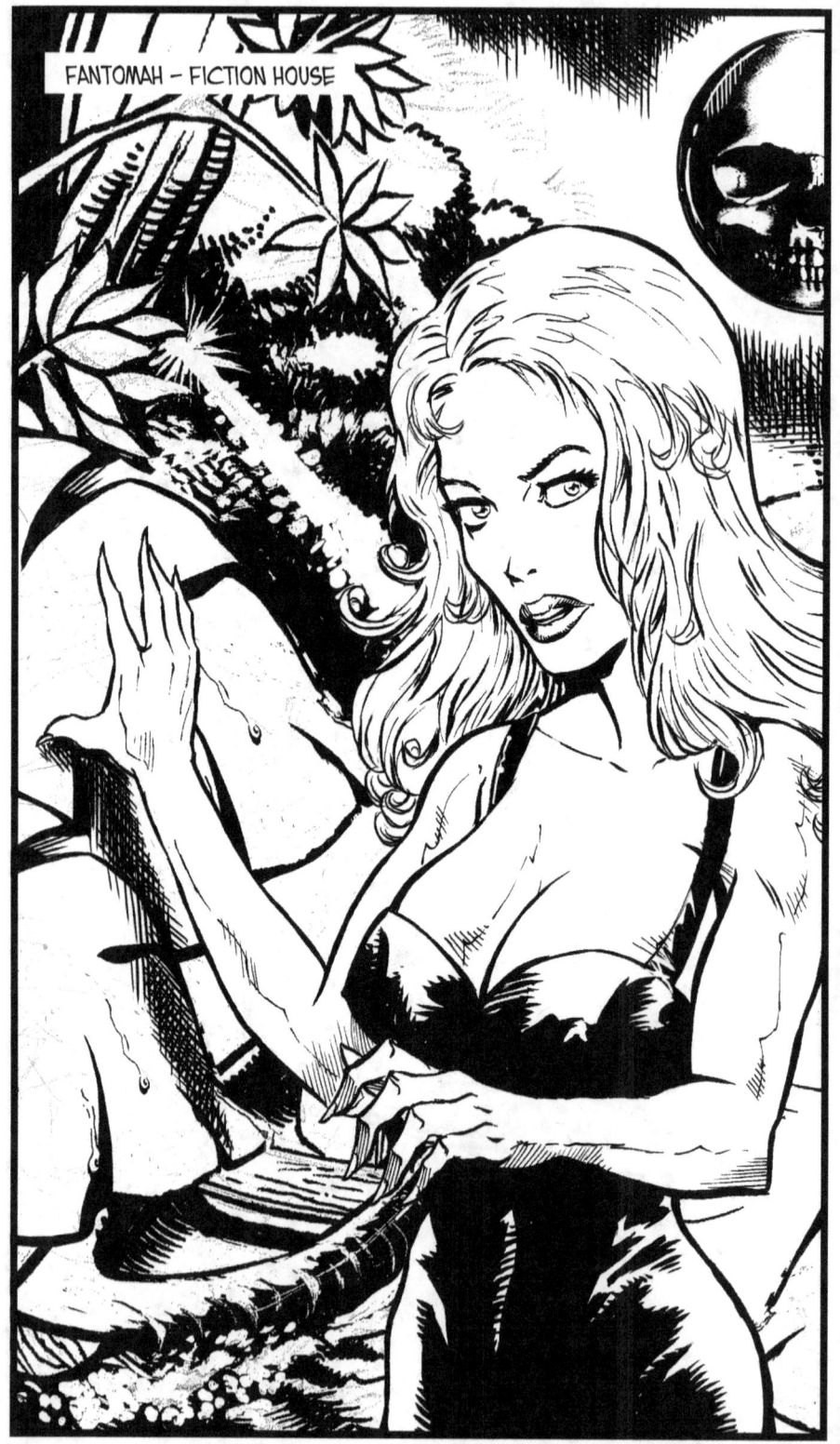

FANTOMAH – FICTION HOUSE

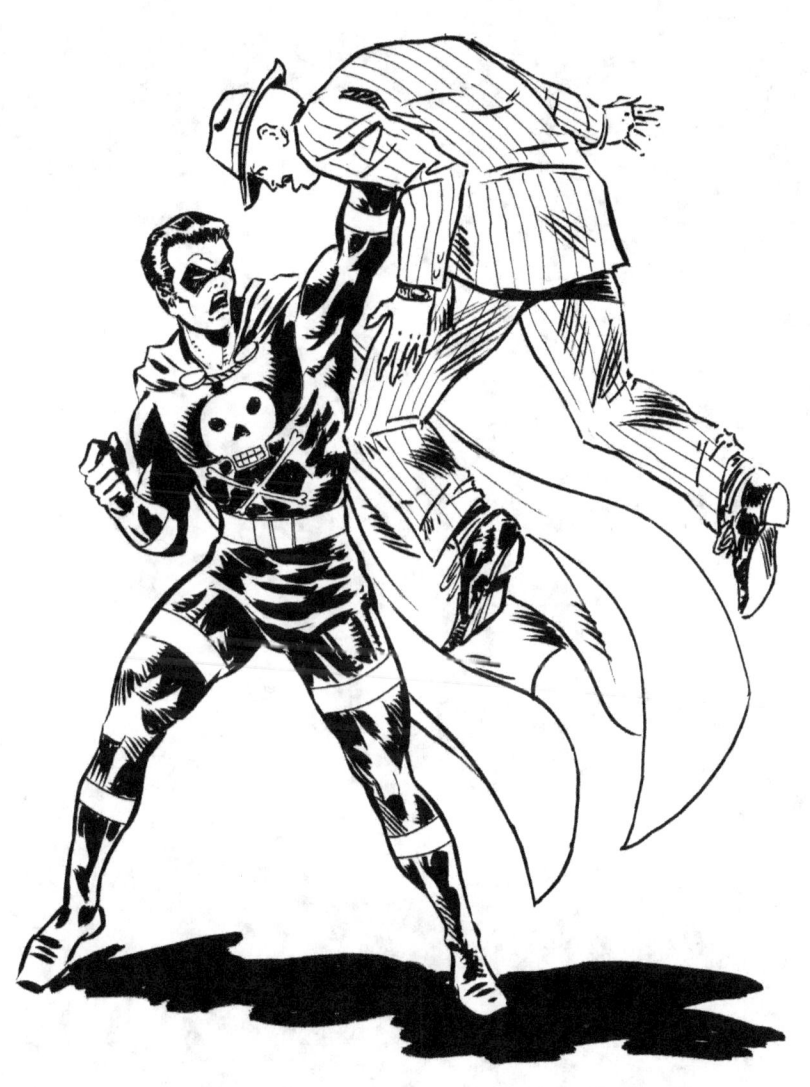

BLACK TERROR - NEDOR

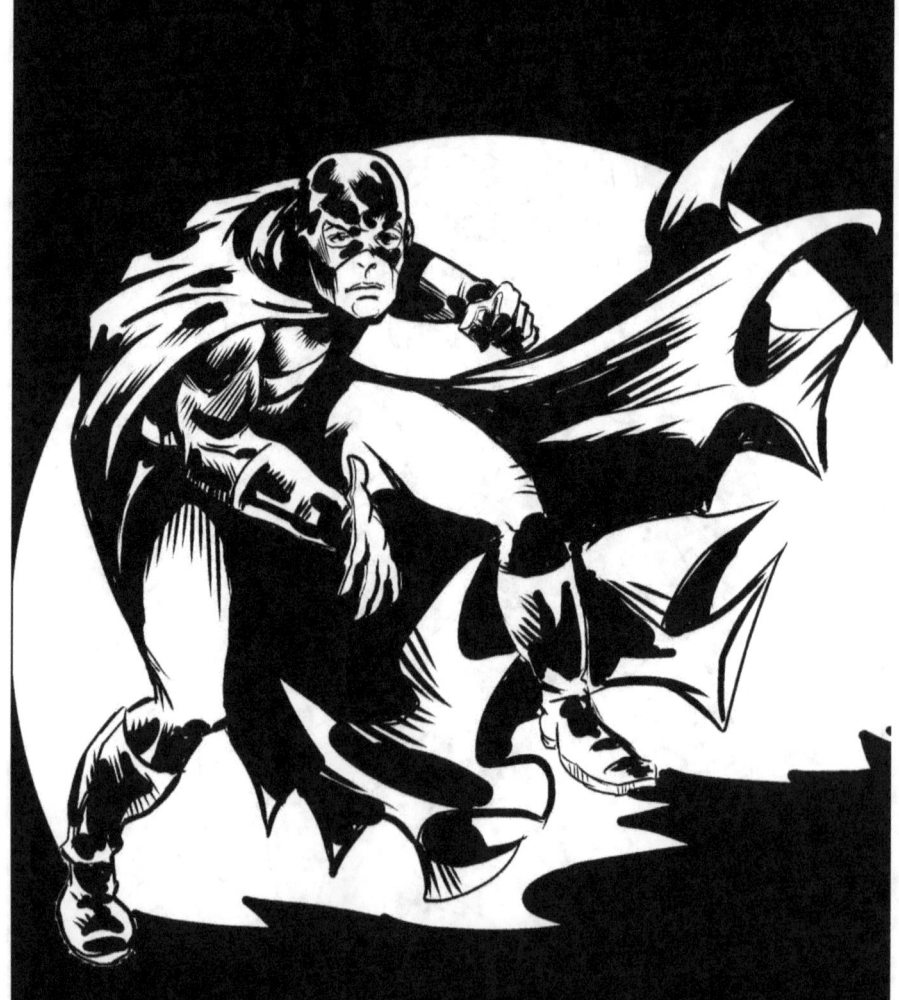

BLACK BAT - NEDOR

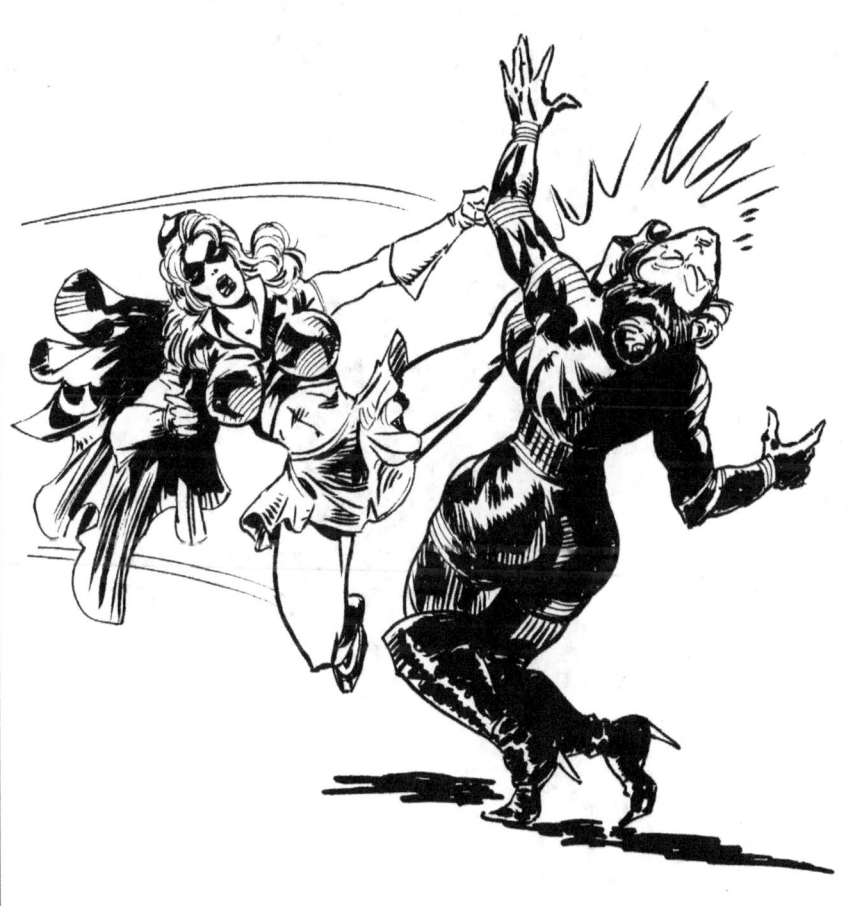

MISS MASQUE – NEDOR

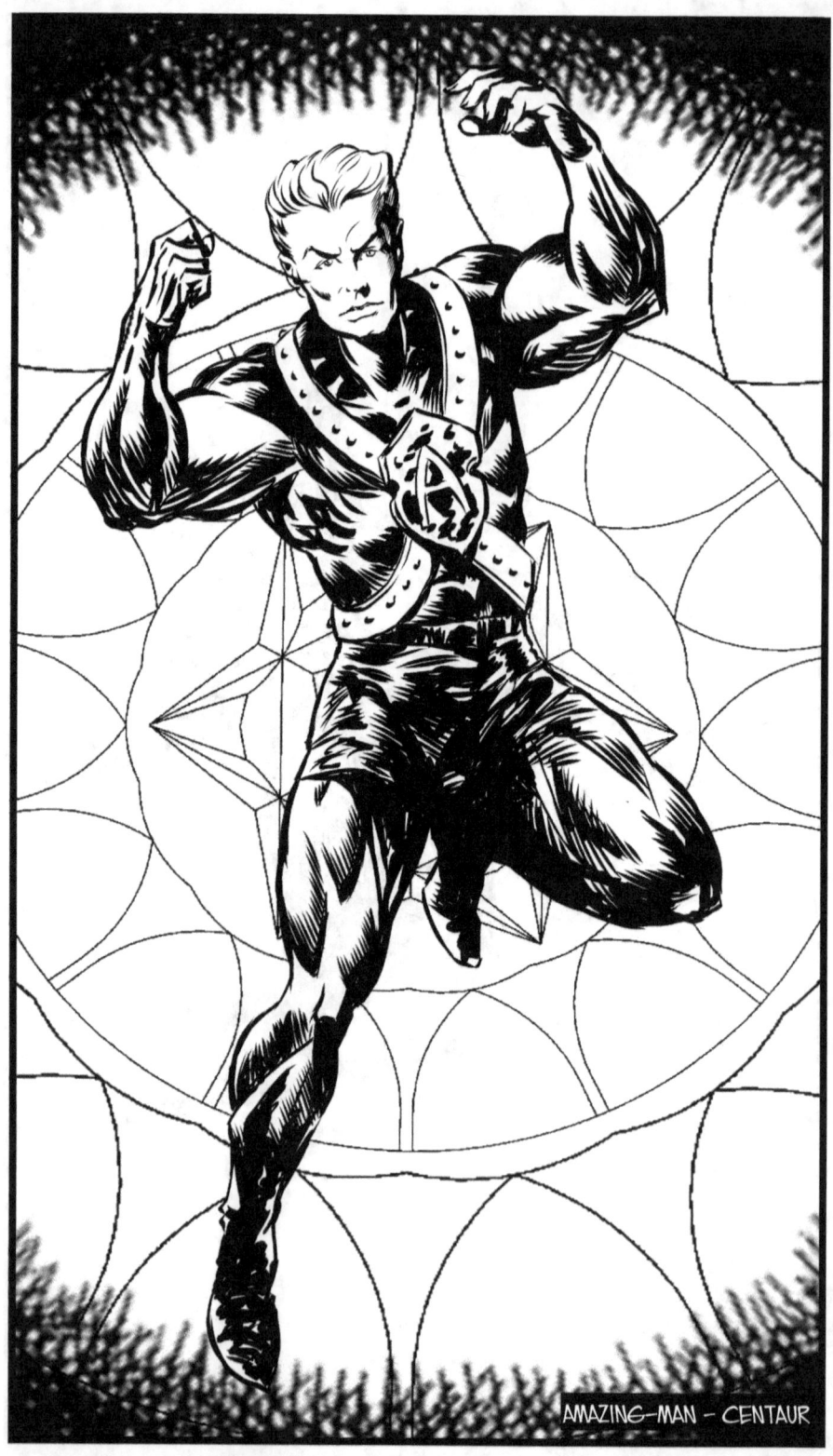

AMAZING-MAN - CENTAUR

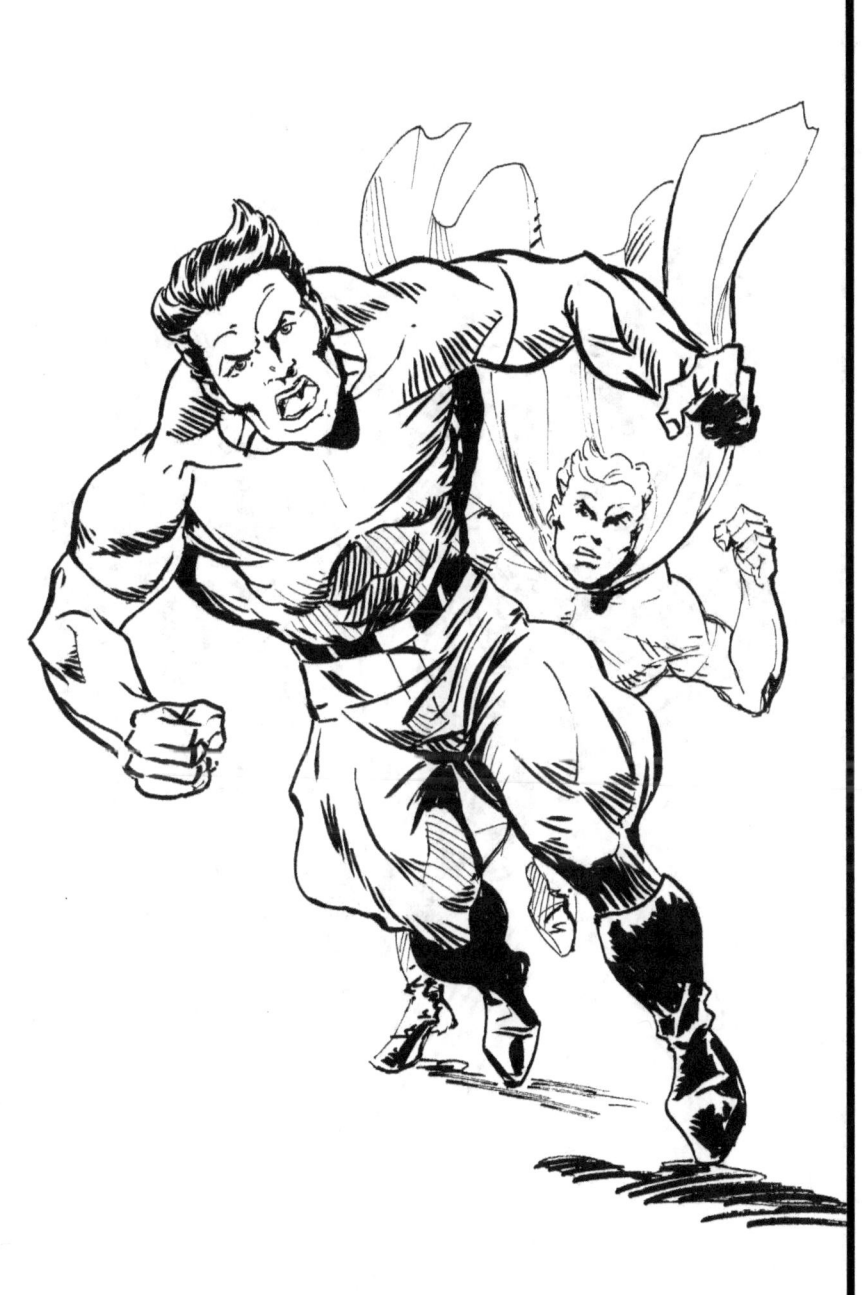

DOC STRANGE & MIKE - NEDOR

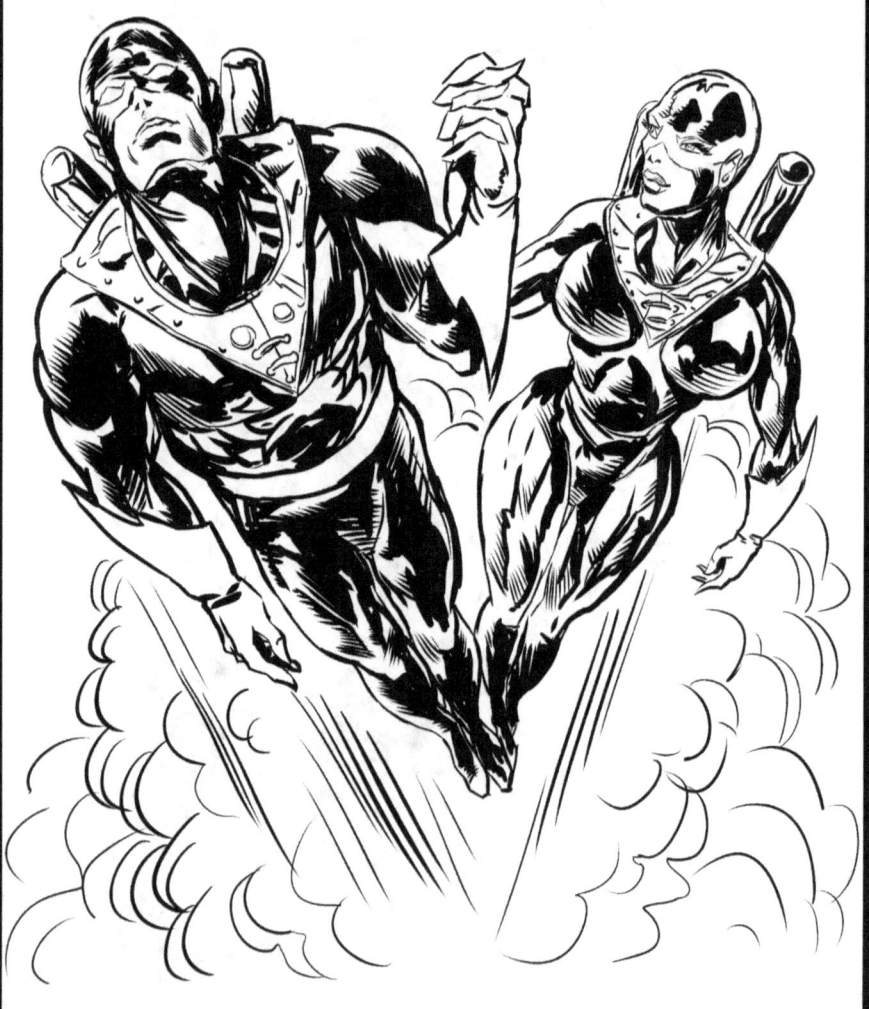

ROCKETMAN & ROCKETGIRL - CHESLER

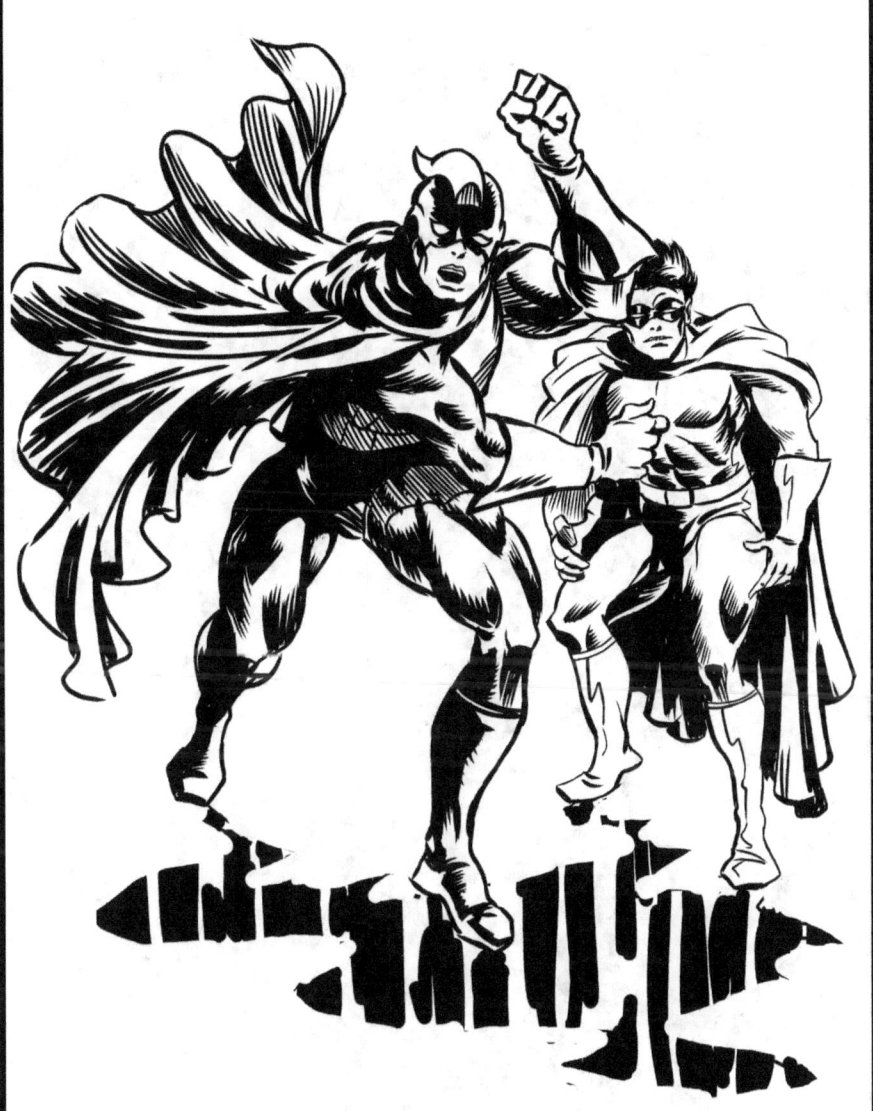

AMERICAN EAGLE & EAGLET - NEDOR

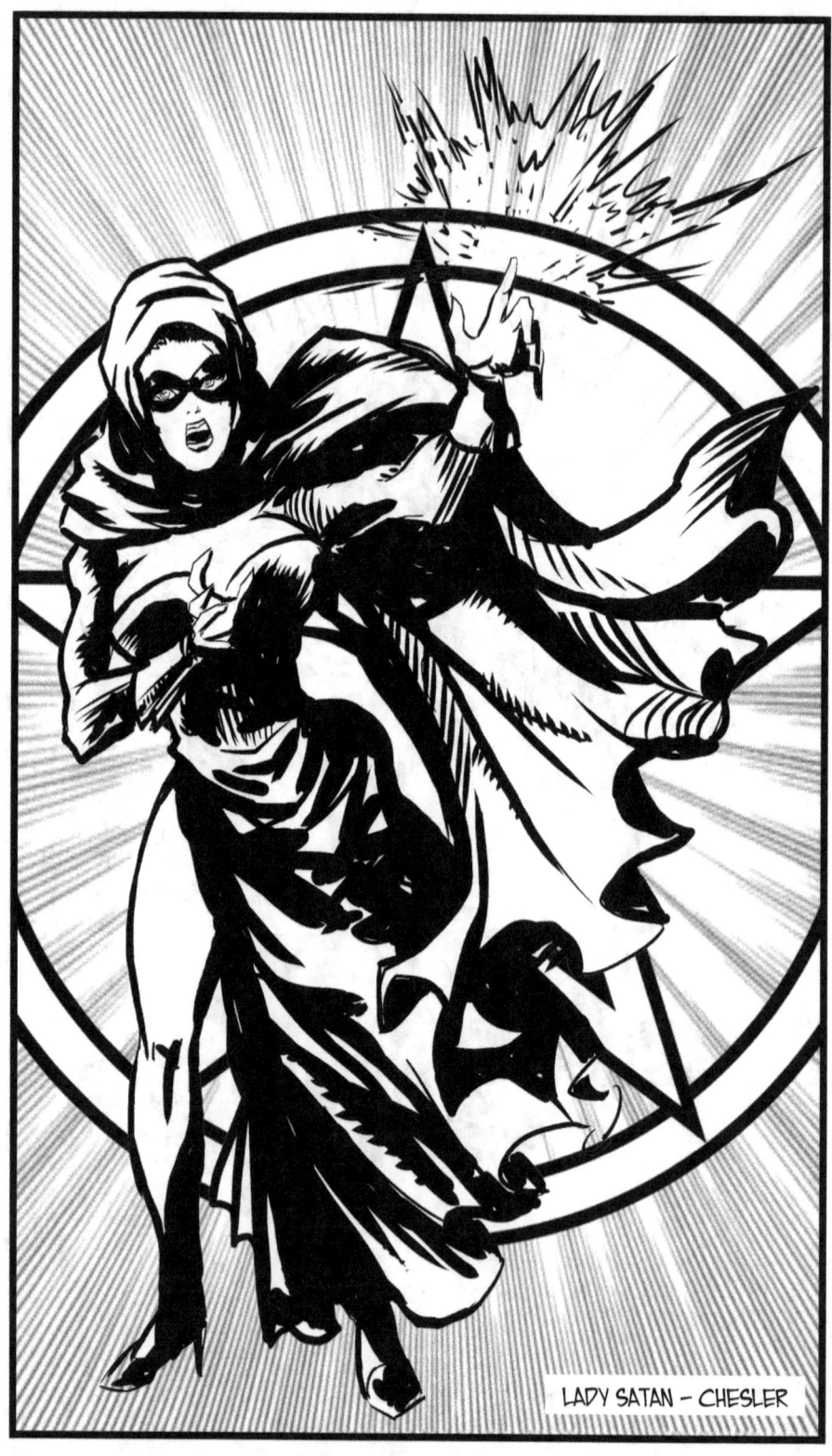

LADY SATAN - CHESLER

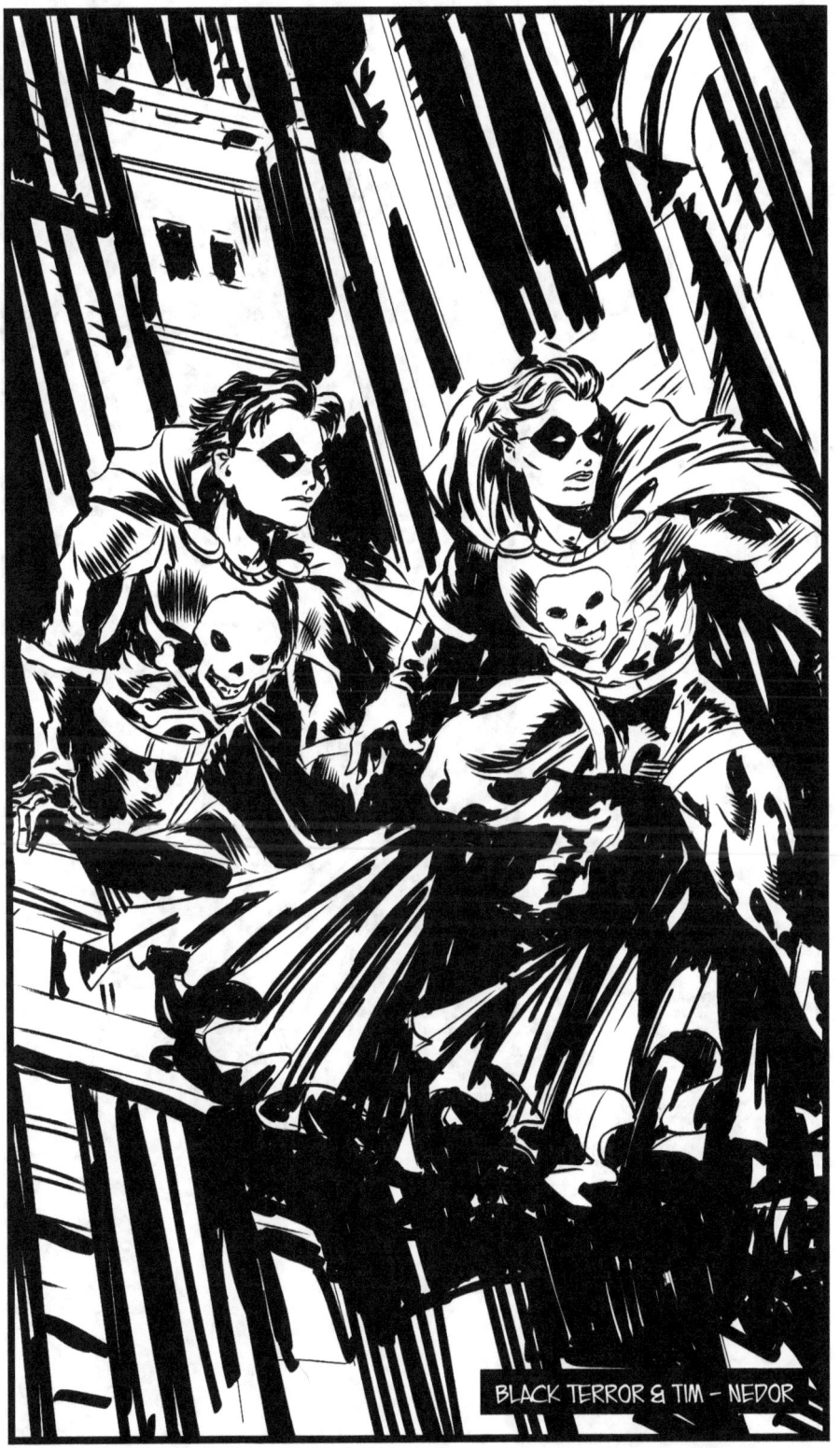

BLACK TERROR & TIM — NEDOR

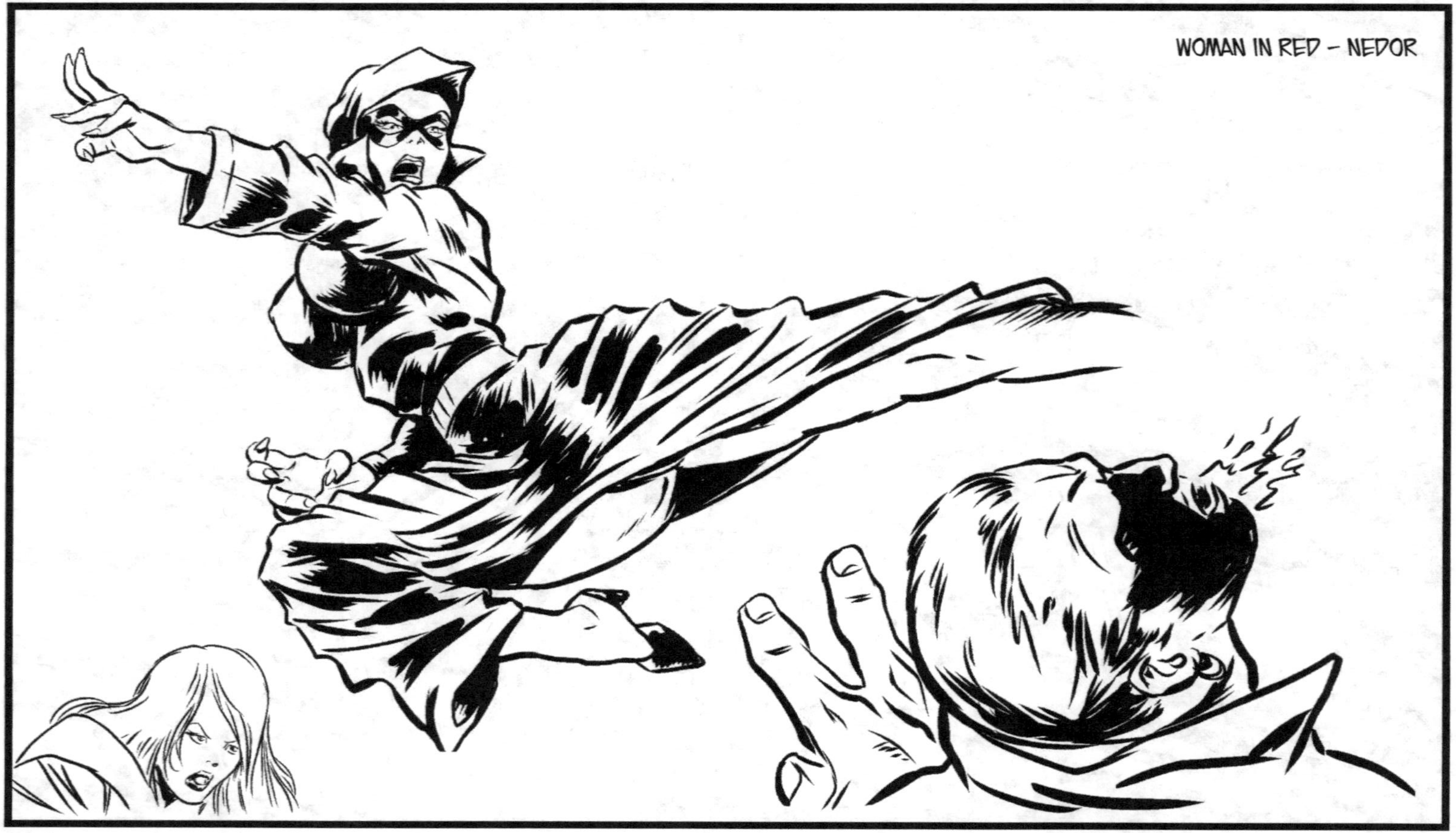
WOMAN IN RED – NEDOR

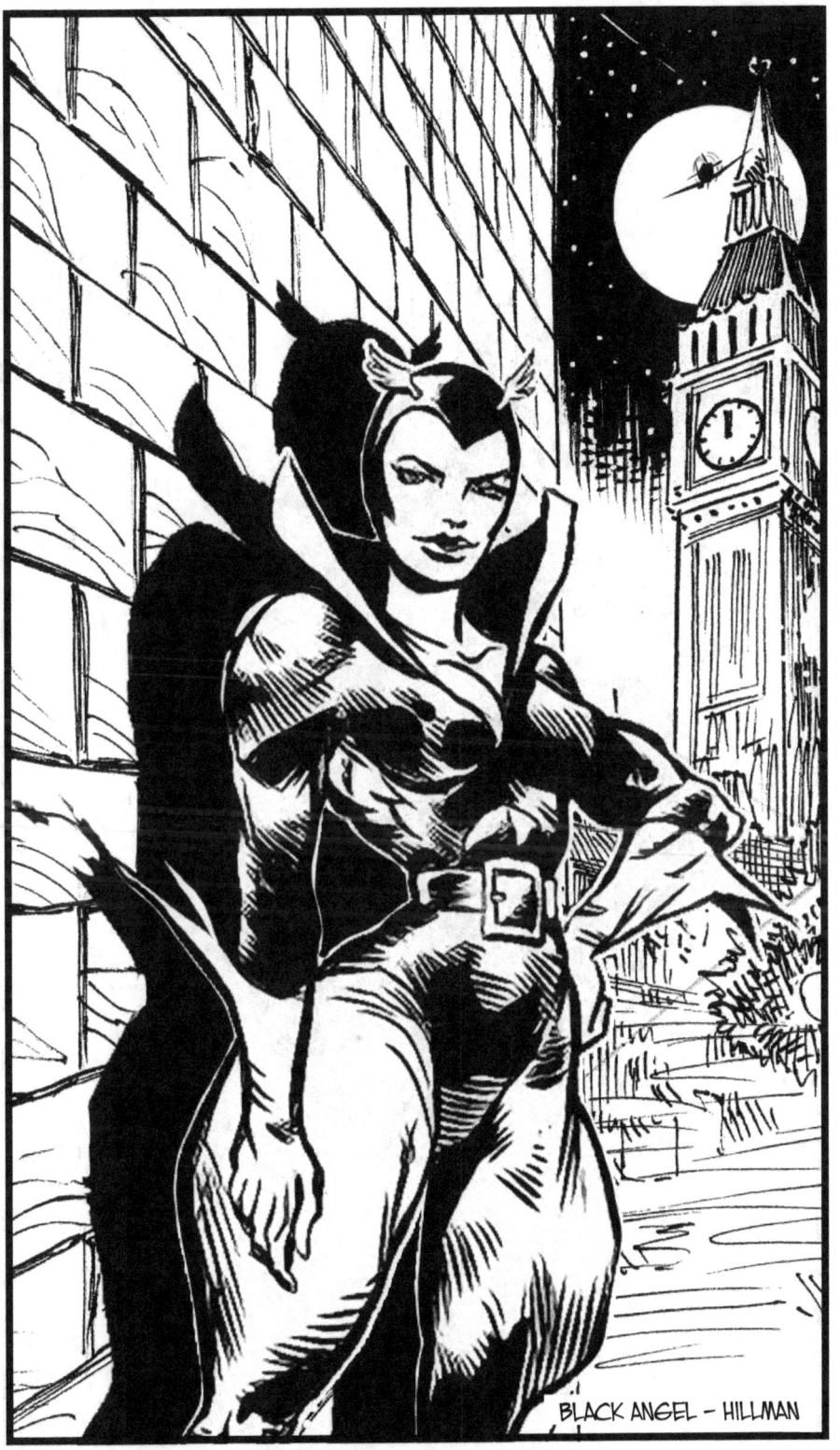

BLACK ANGEL – HILLMAN

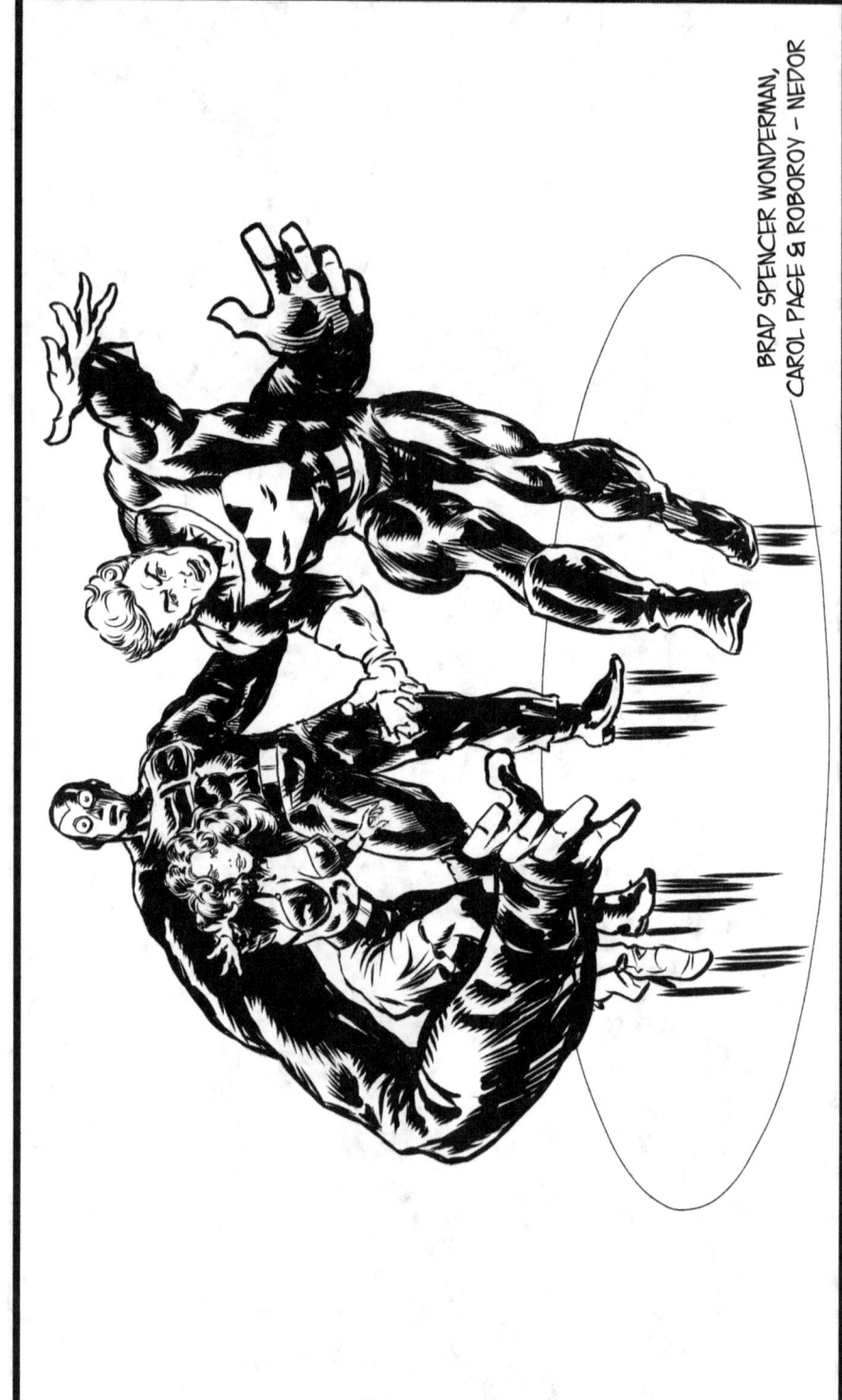

BRAD SPENCER WONDERMAN,
CAROL PAGE & ROBOROY – NEDOR

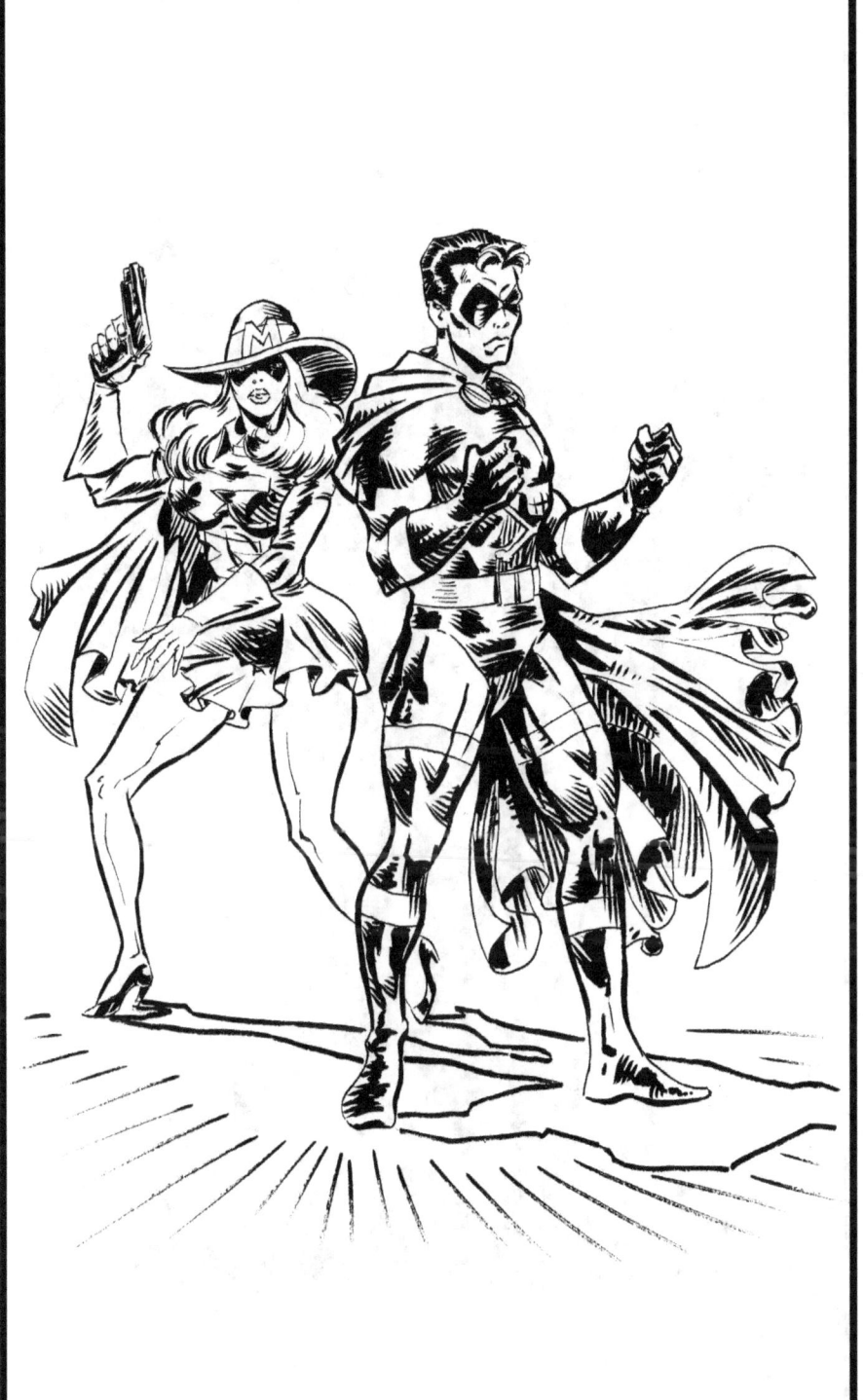

BLACK TERROR & MISS MASQUE — NEDOR

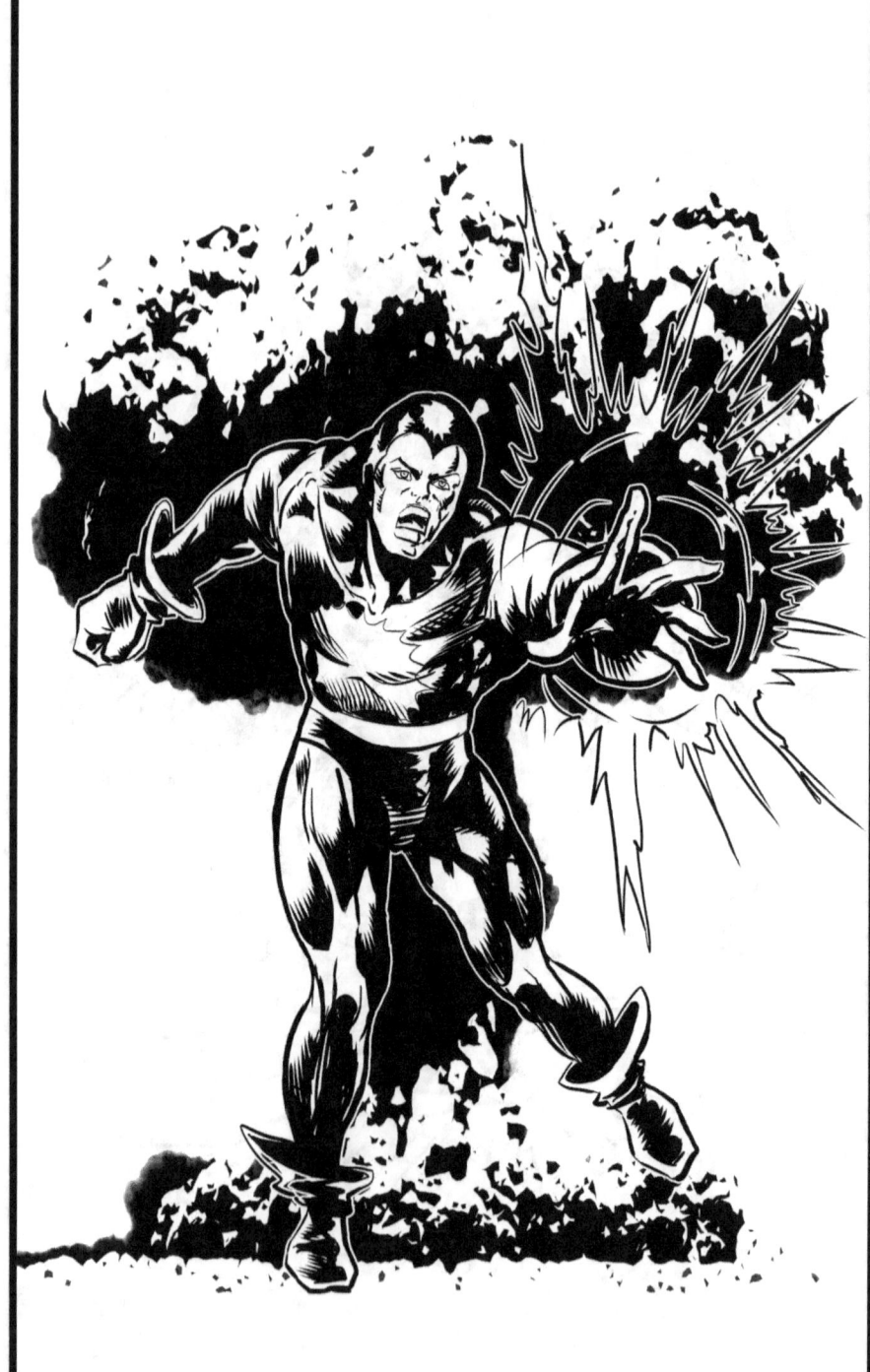

ATOMIC THUNDERBOLT - REGOR

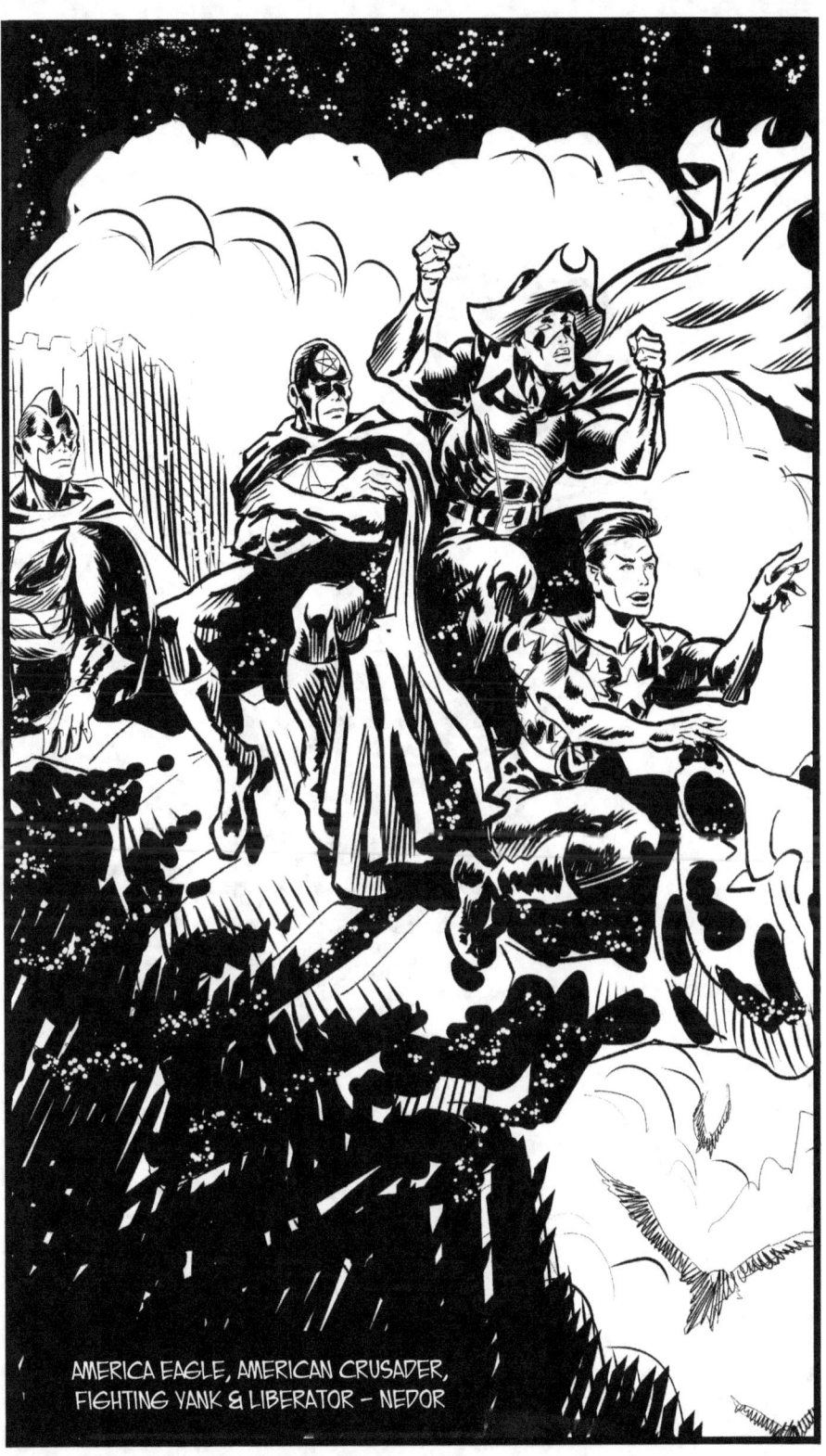

AMERICA EAGLE, AMERICAN CRUSADER,
FIGHTING YANK & LIBERATOR - NEDOR

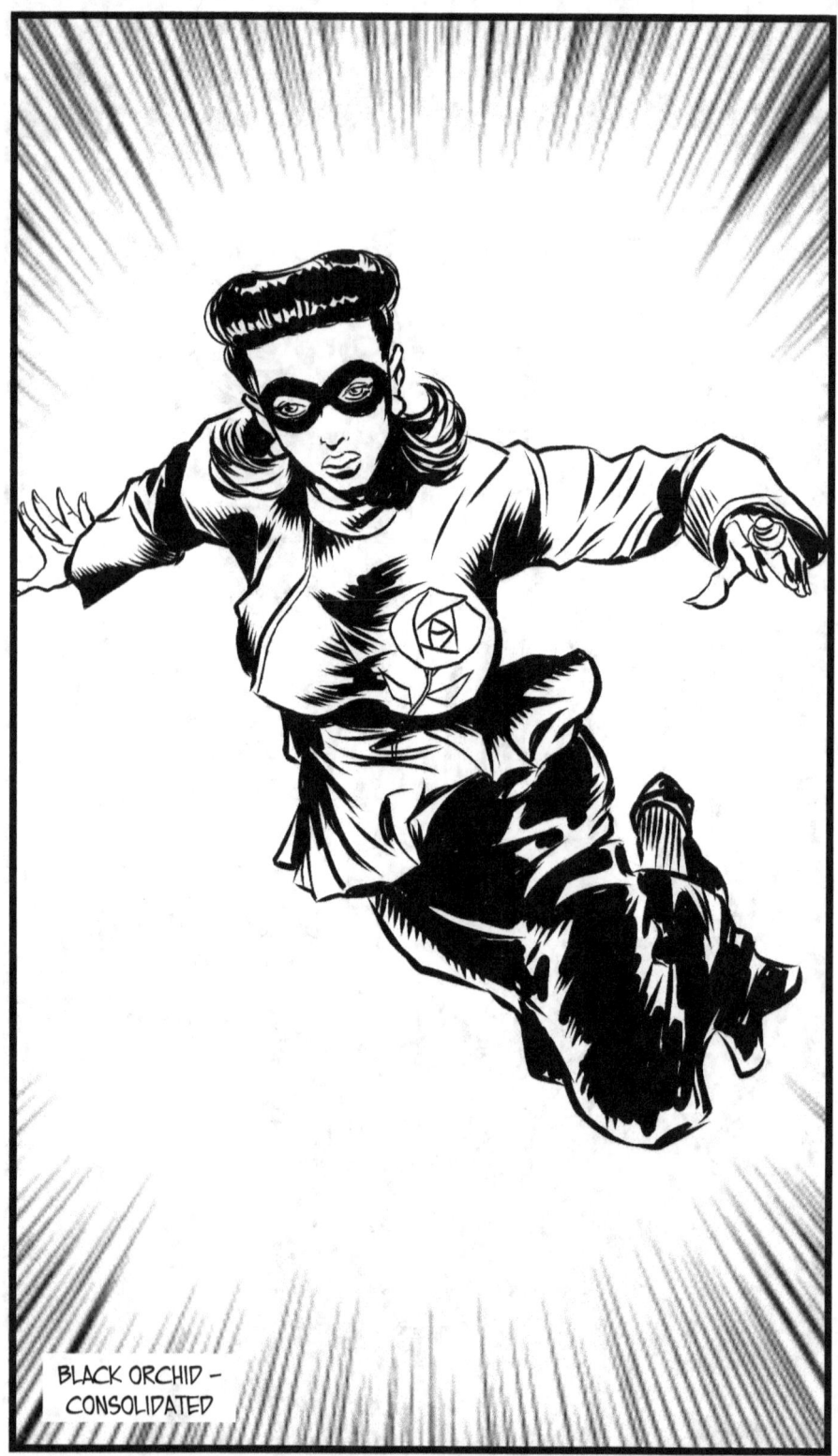

BLACK ORCHID –
CONSOLIDATED

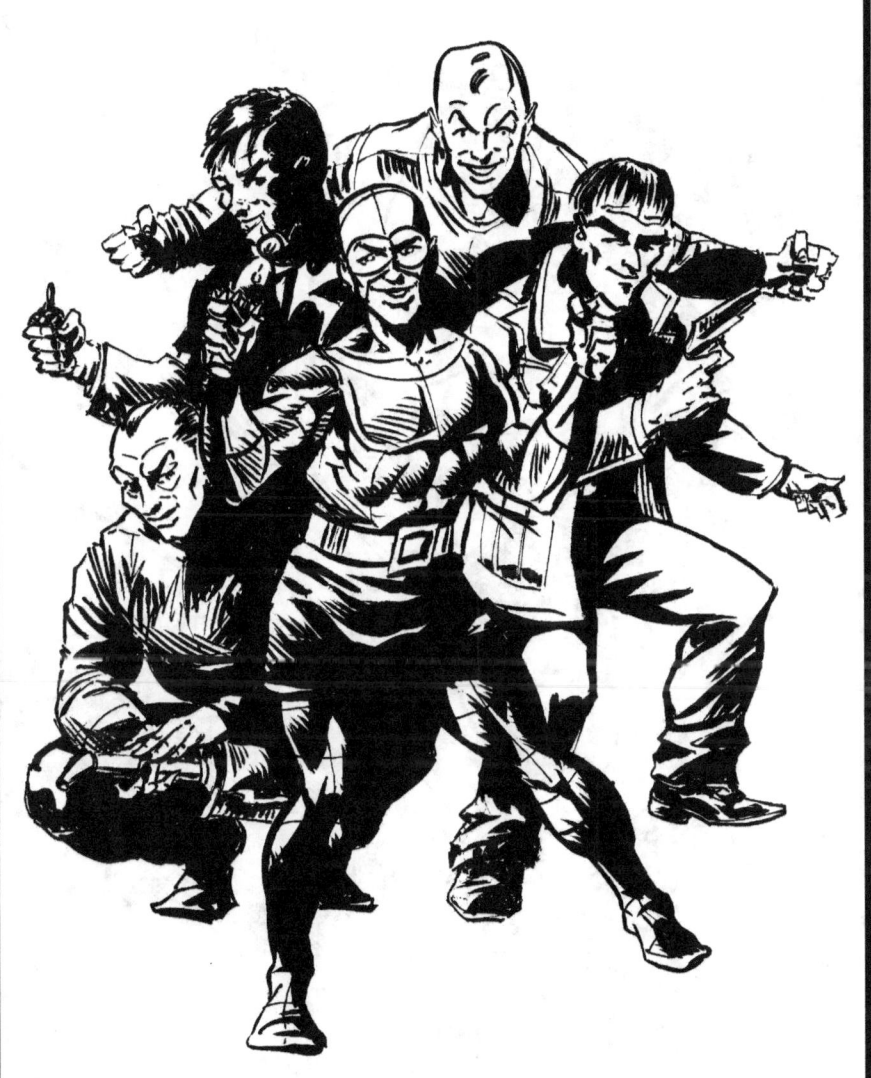

BLACK TERROR'S VILLAINS - NEDOR

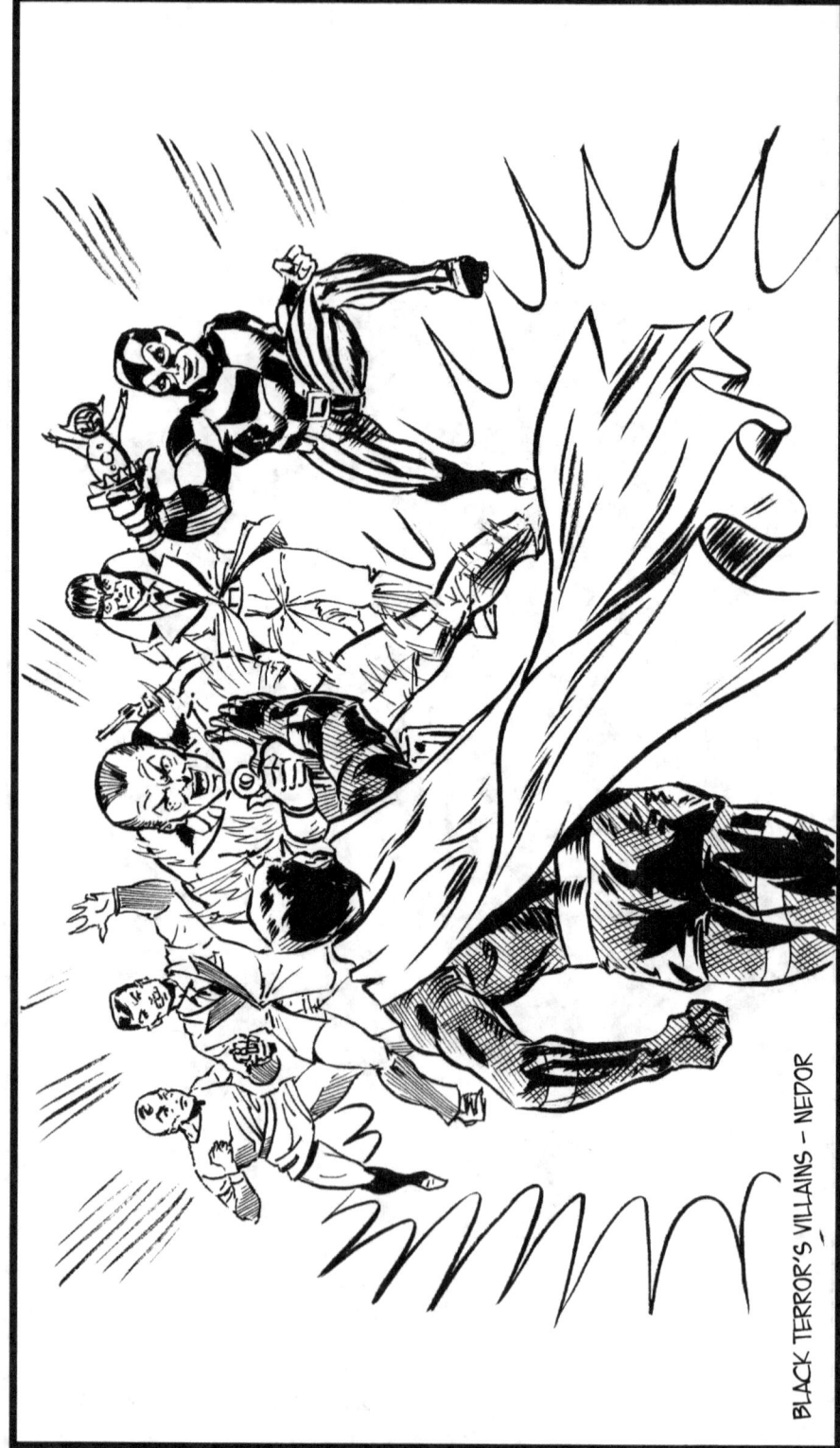

BLACK TERROR'S VILLAINS – NEDOR

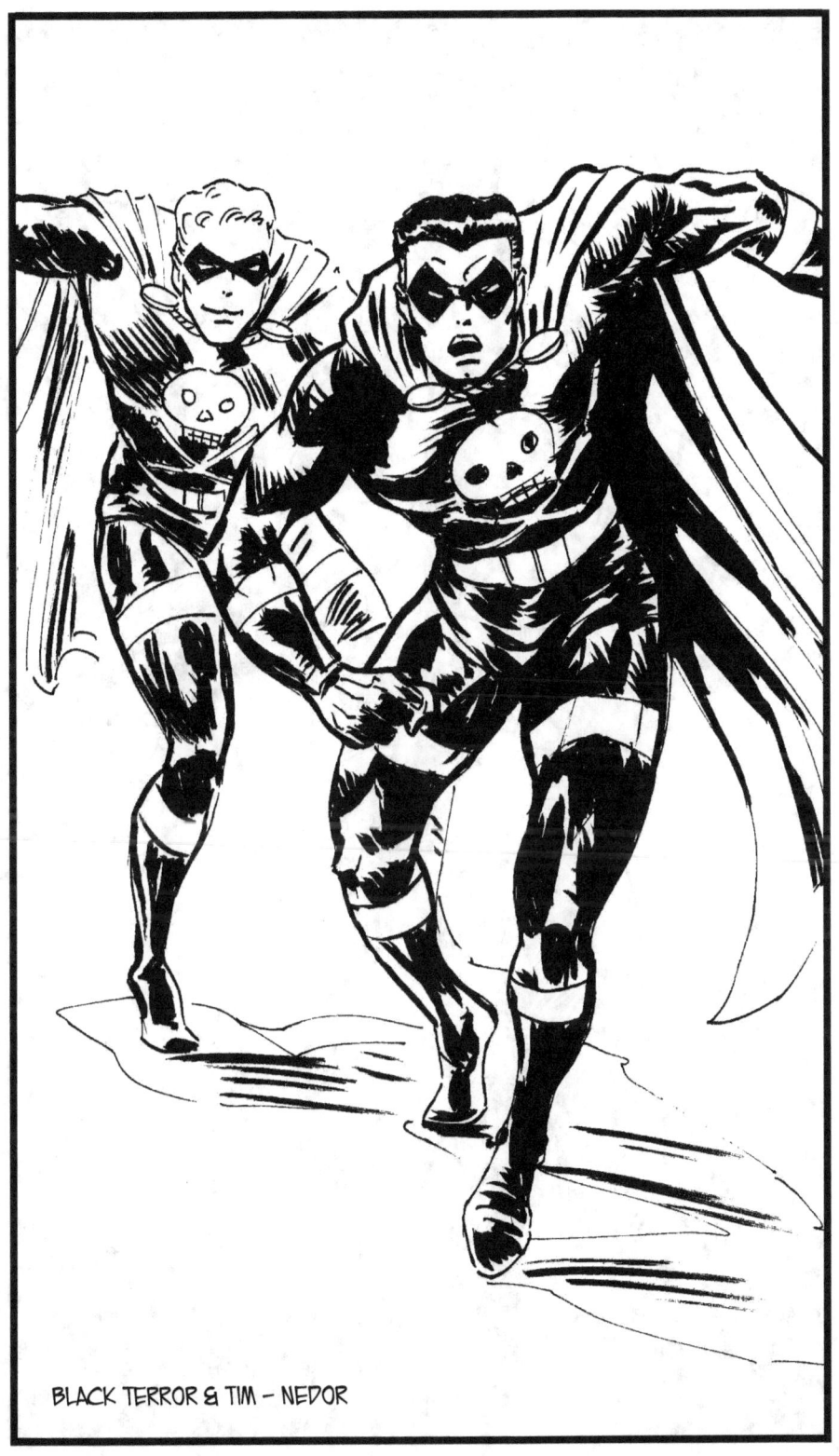

BLACK TERROR & TIM – NEDOR

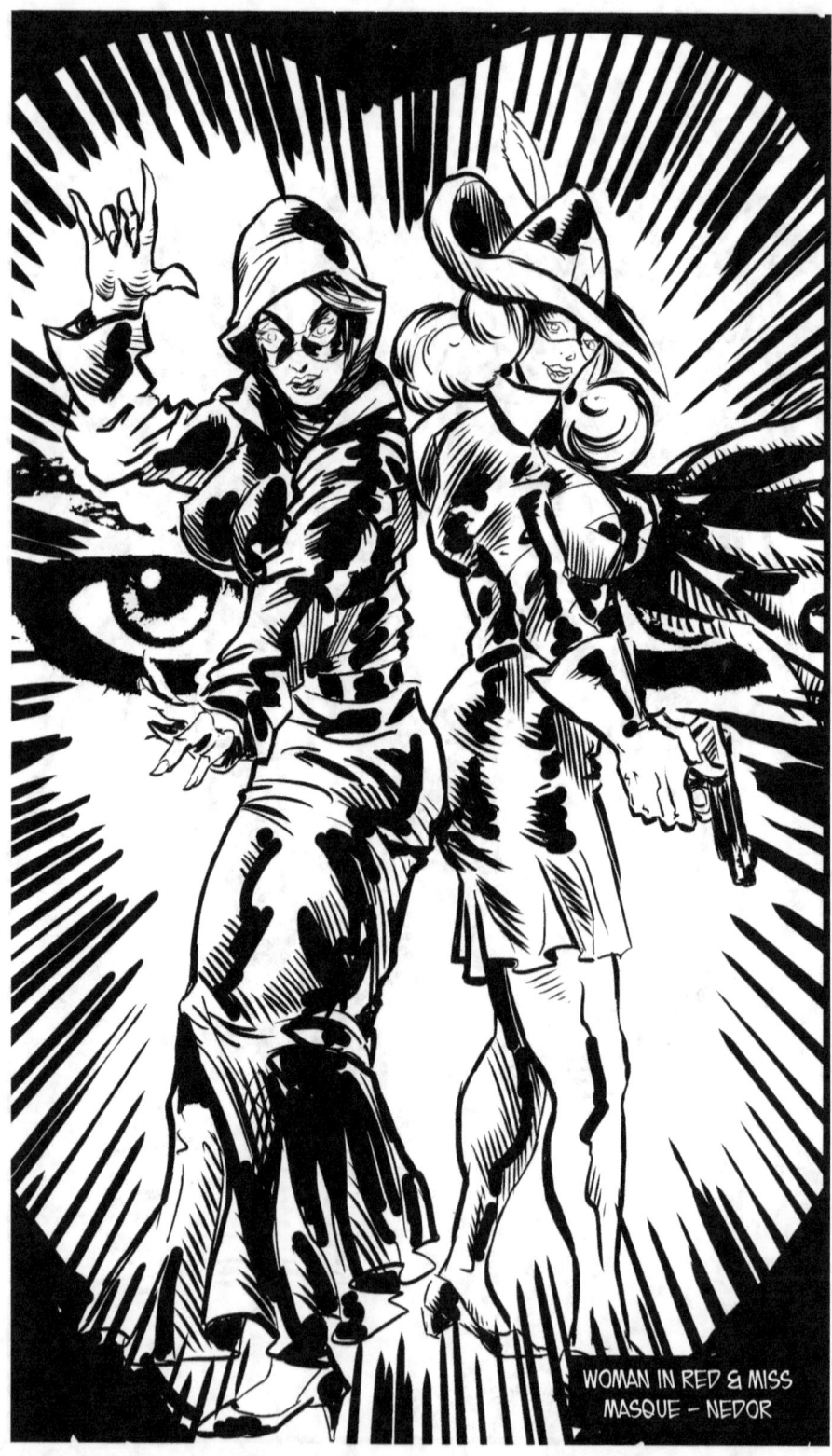

WOMAN IN RED & MISS
MASQUE - NEDOR

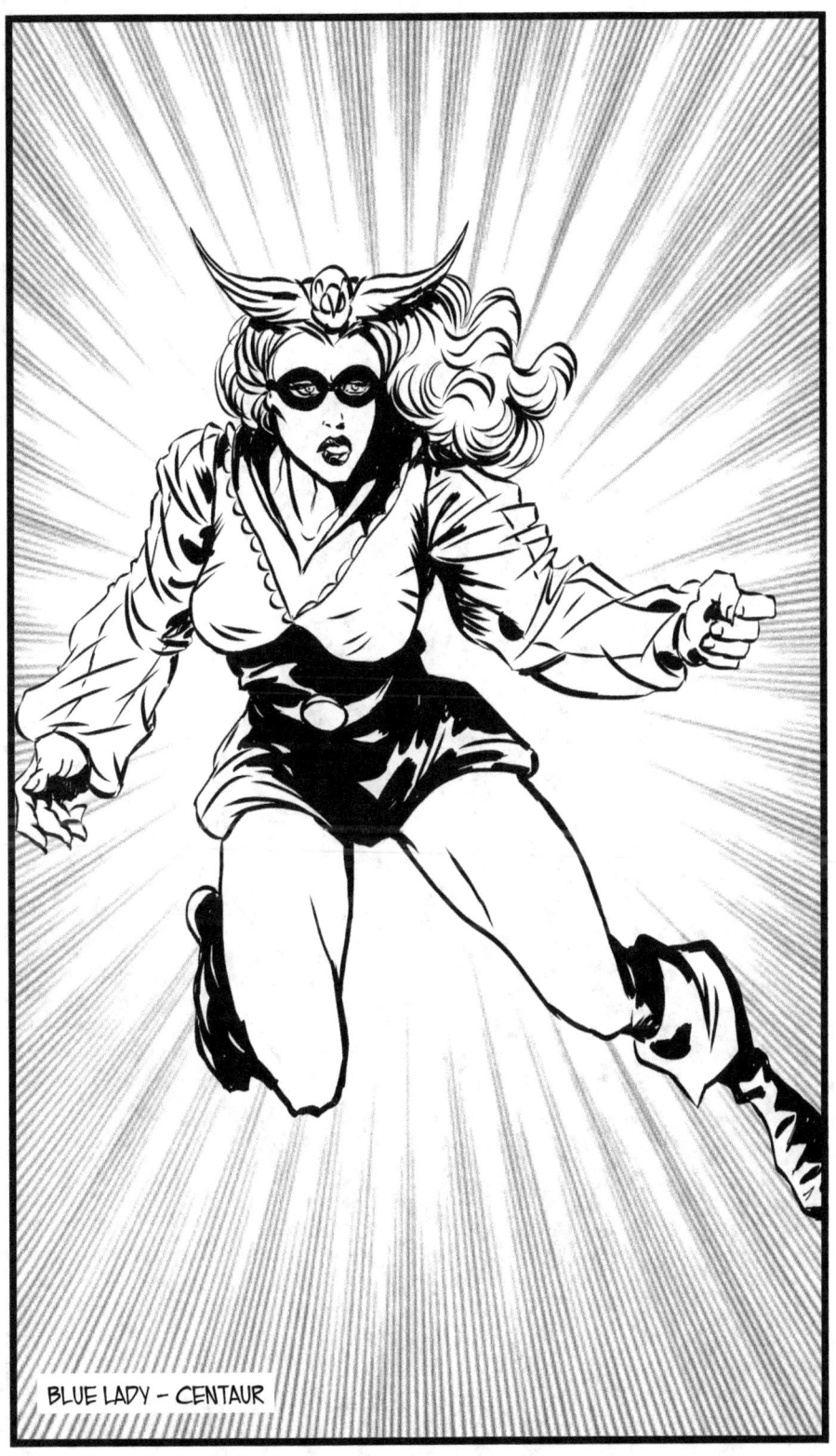

BLUE LADY - CENTAUR

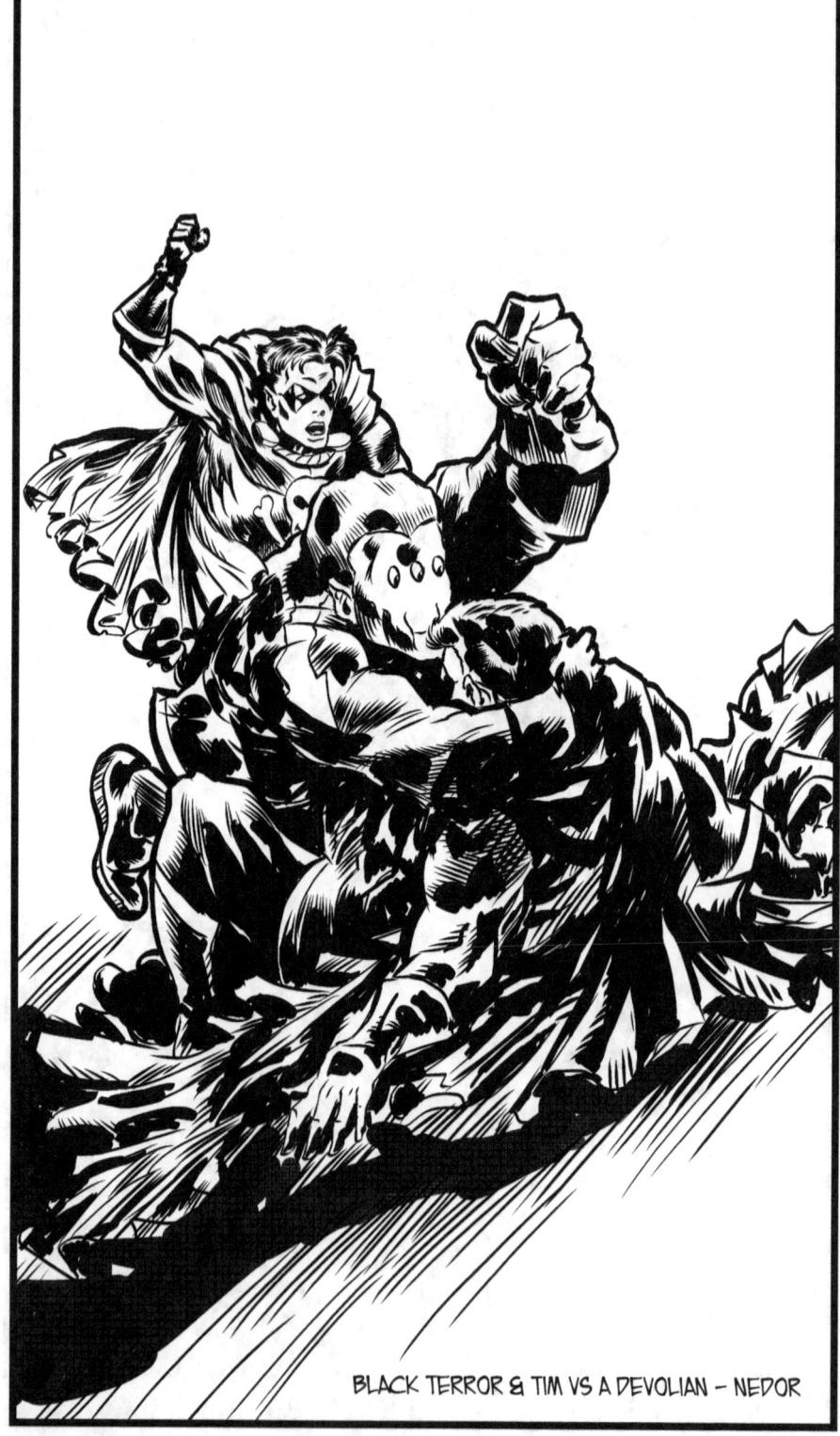

BLACK TERROR & TIM VS A DEVOLIAN - NEDOR

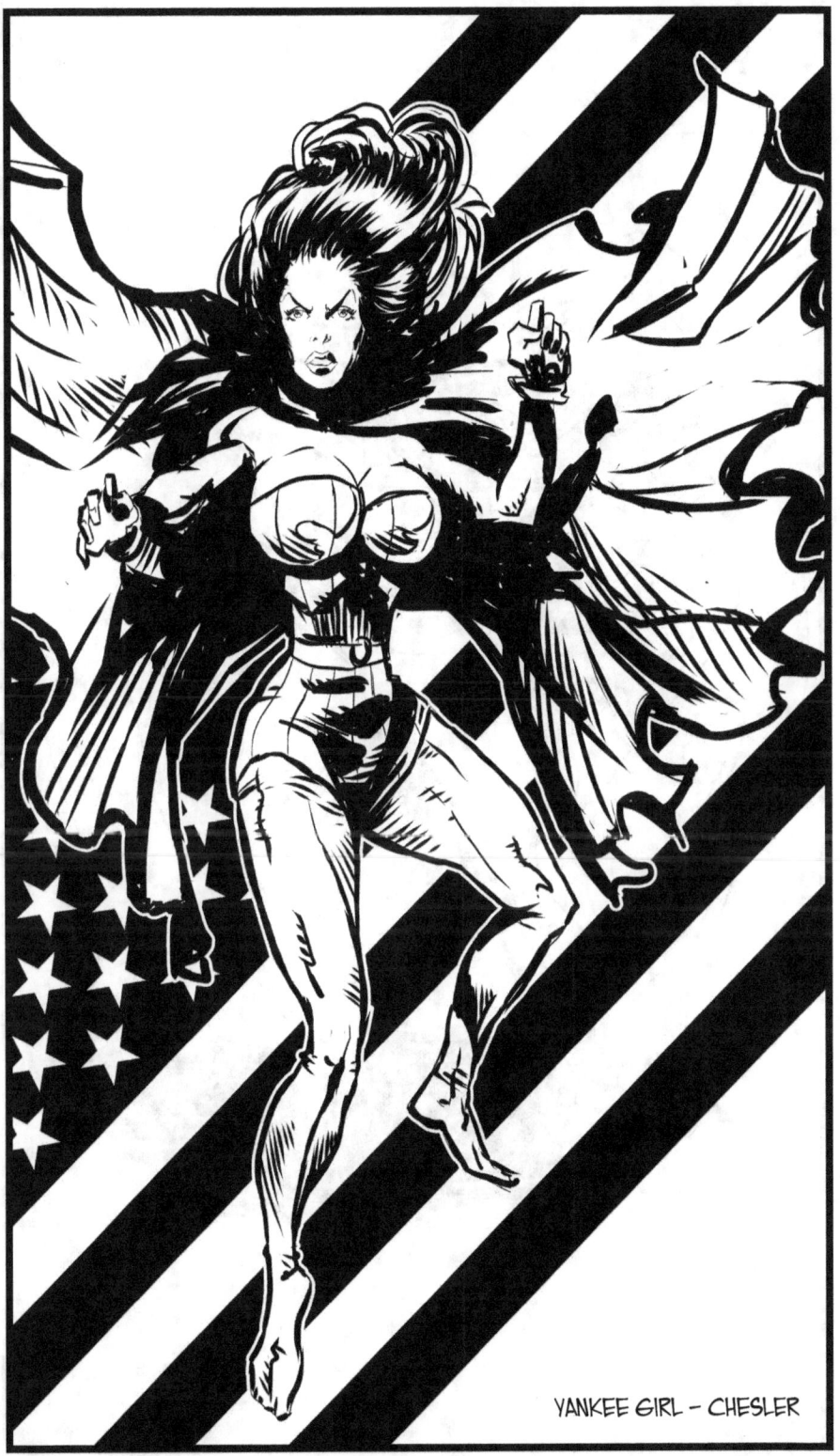

YANKEE GIRL – CHESLER

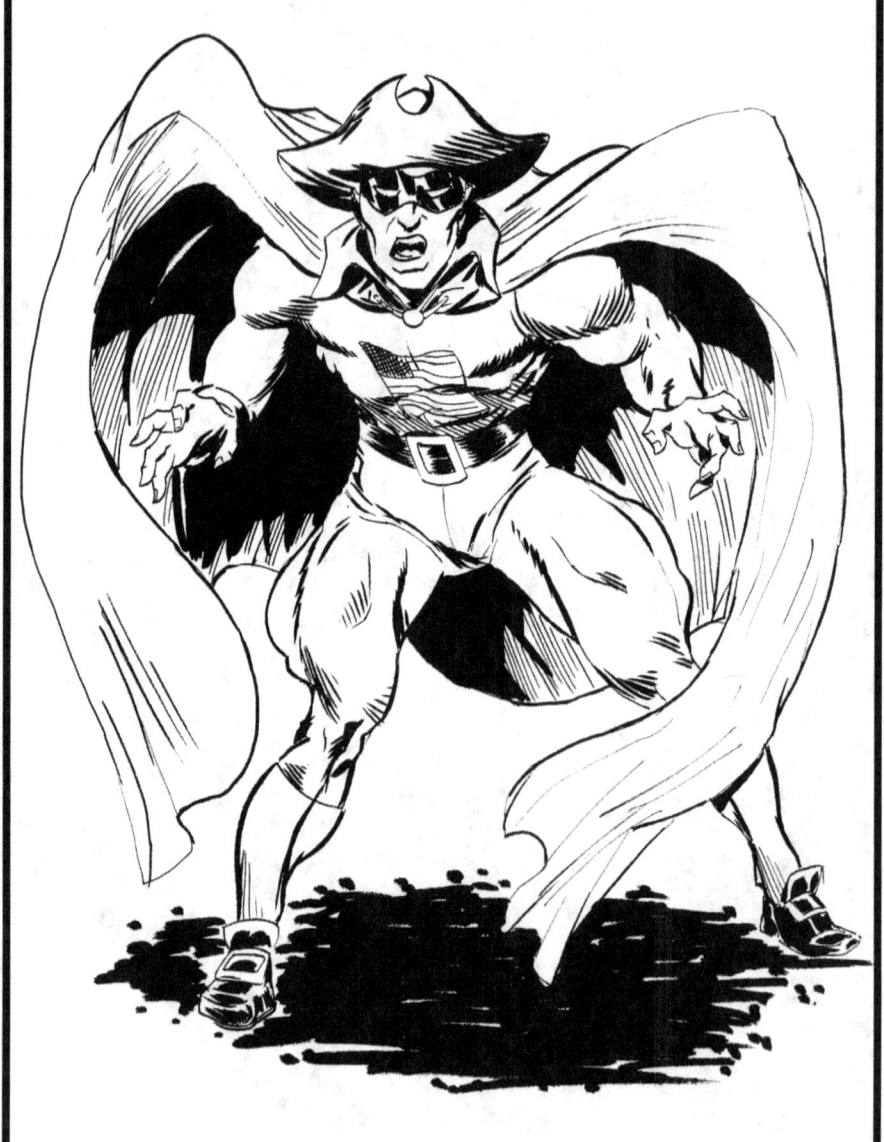

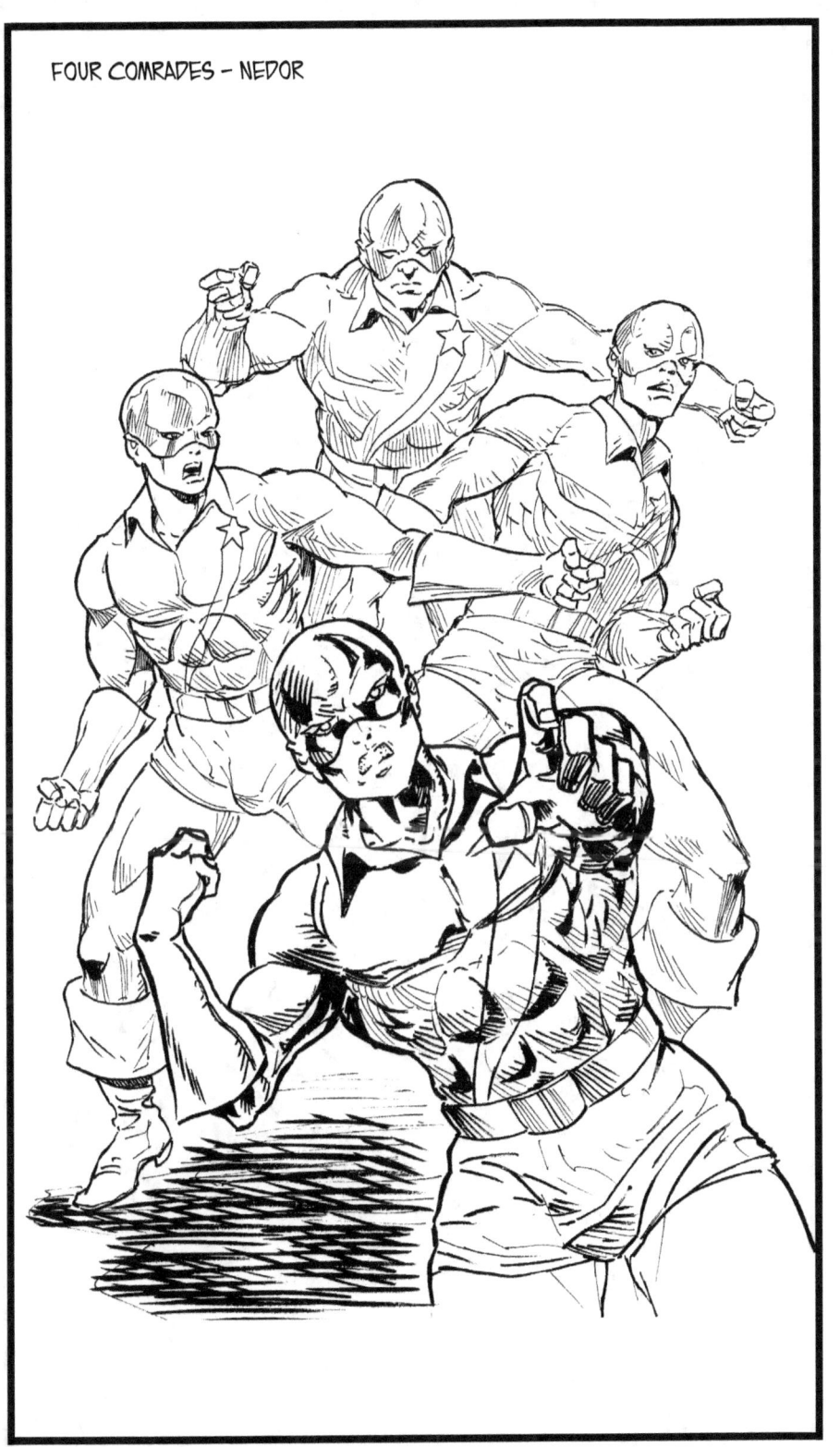

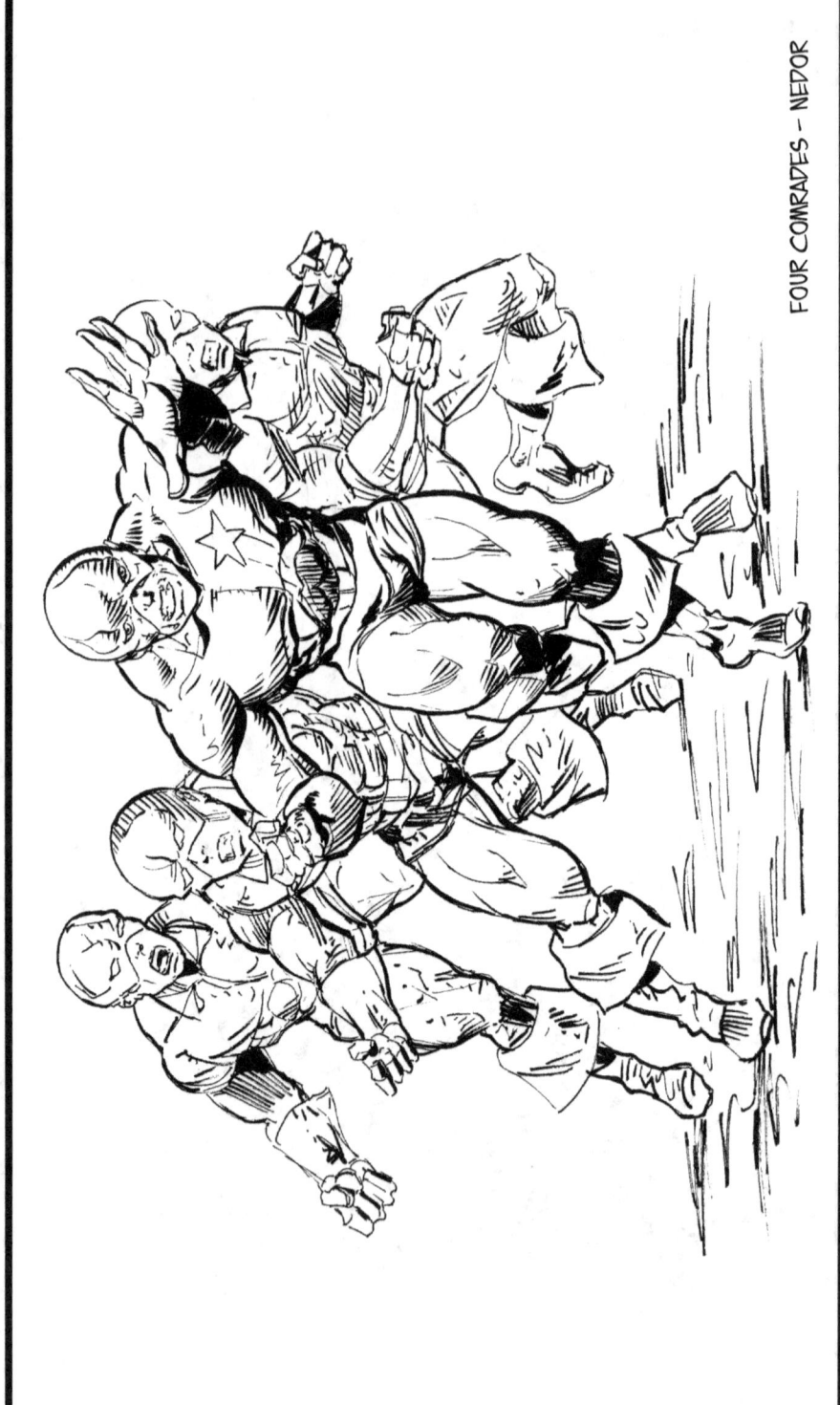

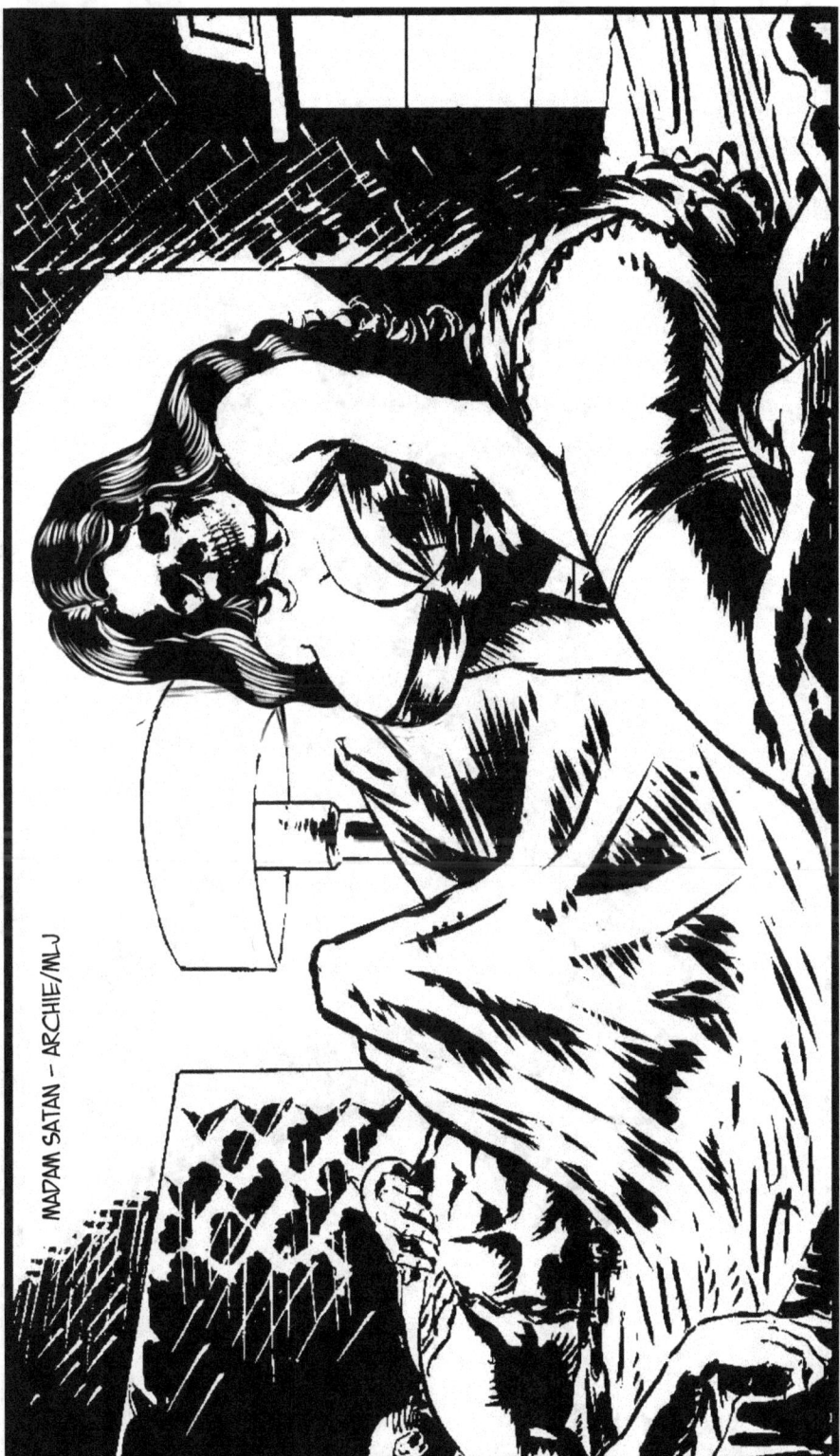

MADAM SATAN – ARCHIE/MLJ

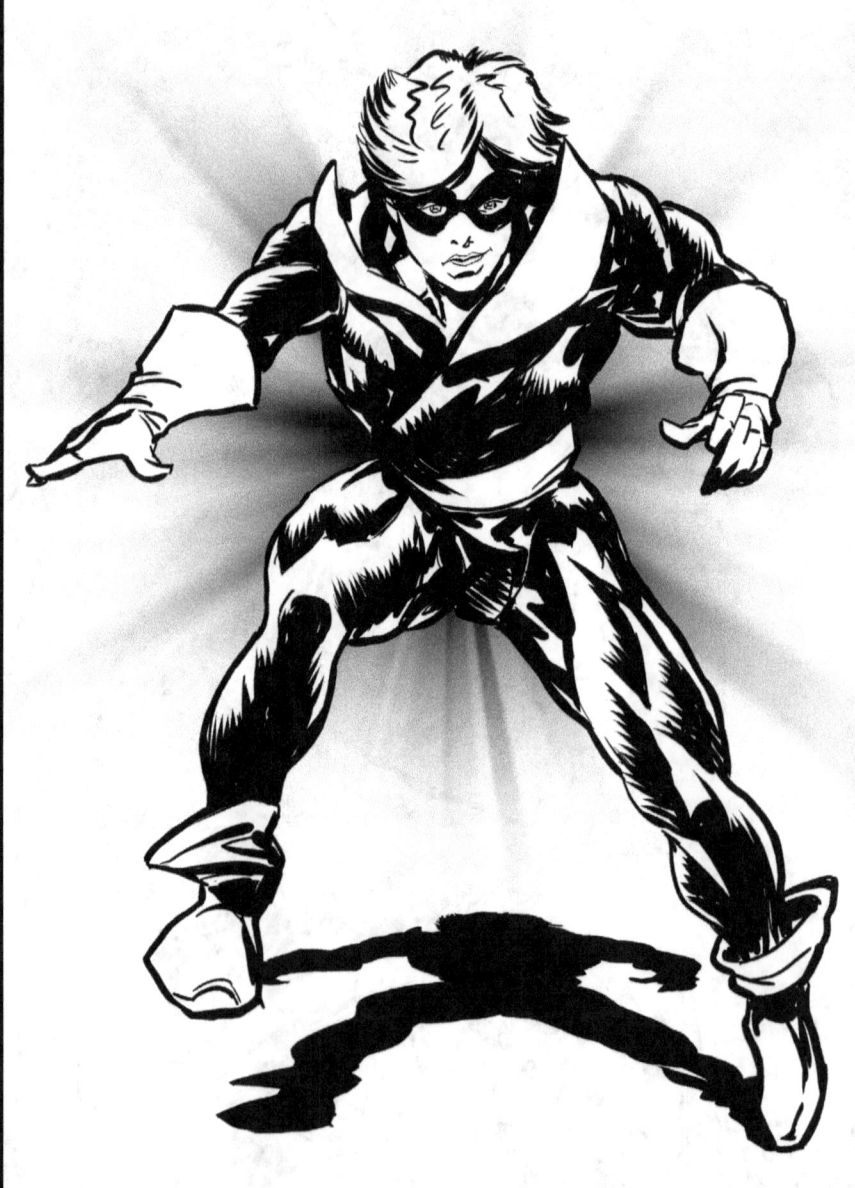

JOHNNY REBEL - CHESLER

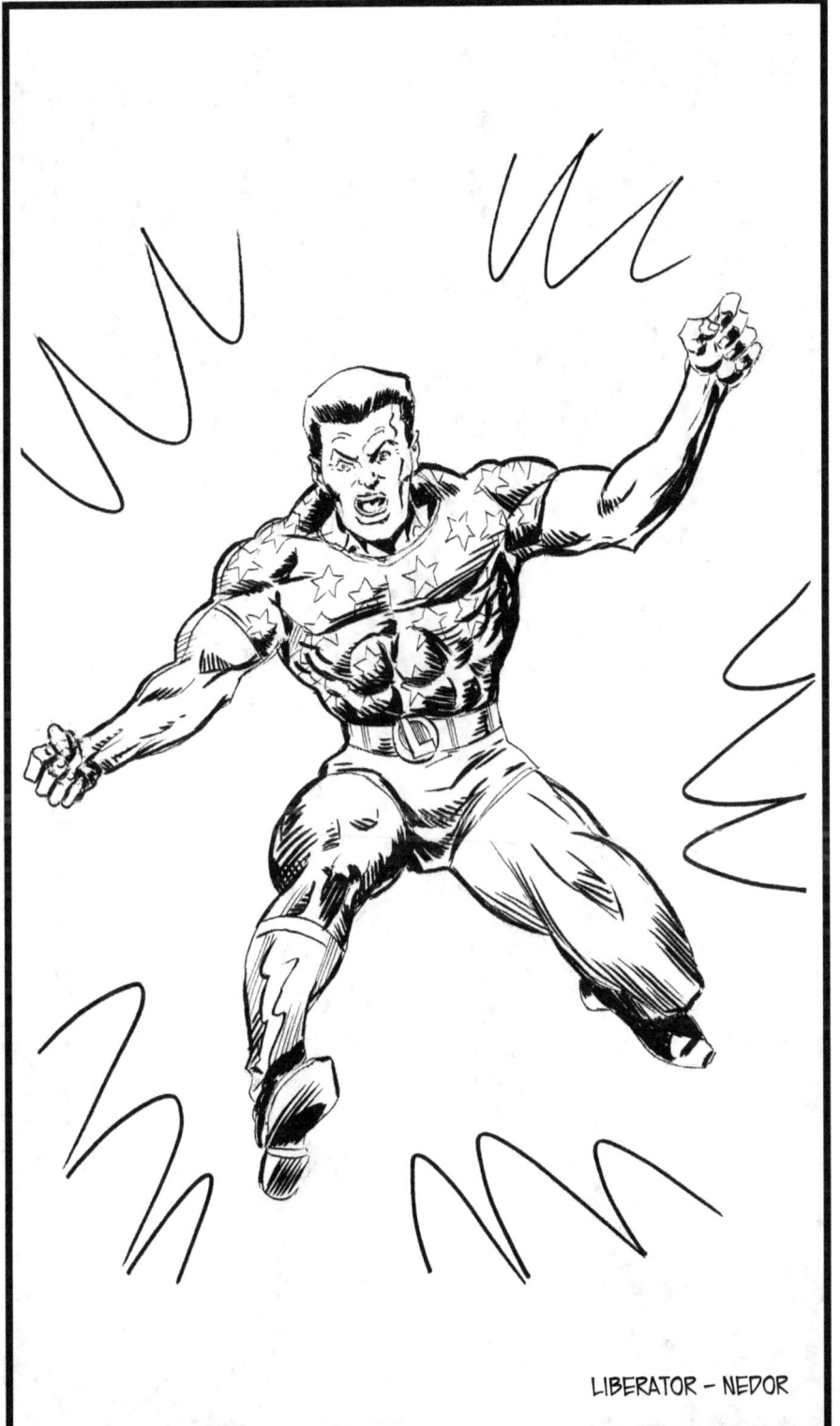

LIBERATOR - NEDOR

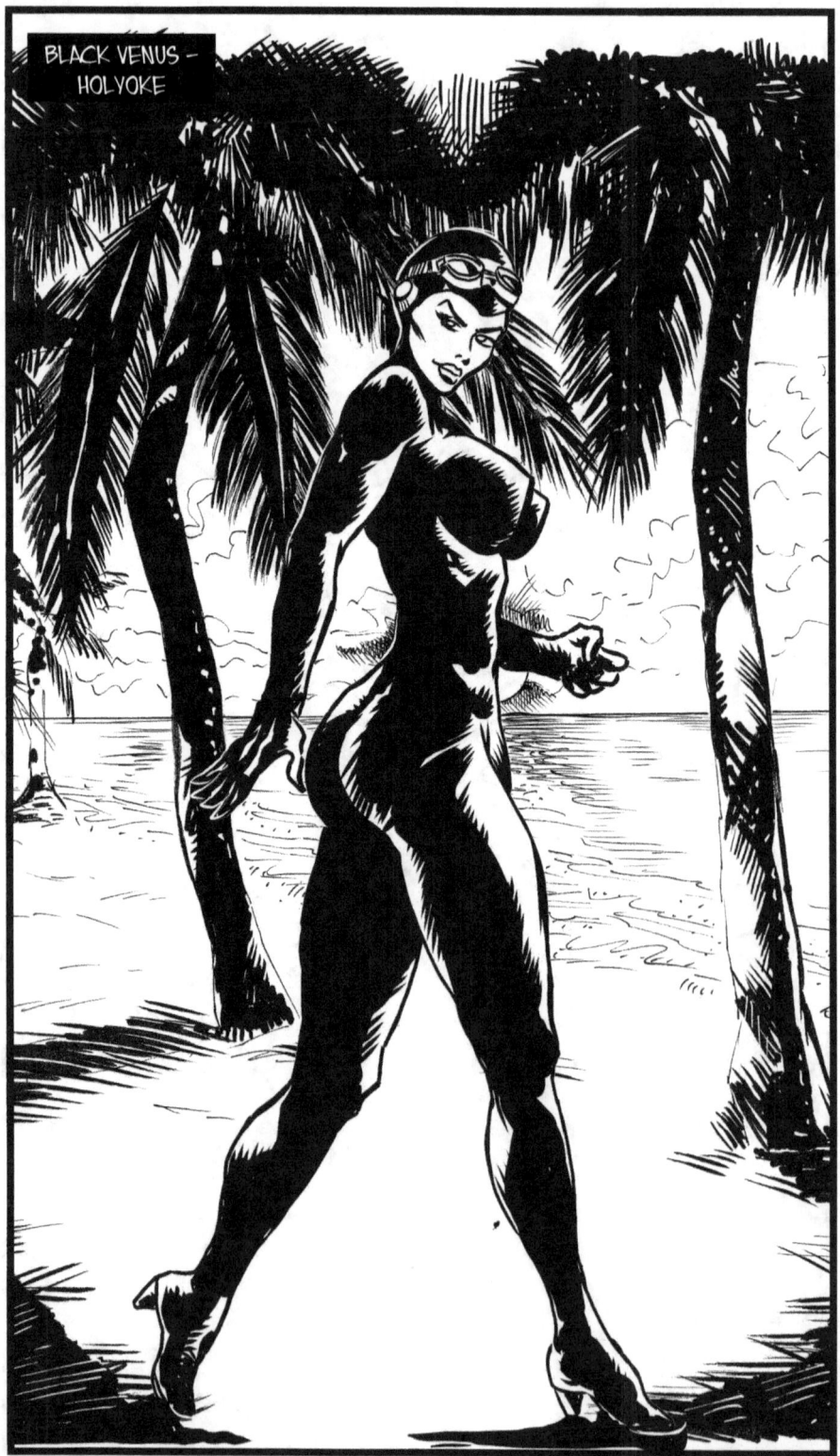

BLACK VENUS – HOLYOKE

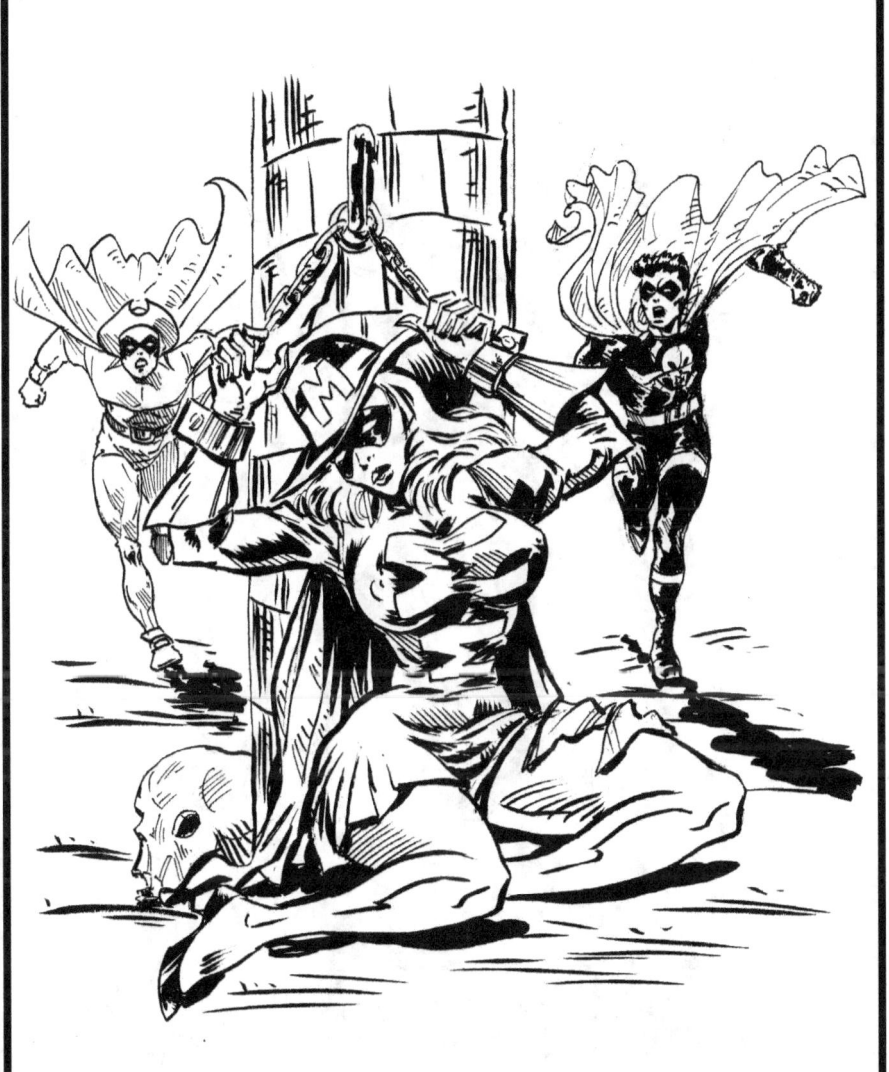

FIGHTING YANK, BLACK TERROR &
MISS MASQUE - NEDOR

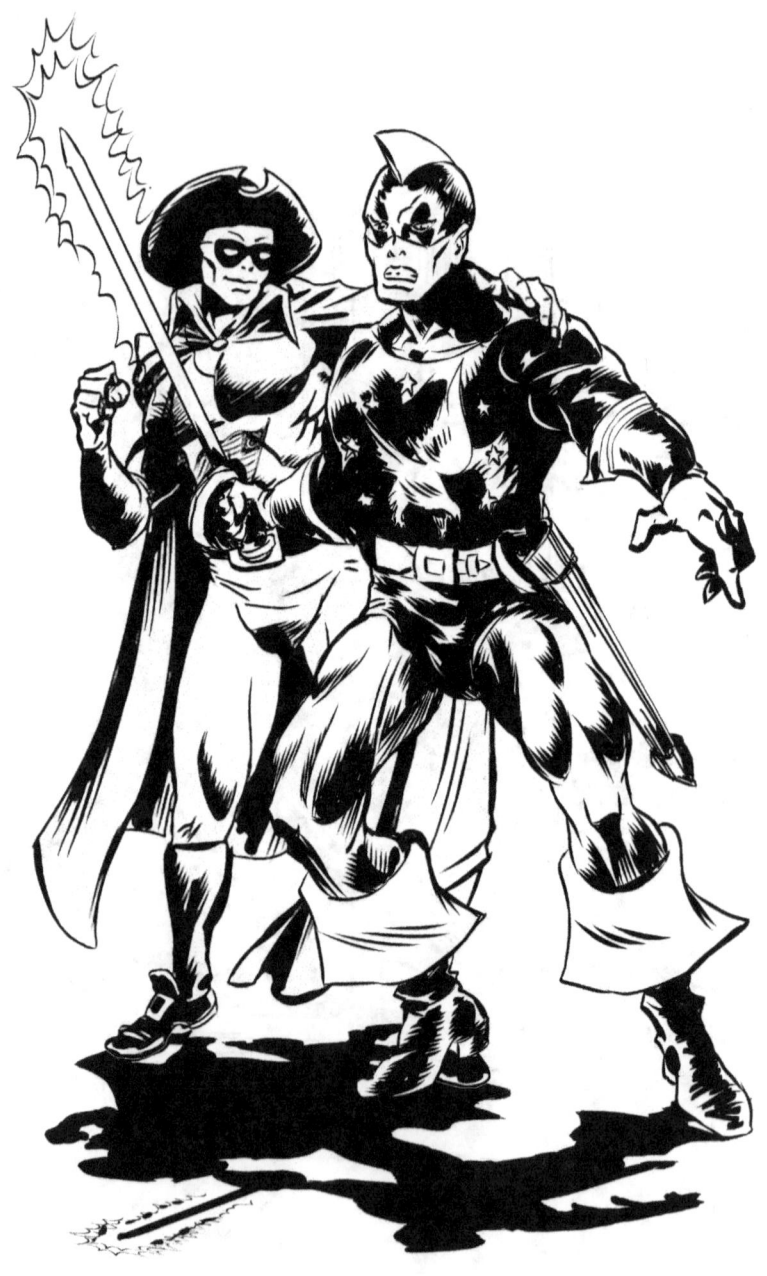

PHANTOM DETECTIVE - NEDOR

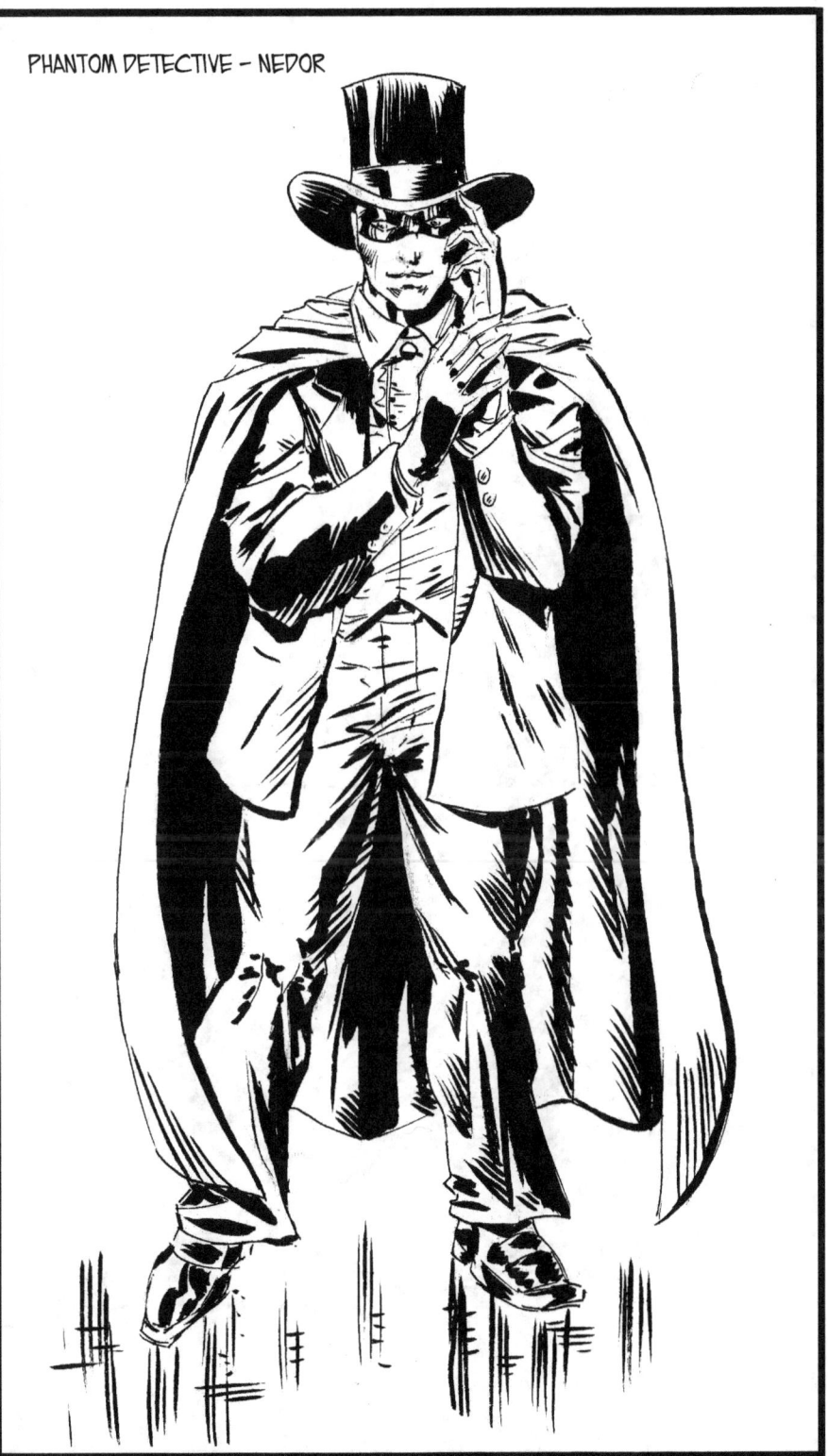

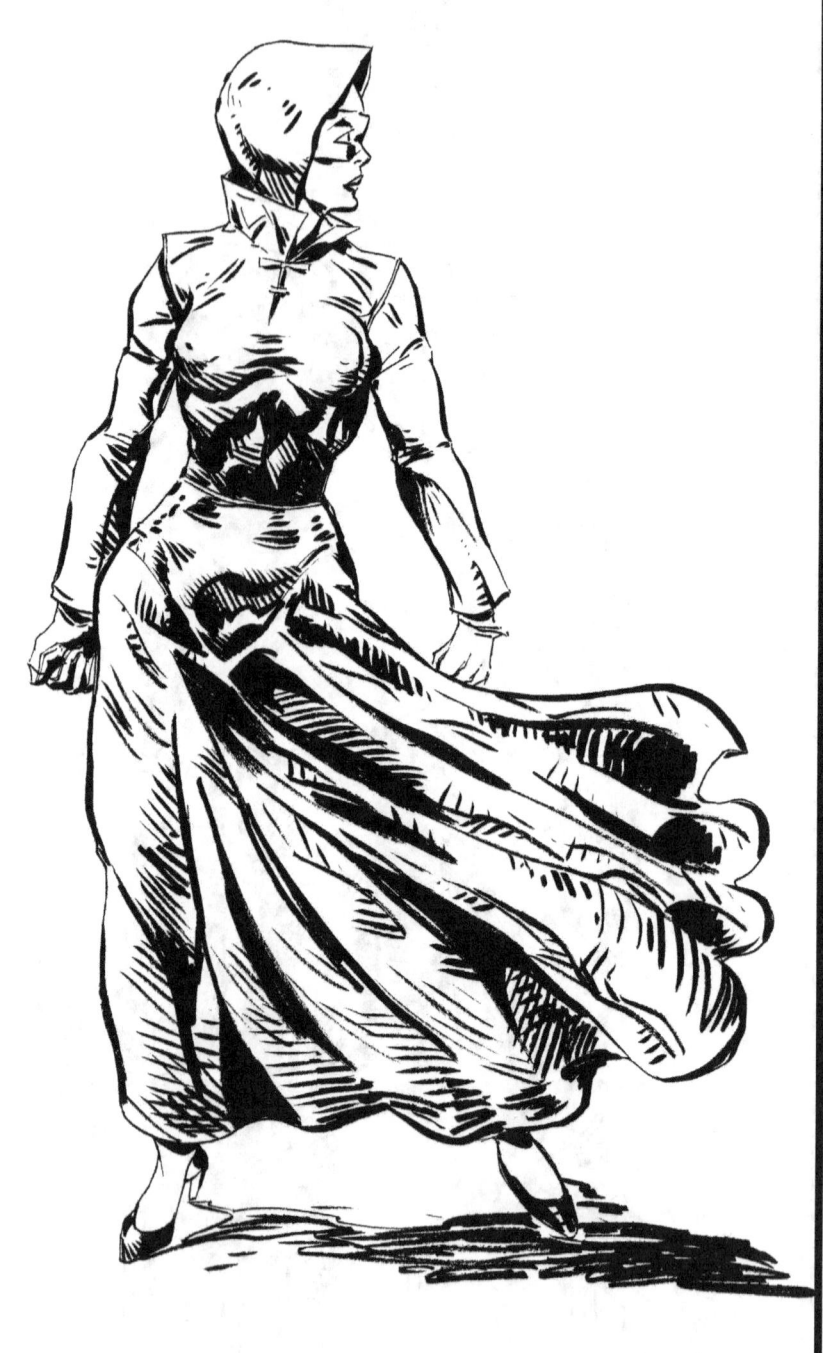

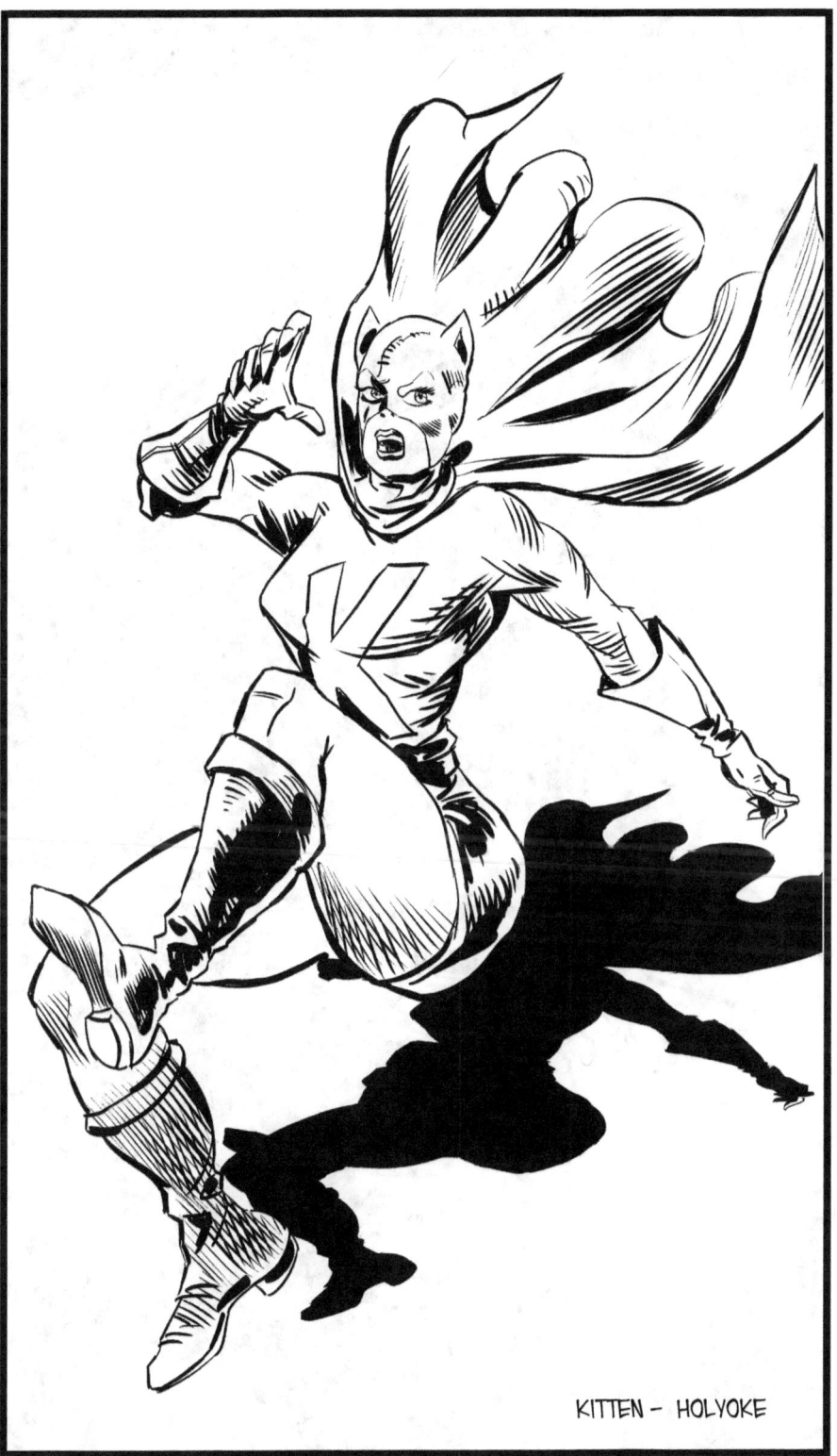

KITTEN - HOLYOKE

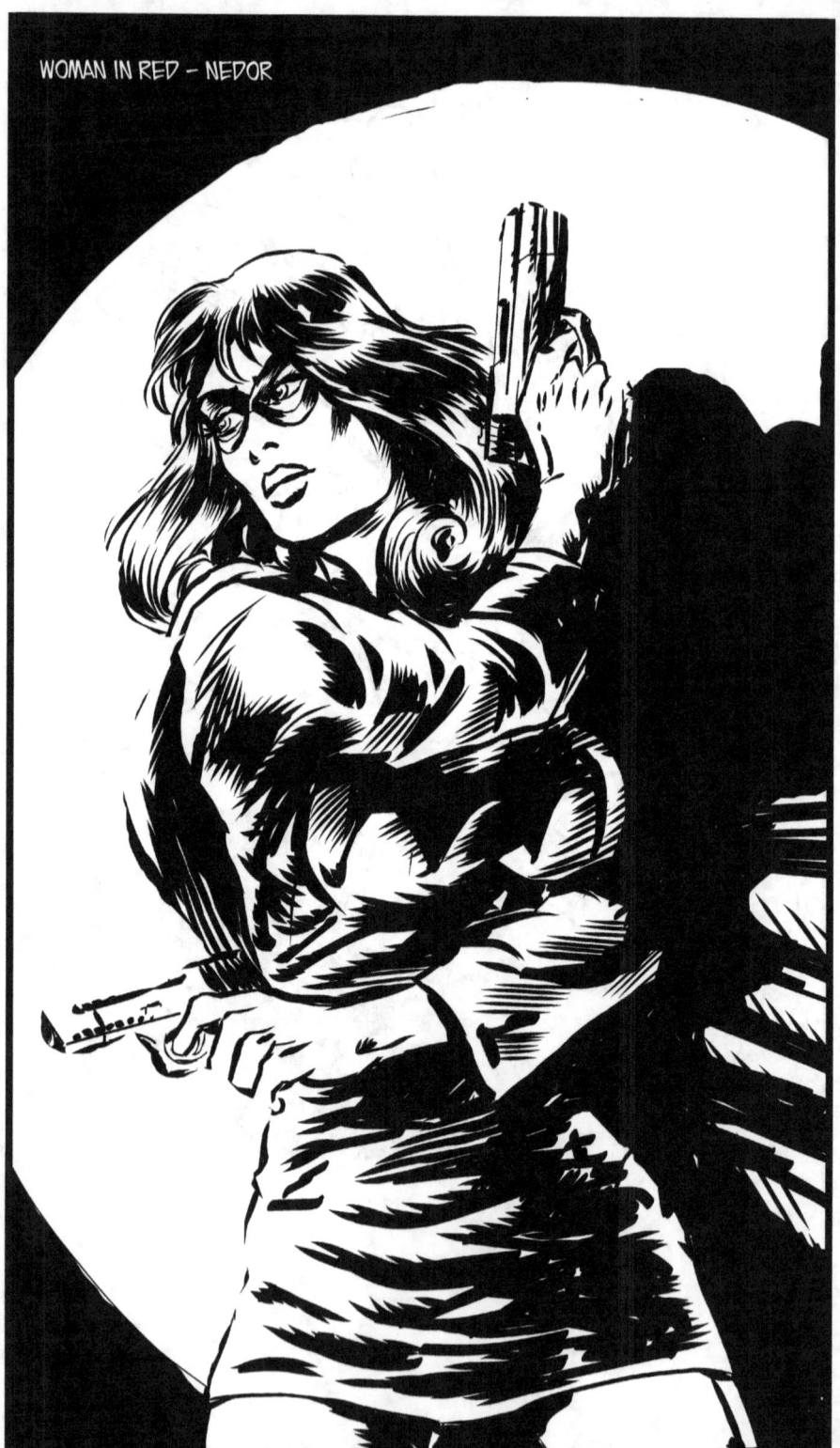

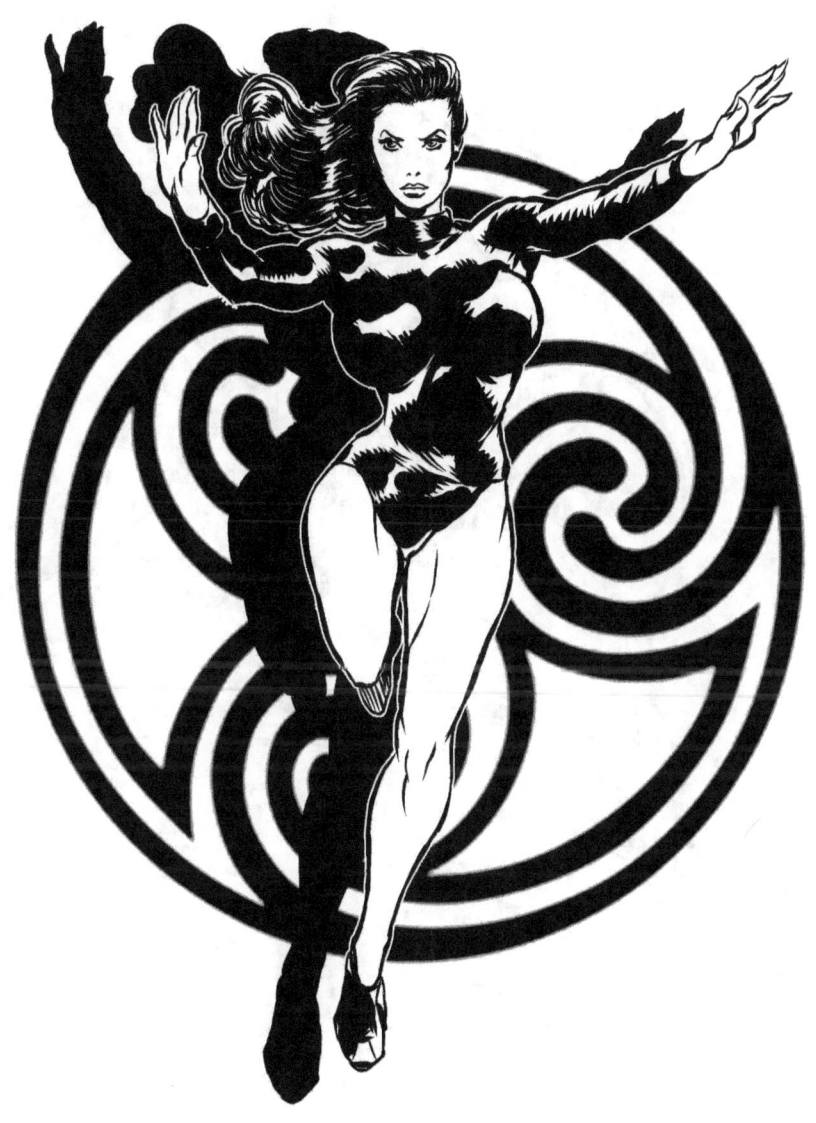

AMAZONA - FICTION HOUSE

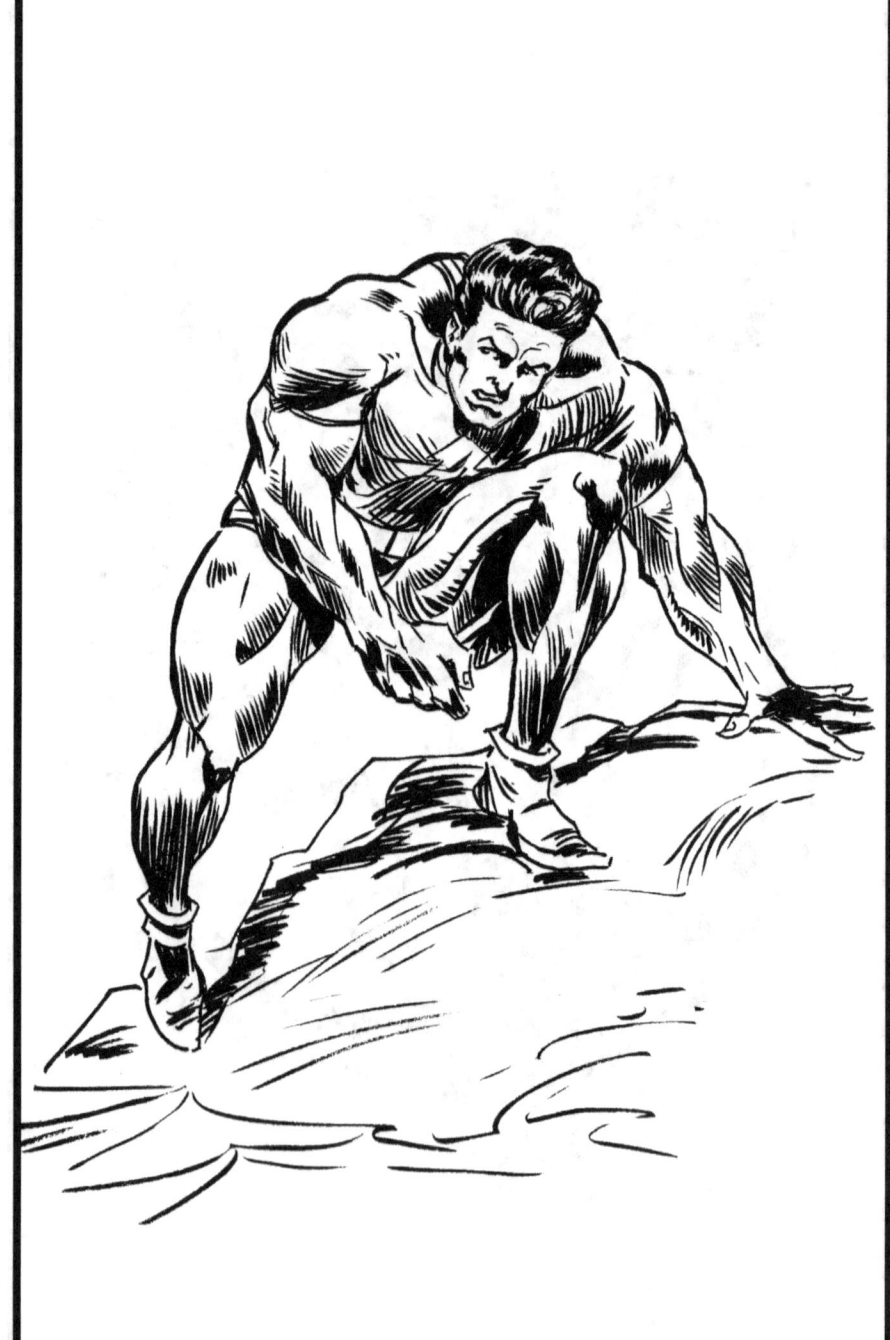

CAPTAIN FUTURE - NEDOR

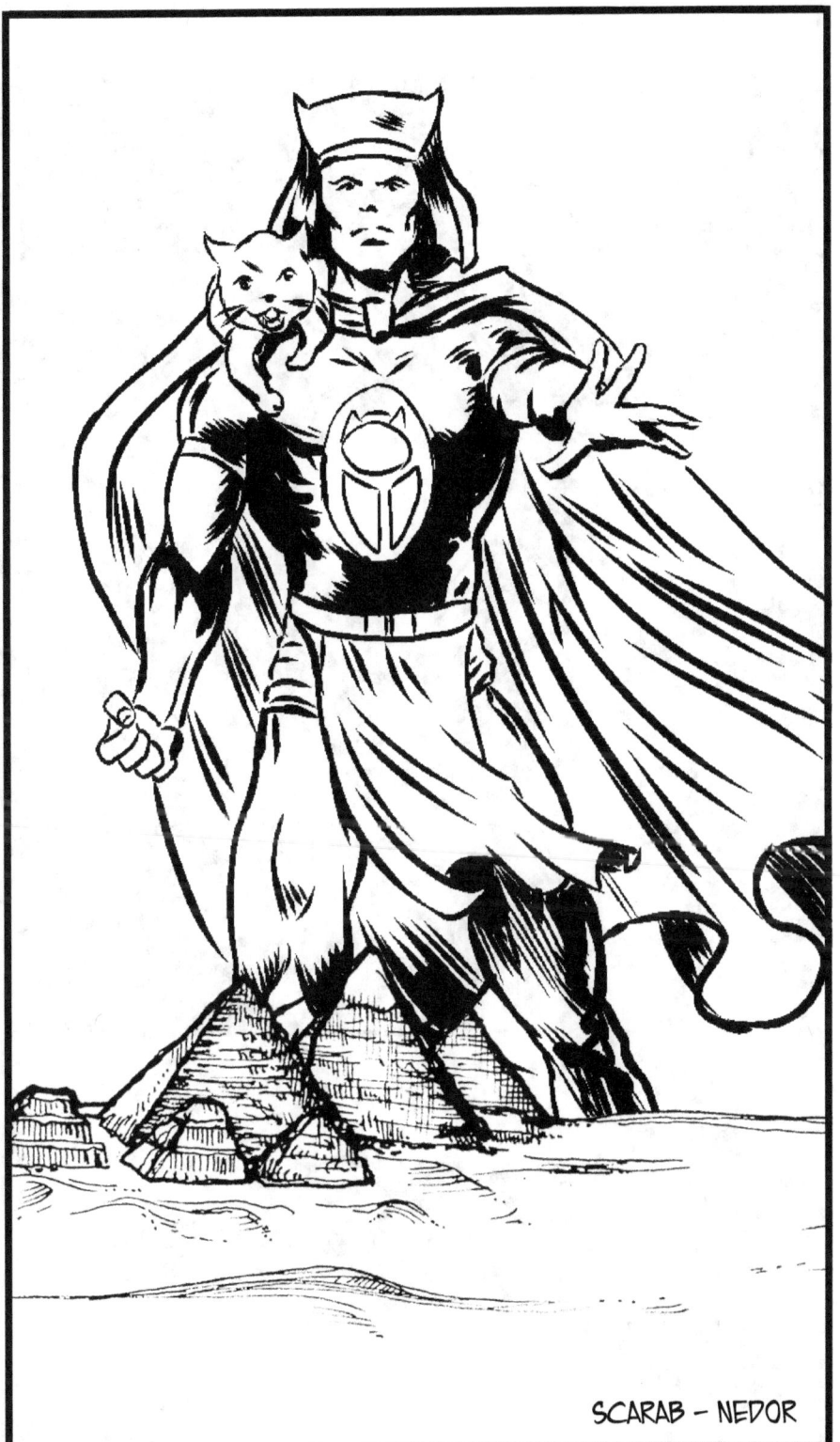

SCARAB - NEDOR

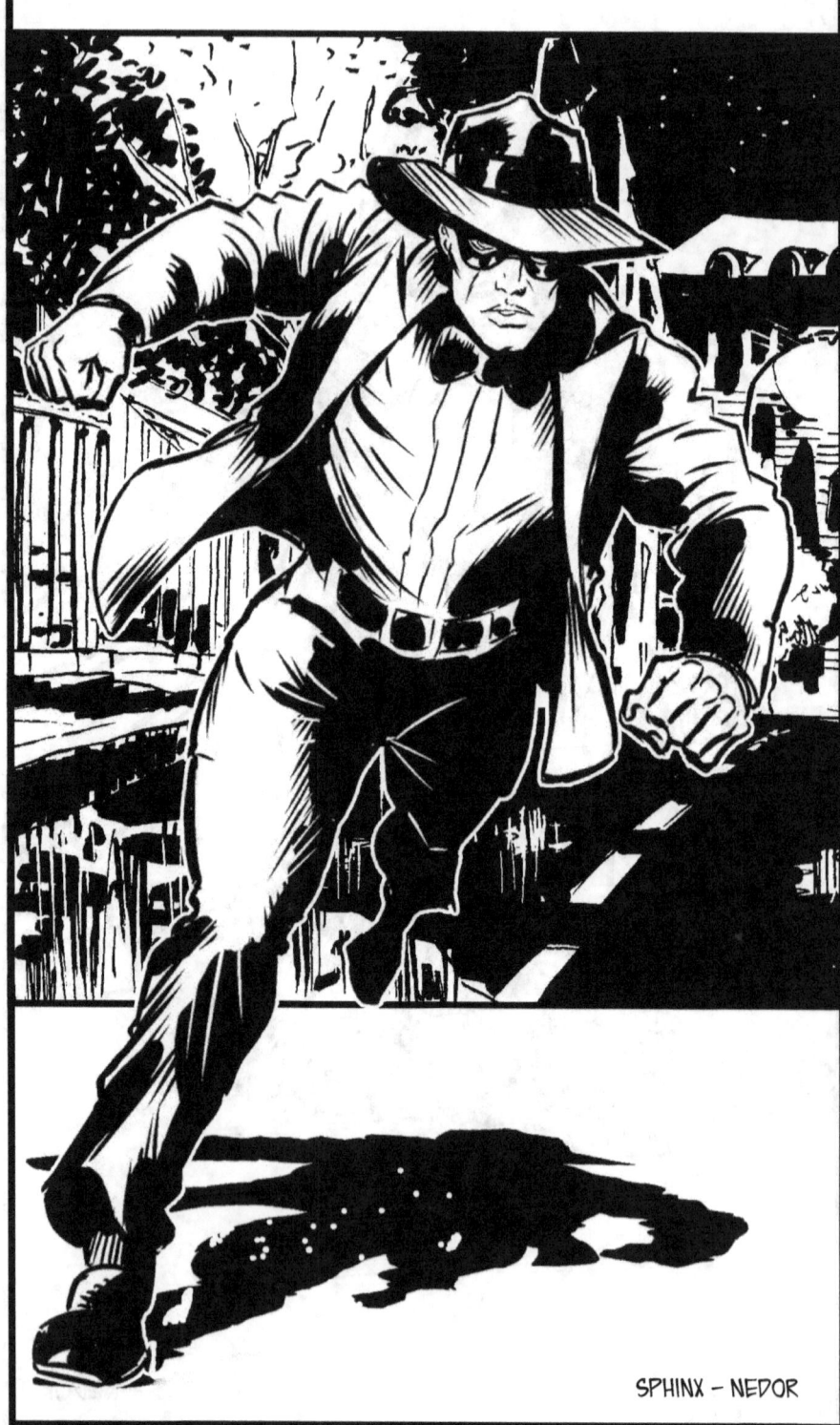

SPHINX - NEDOR

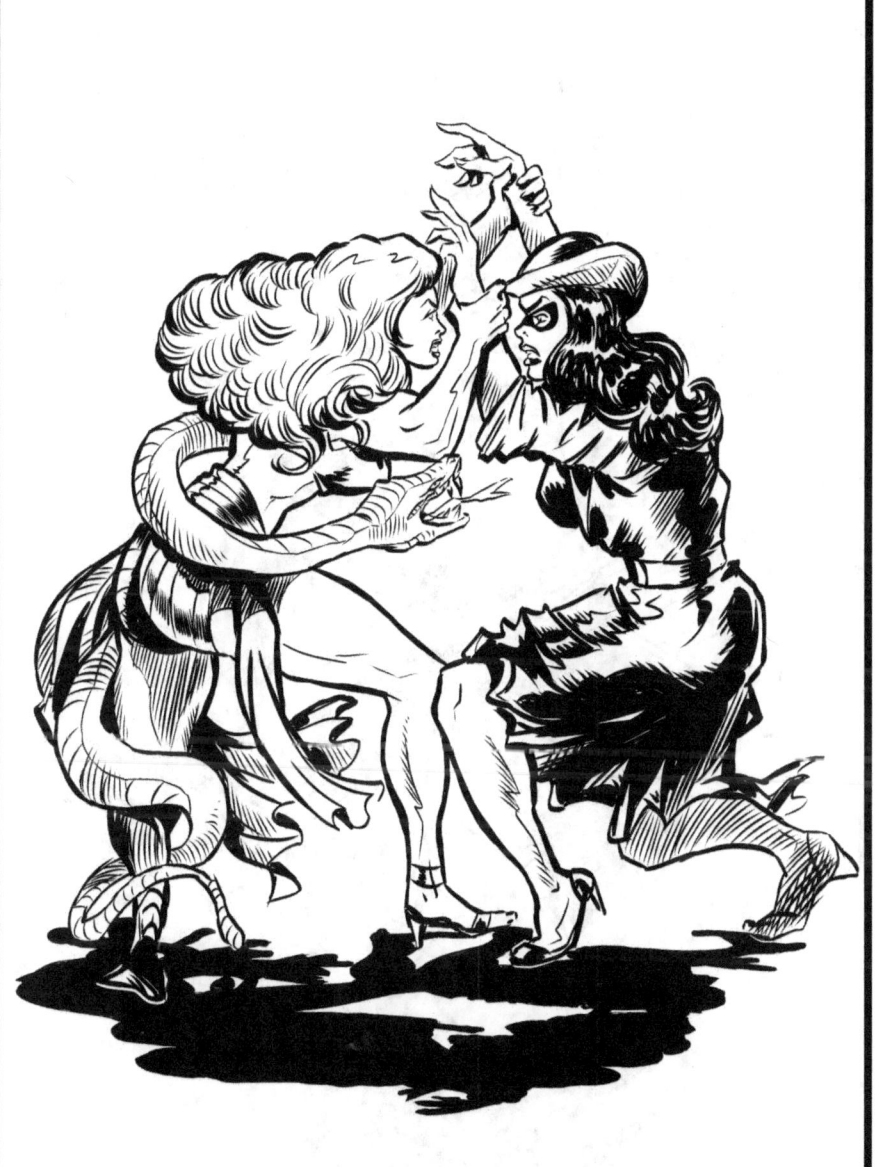

LADY SERPENT VS RED ANN – NEDOR

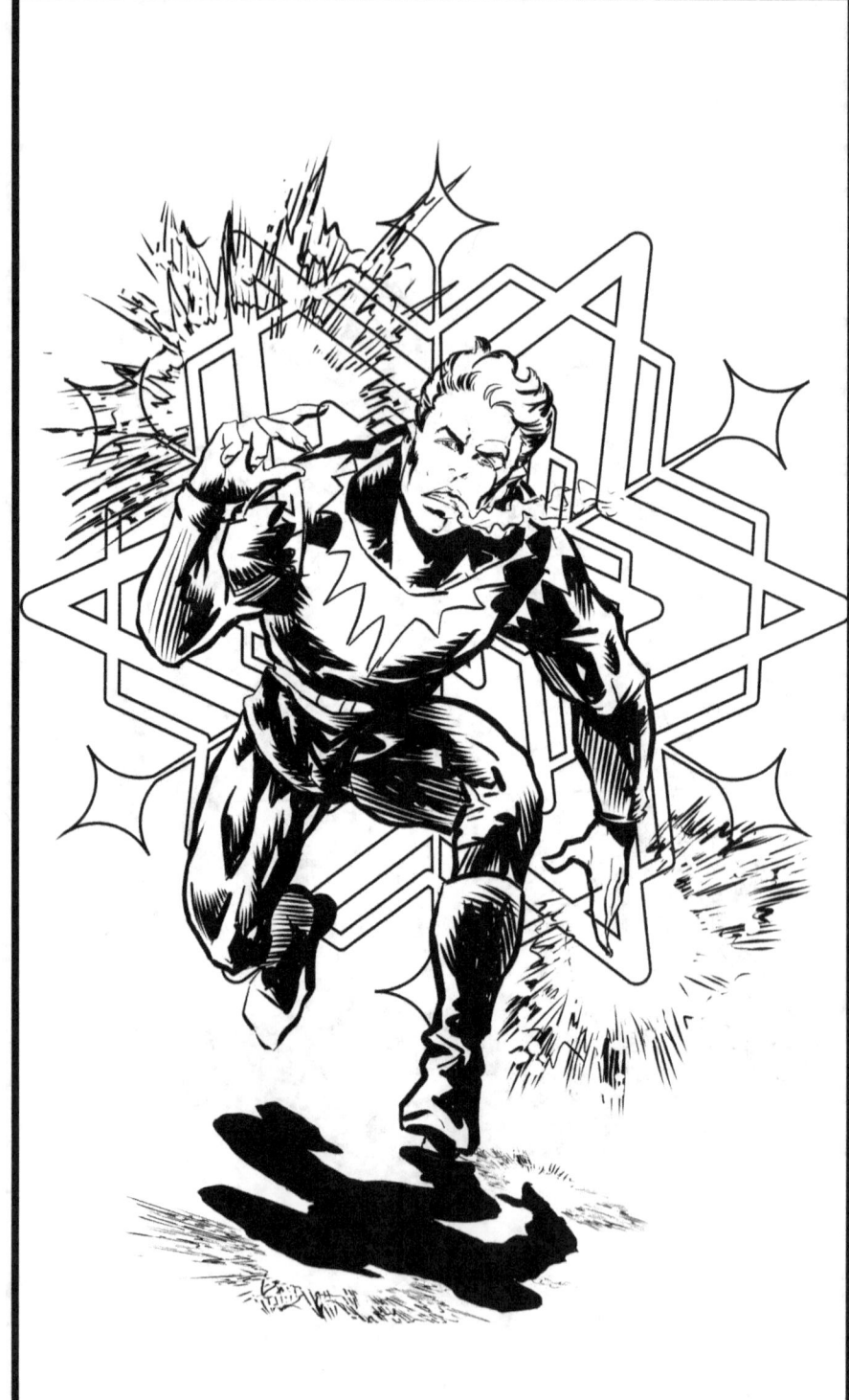

DR. FROST - PRIZE

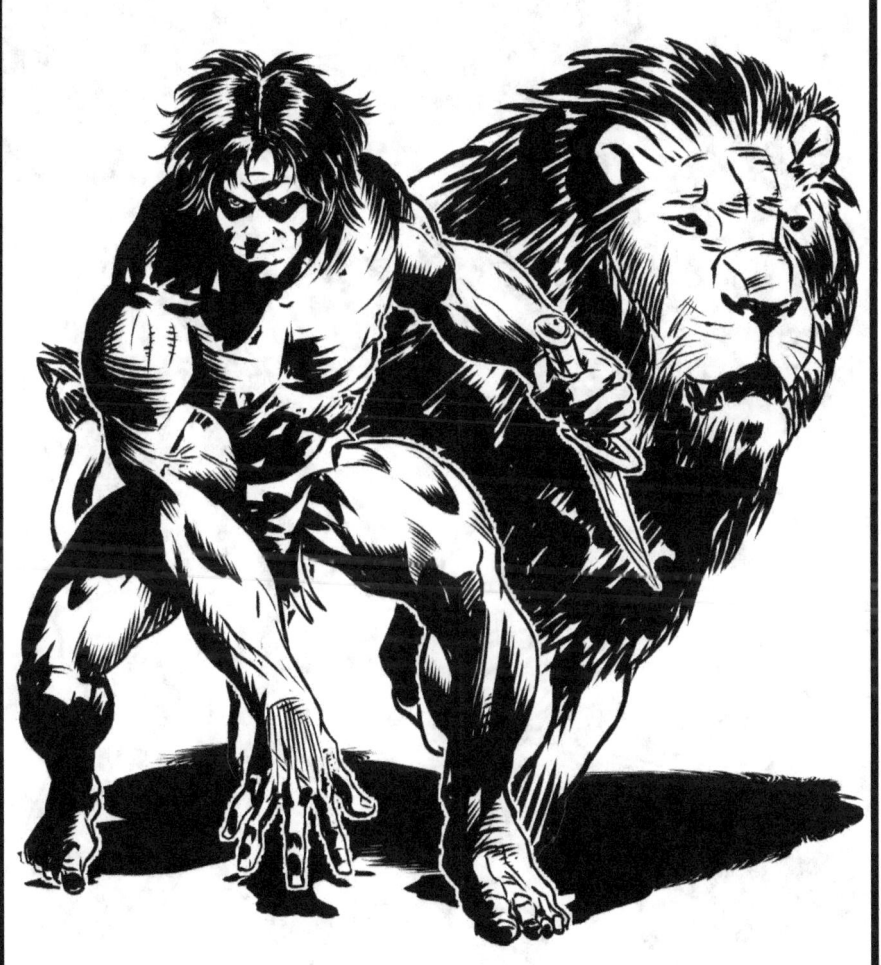

KAZA – AJAX–FARRELL

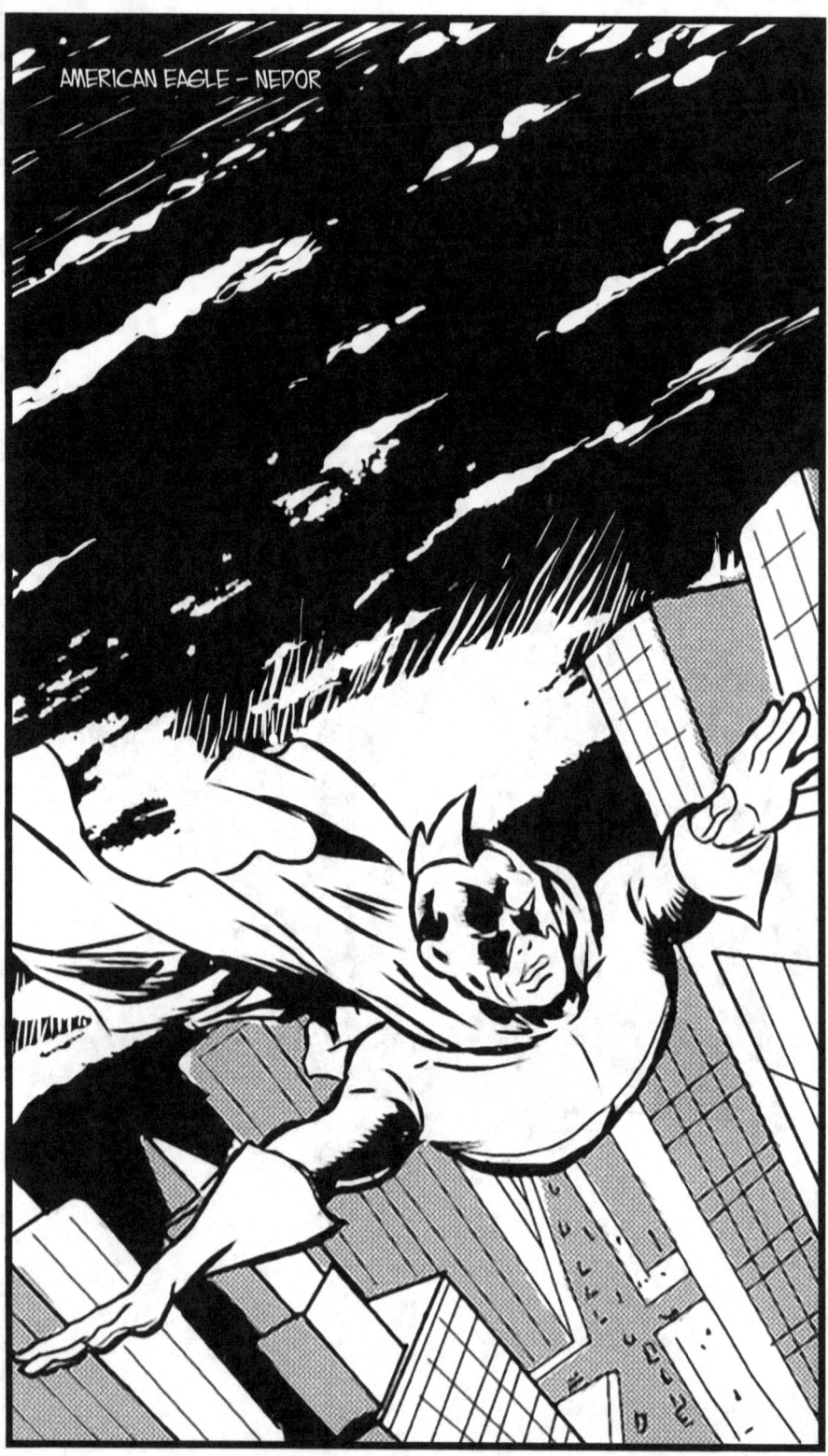

AMERICAN EAGLE - NEDOR

VEILED AVENGERS - CHESLER

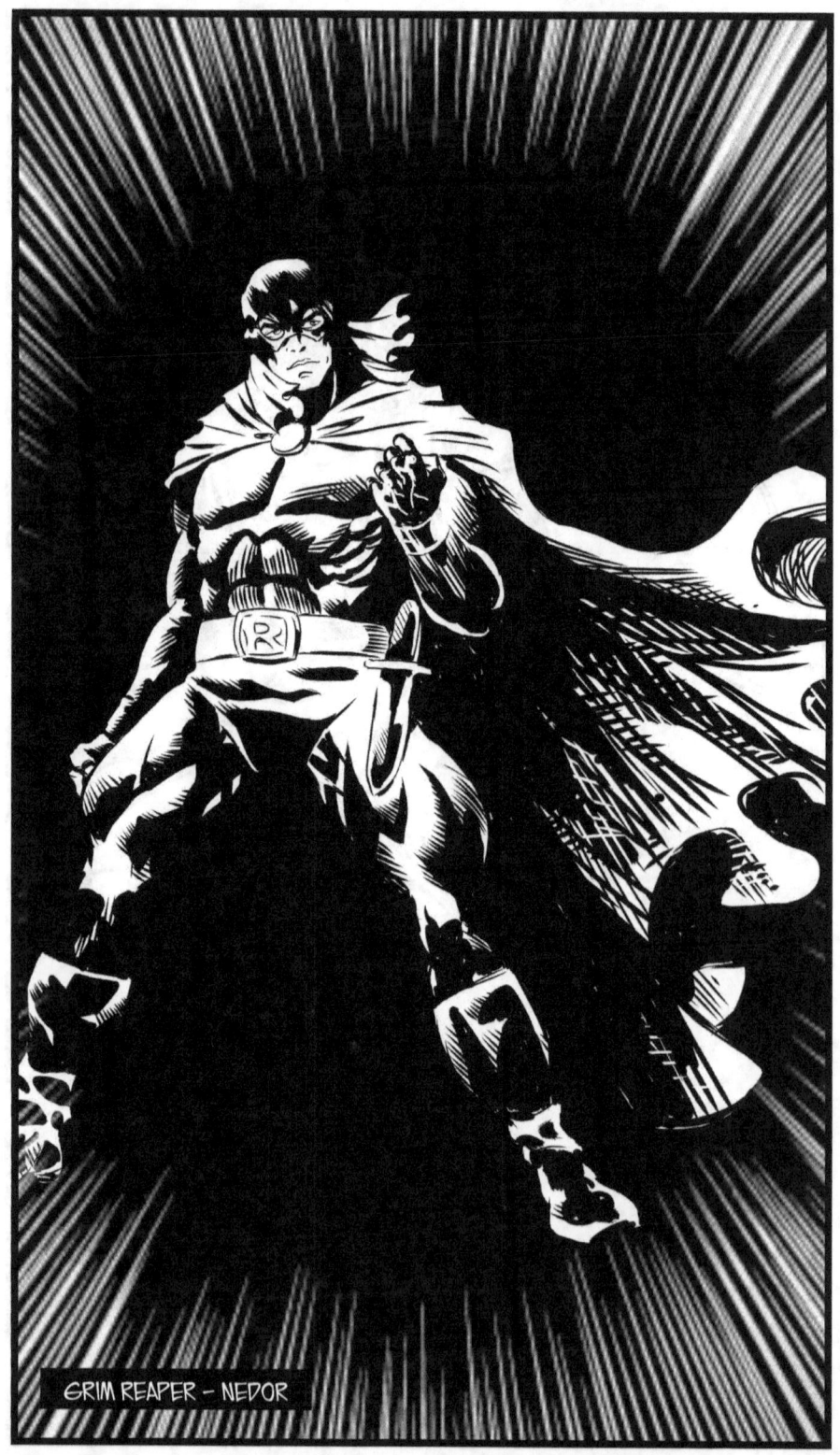

GRIM REAPER - NEDOR

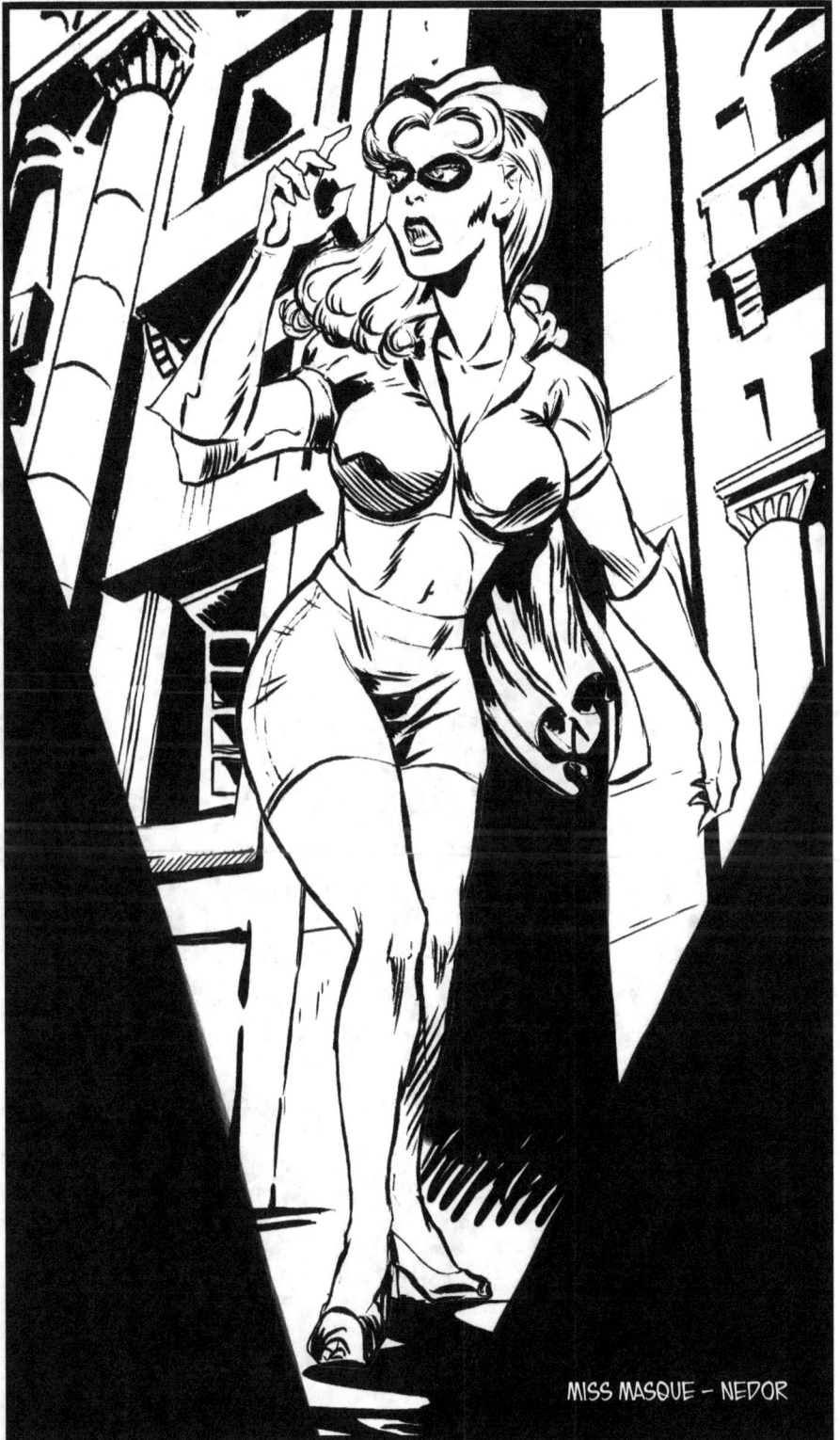

MISS MASQUE - NEDOR

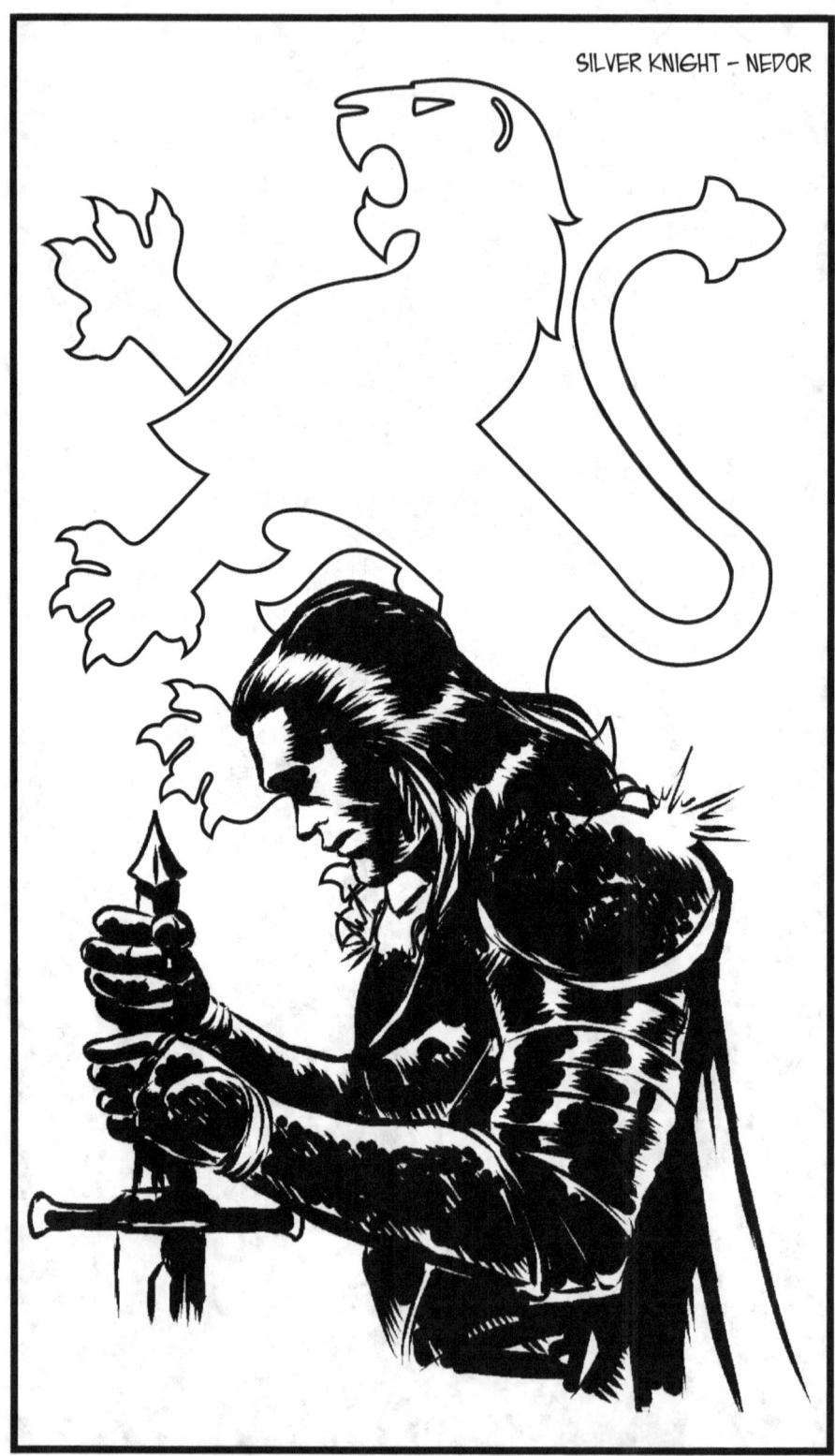

SILVER KNIGHT - NEDOR

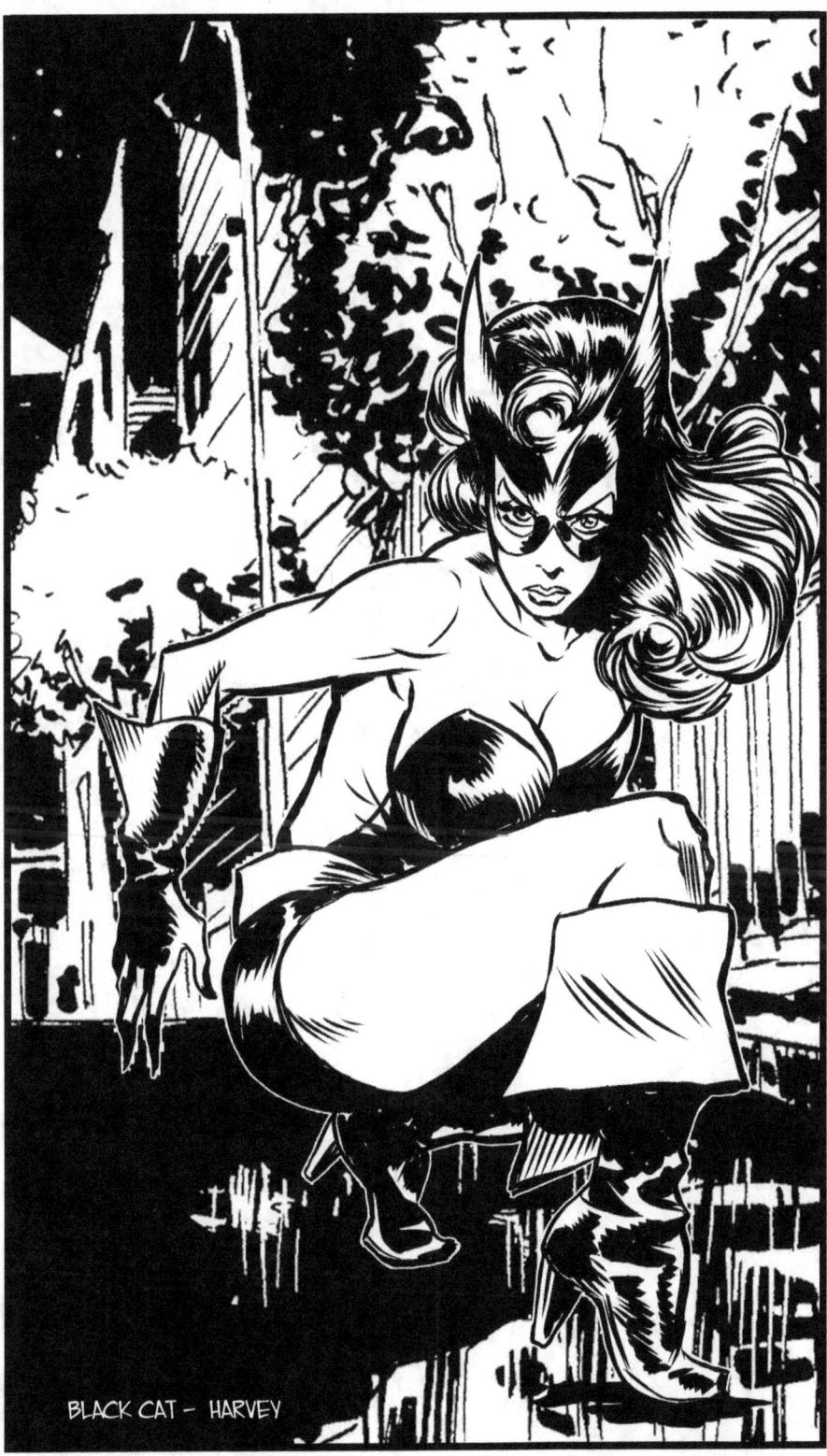

BLACK CAT - HARVEY

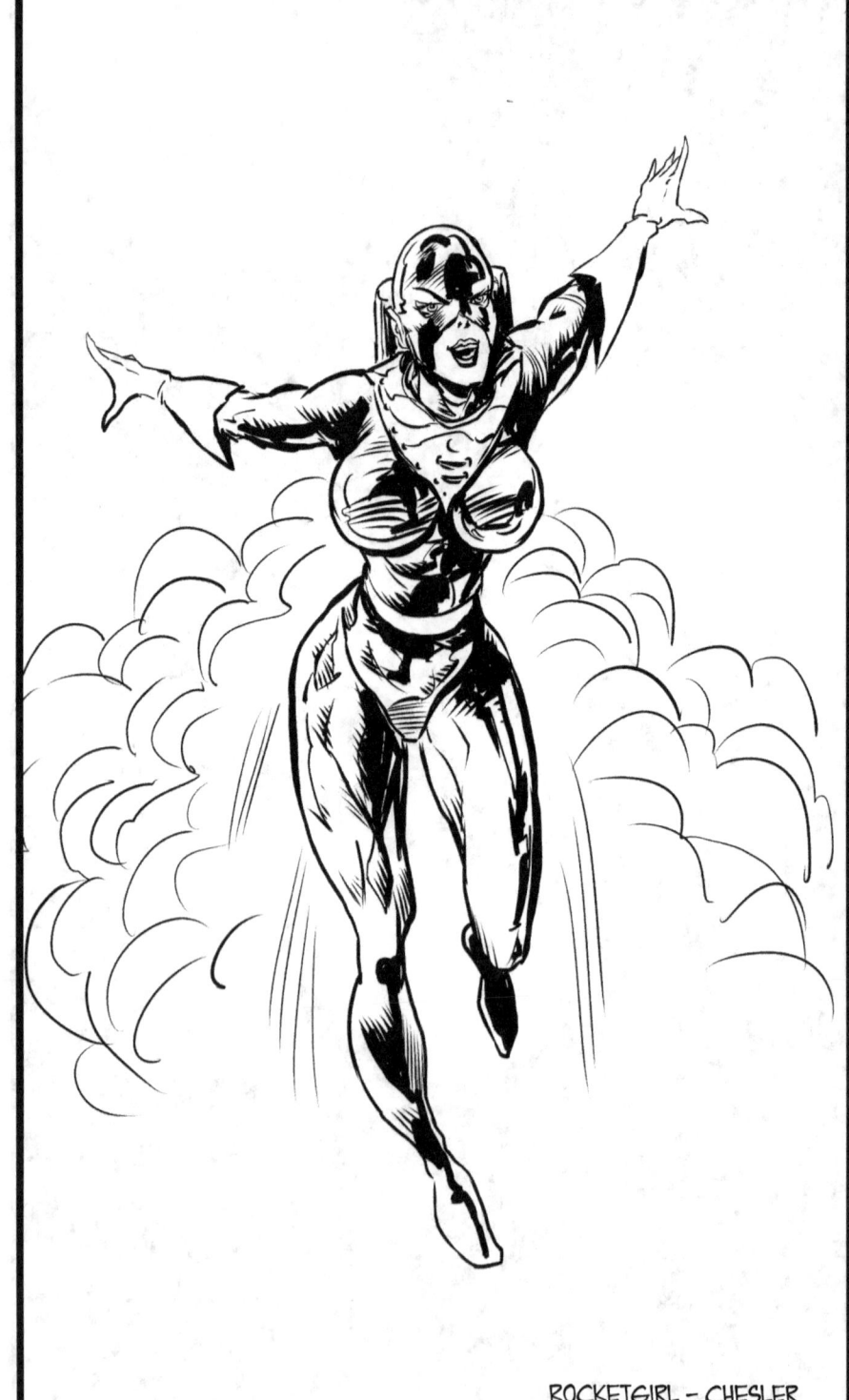

ROCKETGIRL - CHESLER

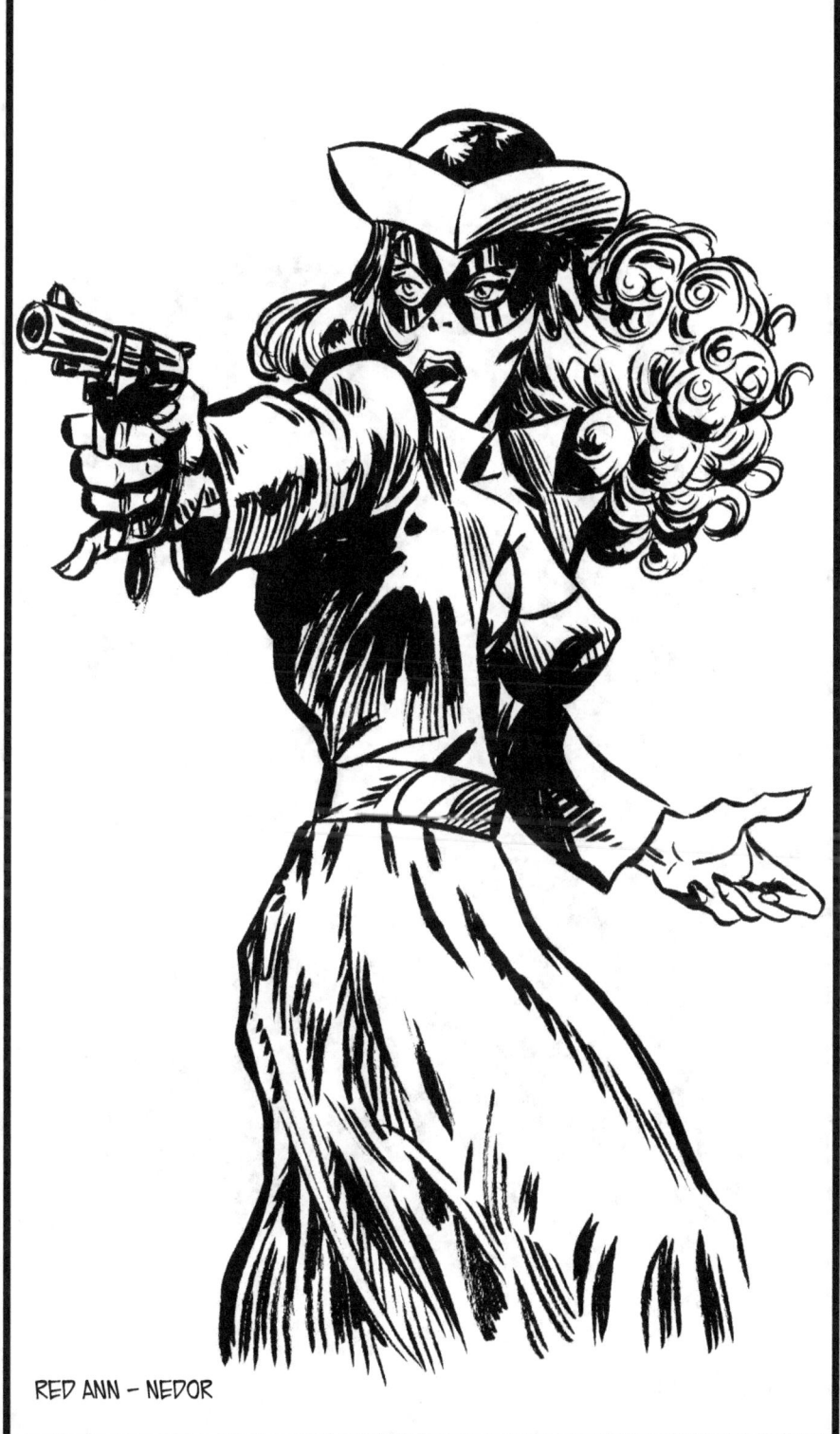

RED ANN - NEDOR

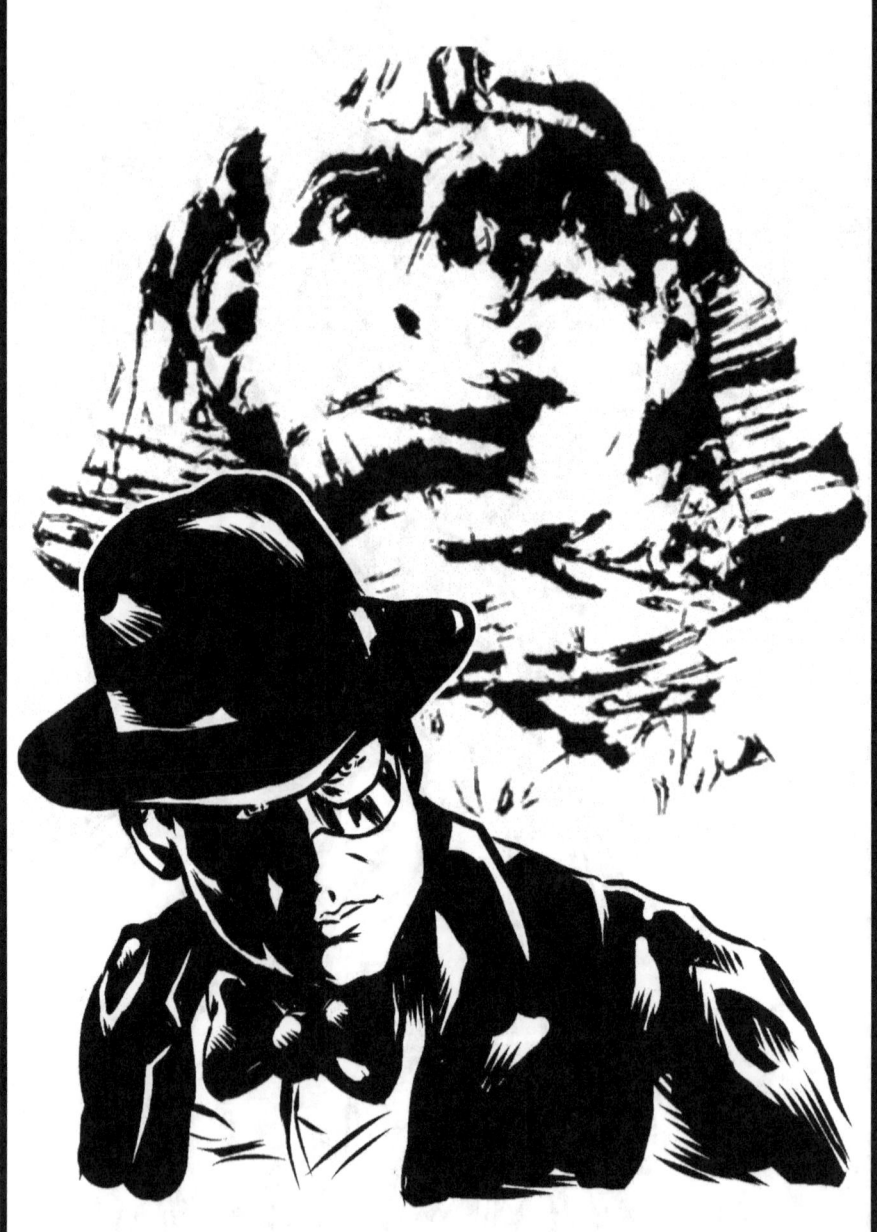

SPHINX – NEDOR

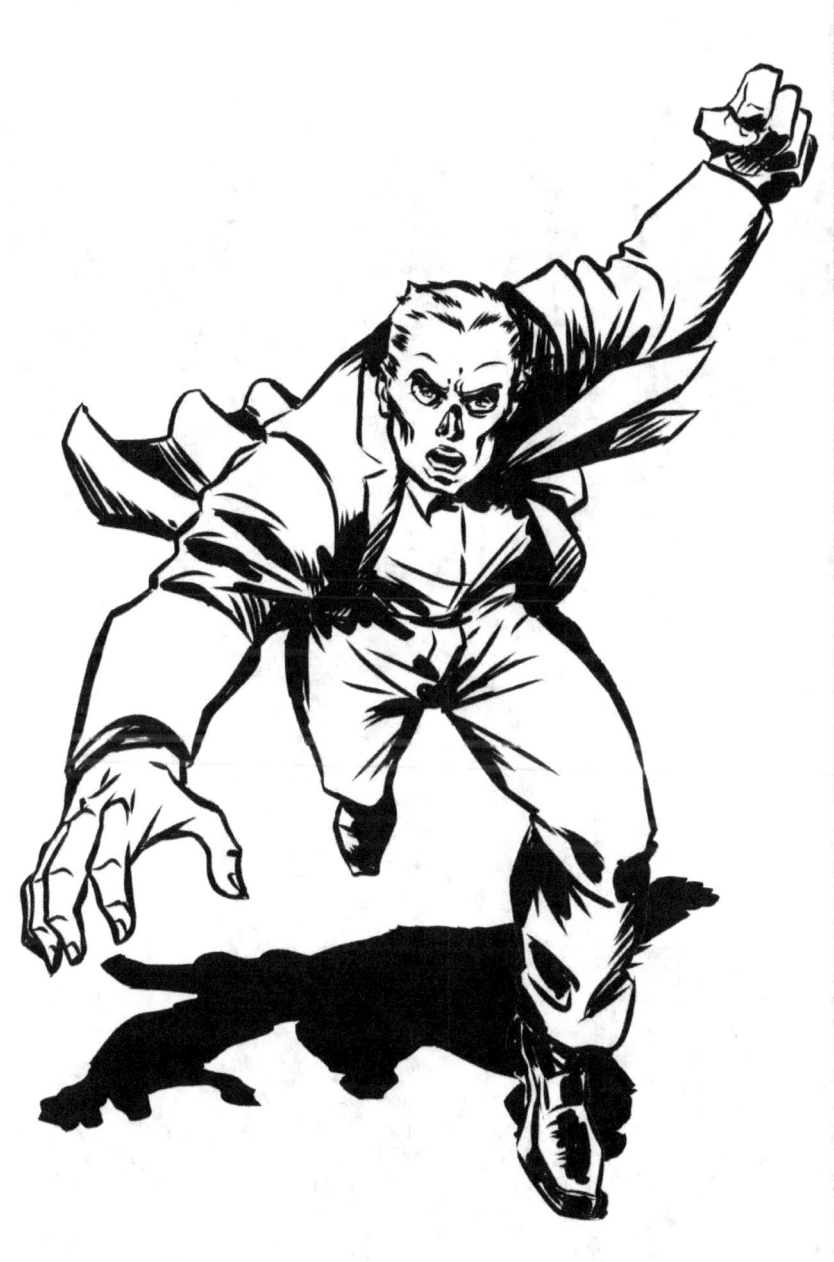

IRON SKULL - CENTAUR

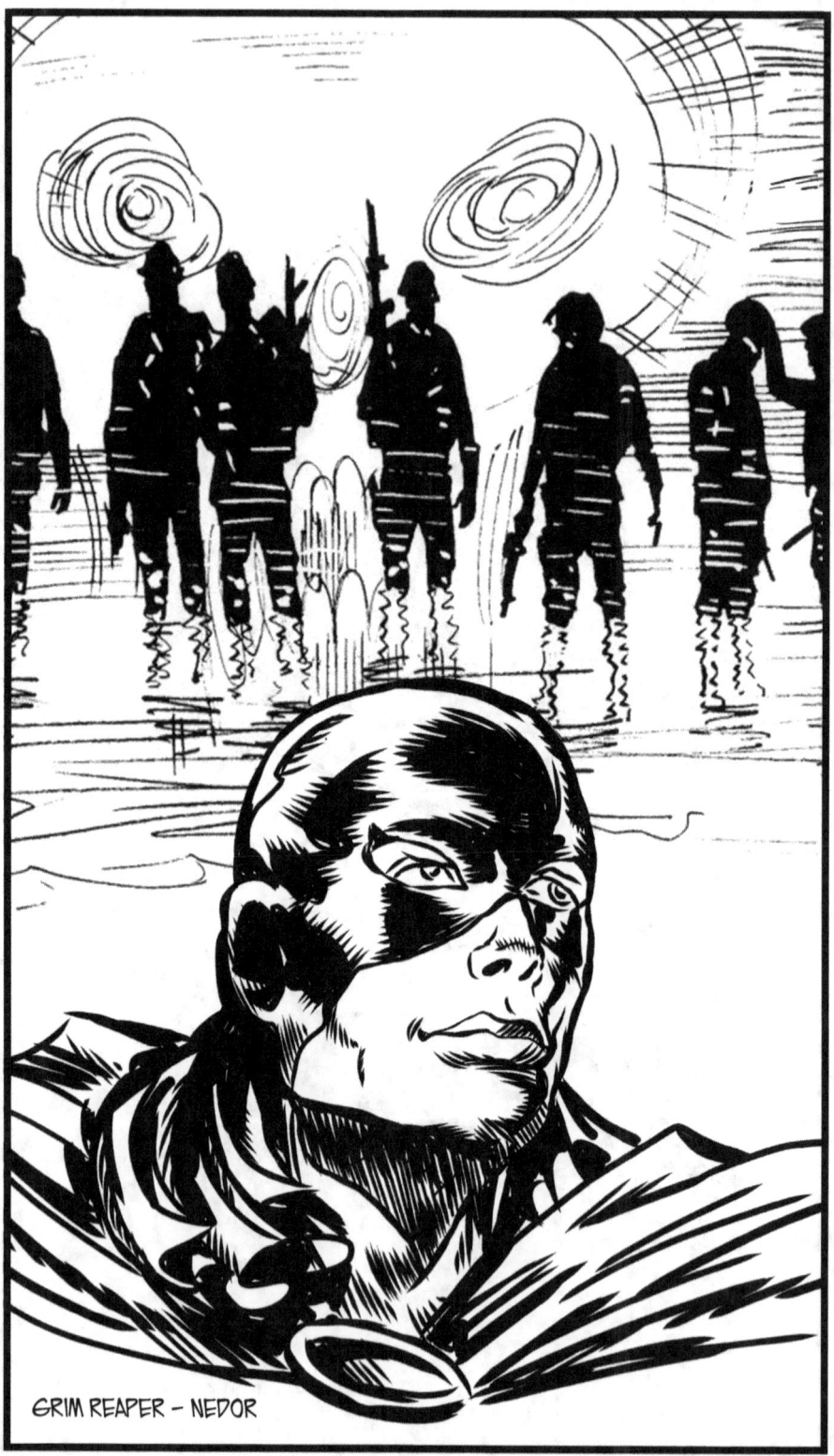

GRIM REAPER – NEDOR

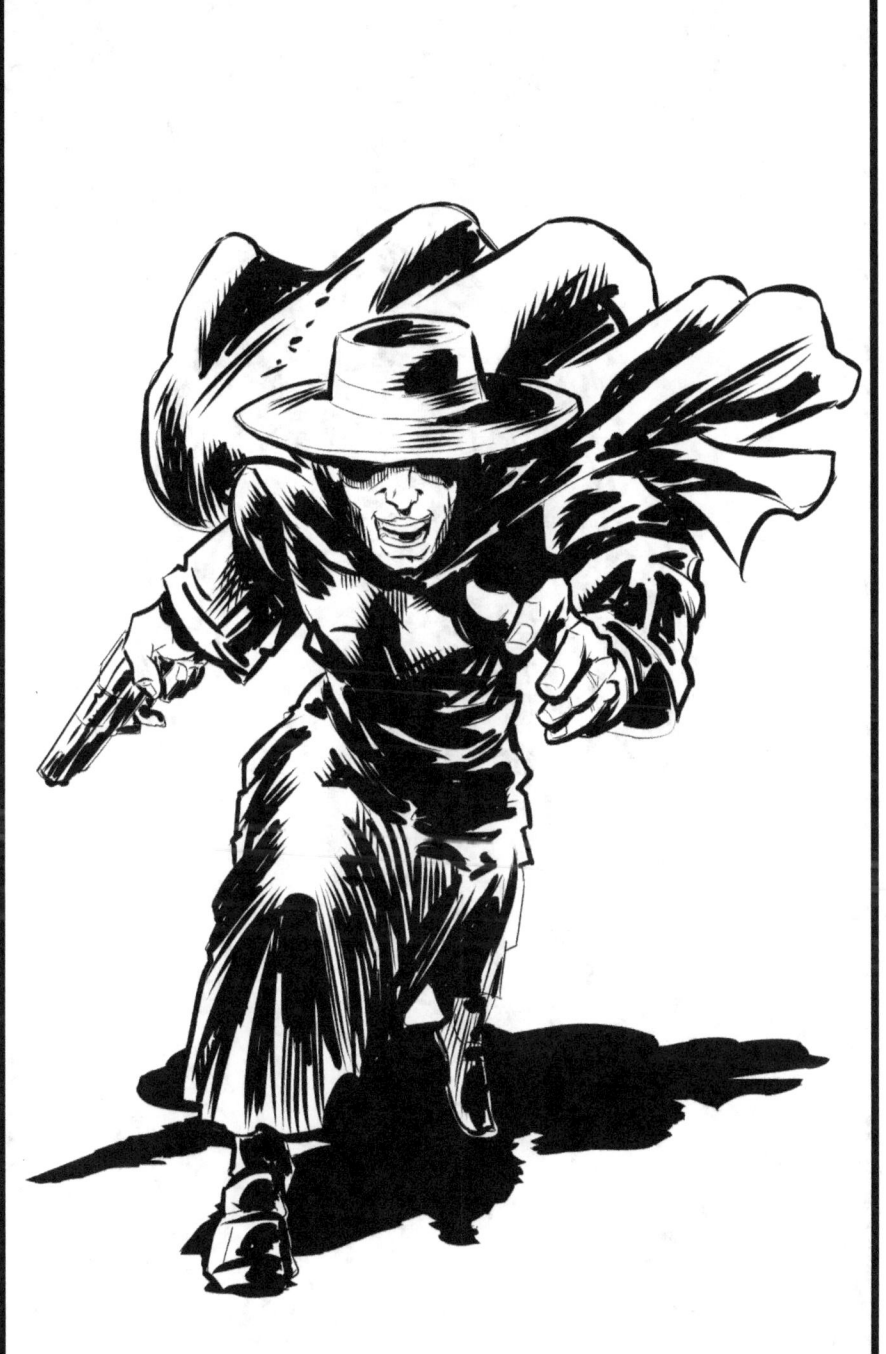

BLACK DWARF - CHESLER

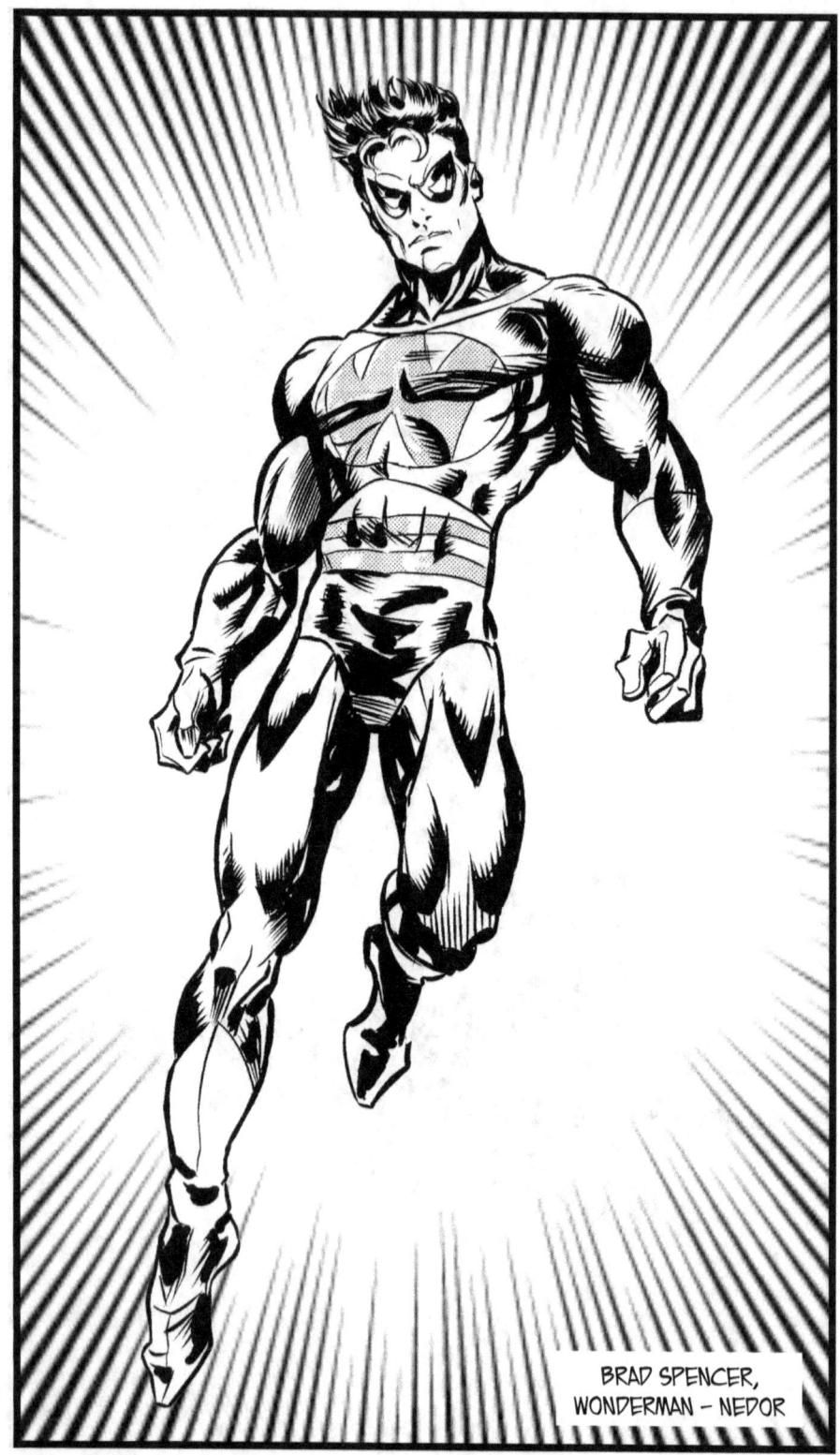

BRAD SPENCER,
WONDERMAN – NEDOR

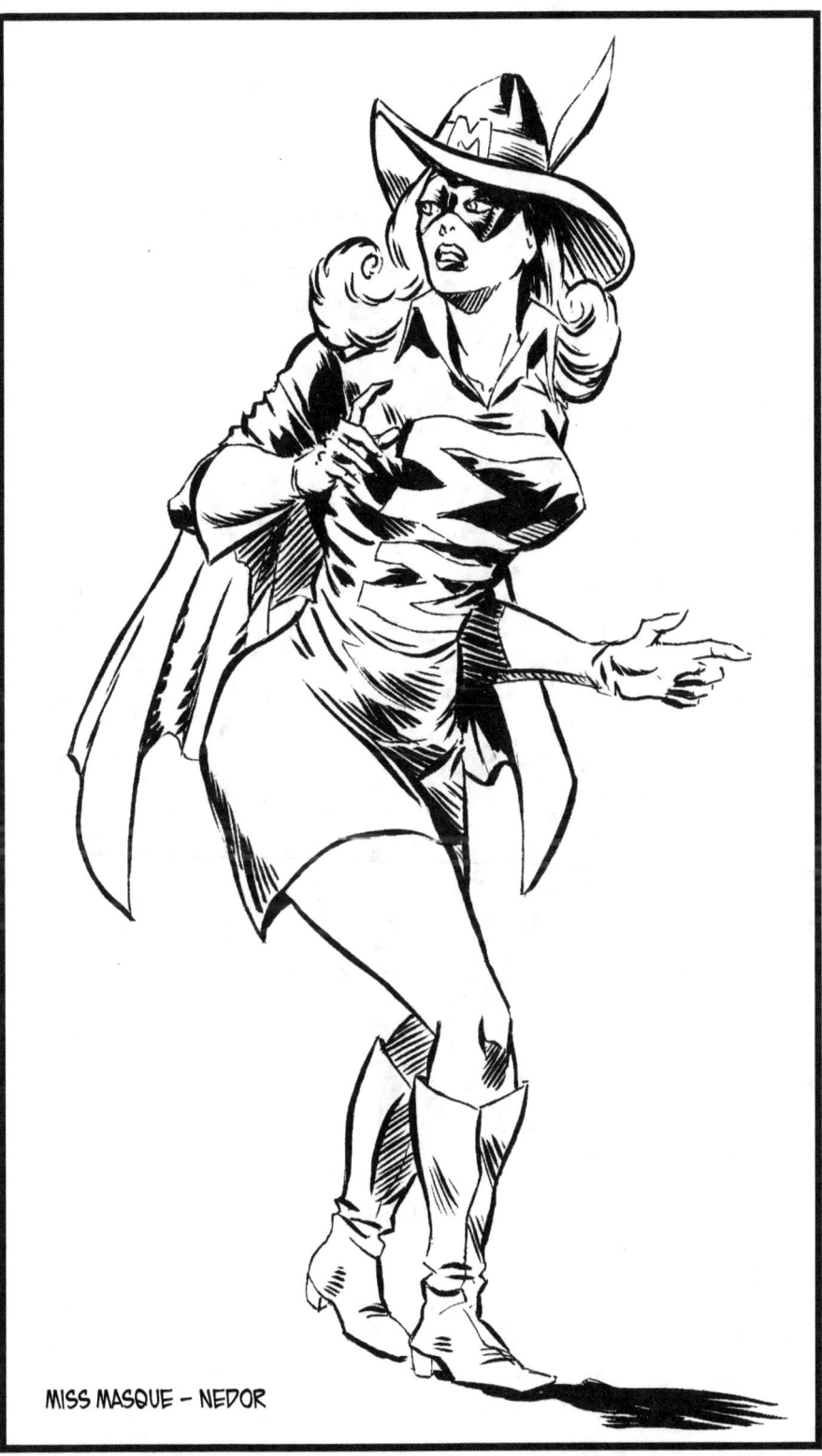

MISS MASQUE – NEDOR

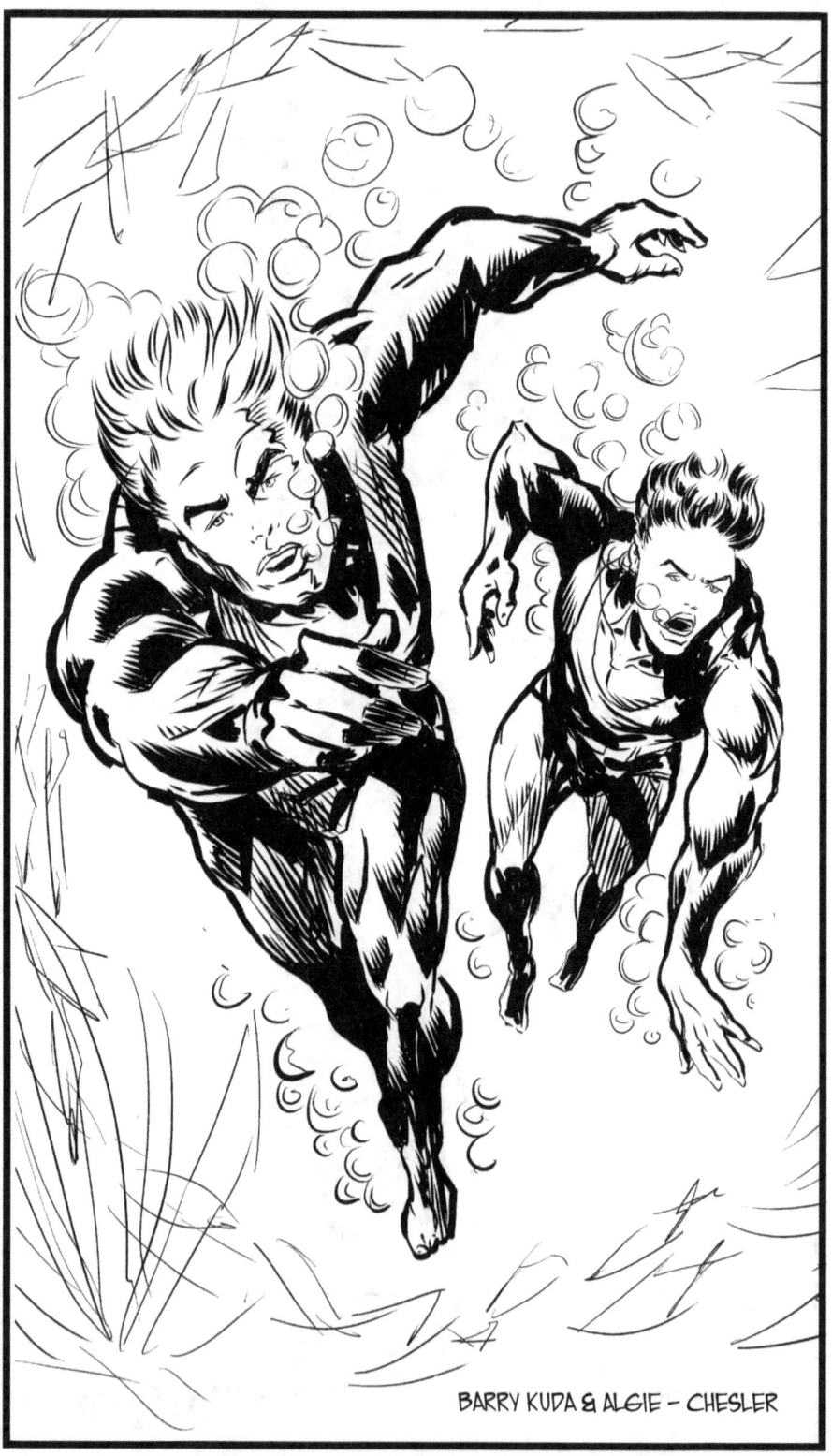

BARRY KUDA & ALGIE - CHESLER

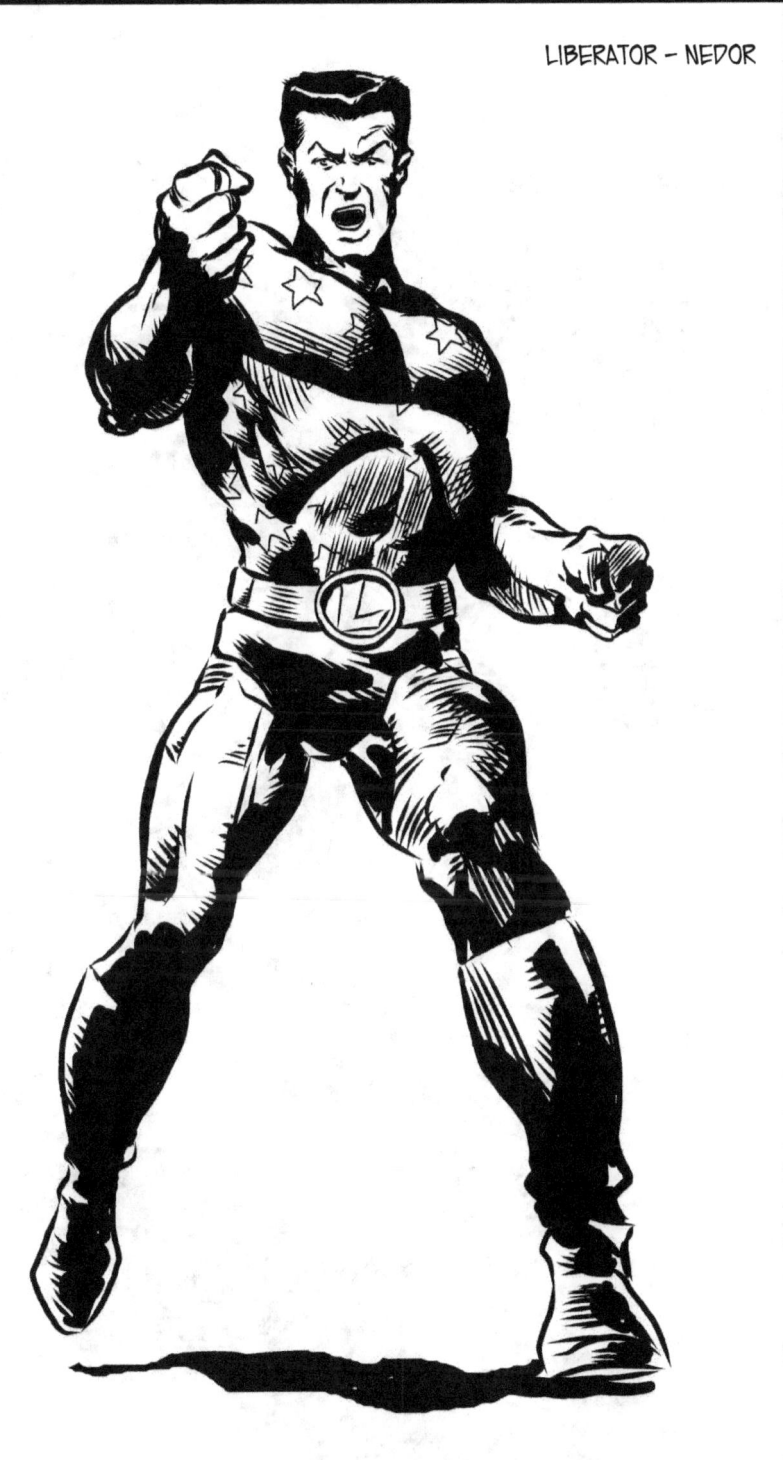

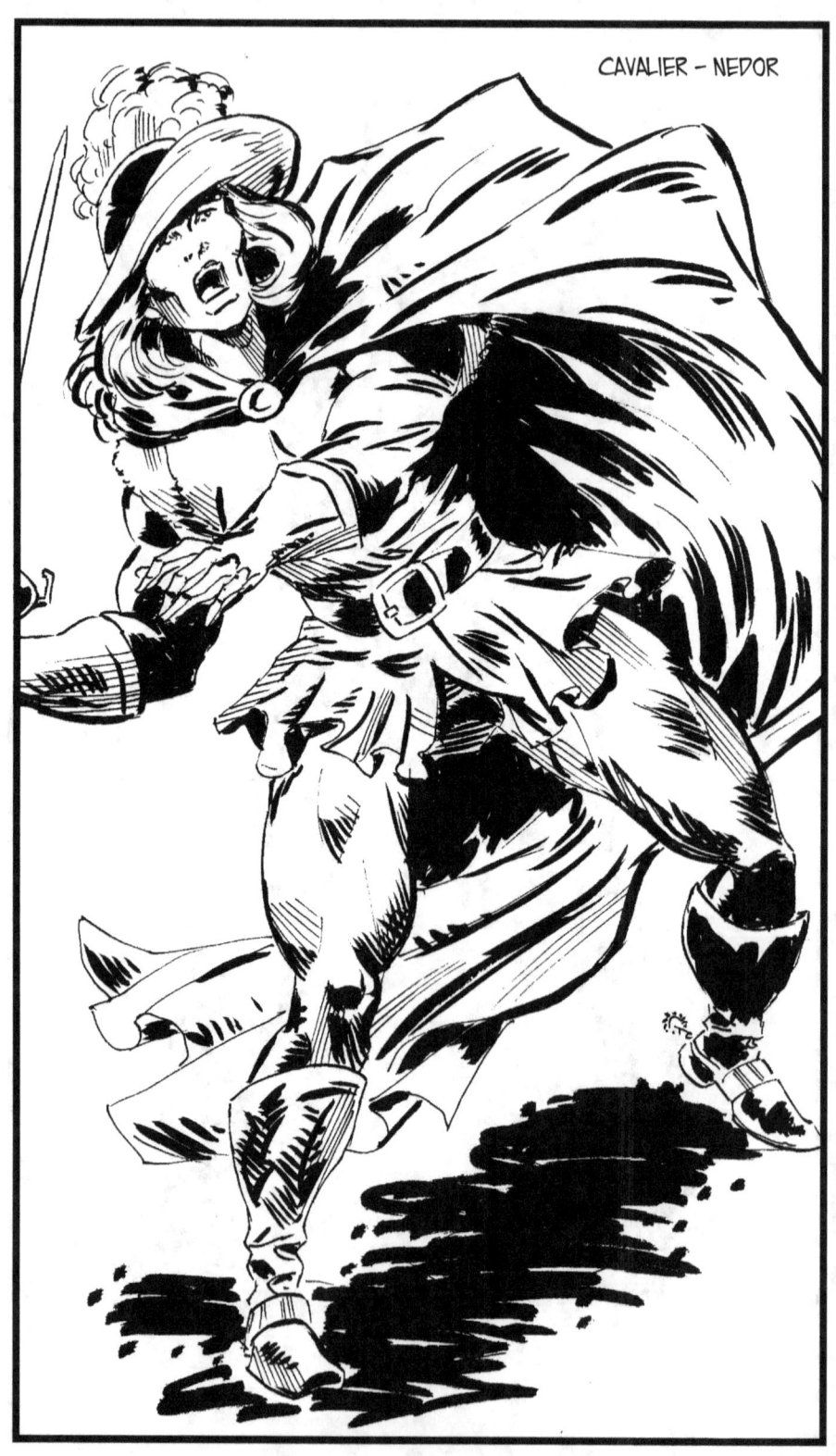

CAVALIER - NEDOR

DR. VAMPIRE - CHESLER

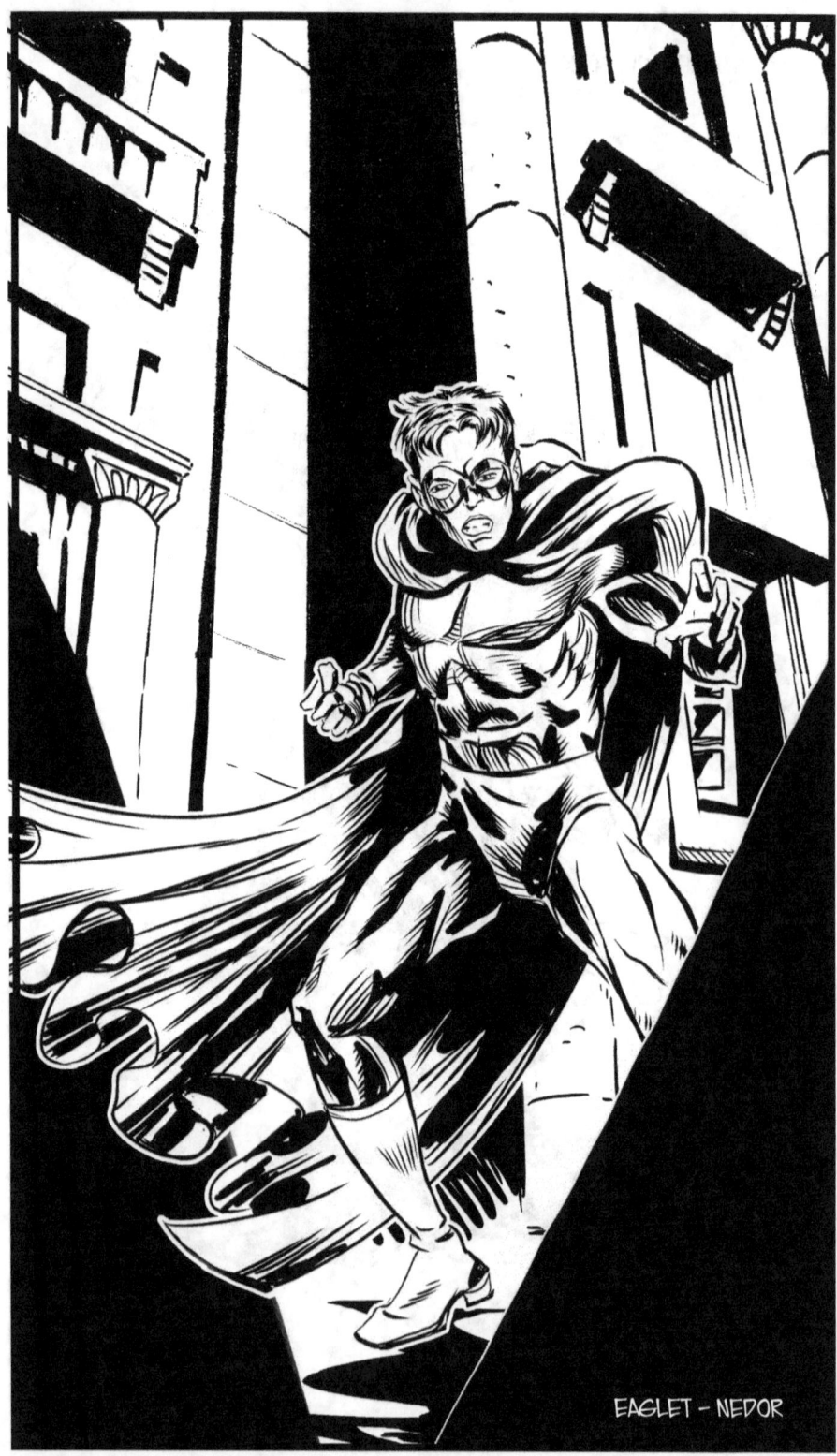

EAGLET - NEDOR

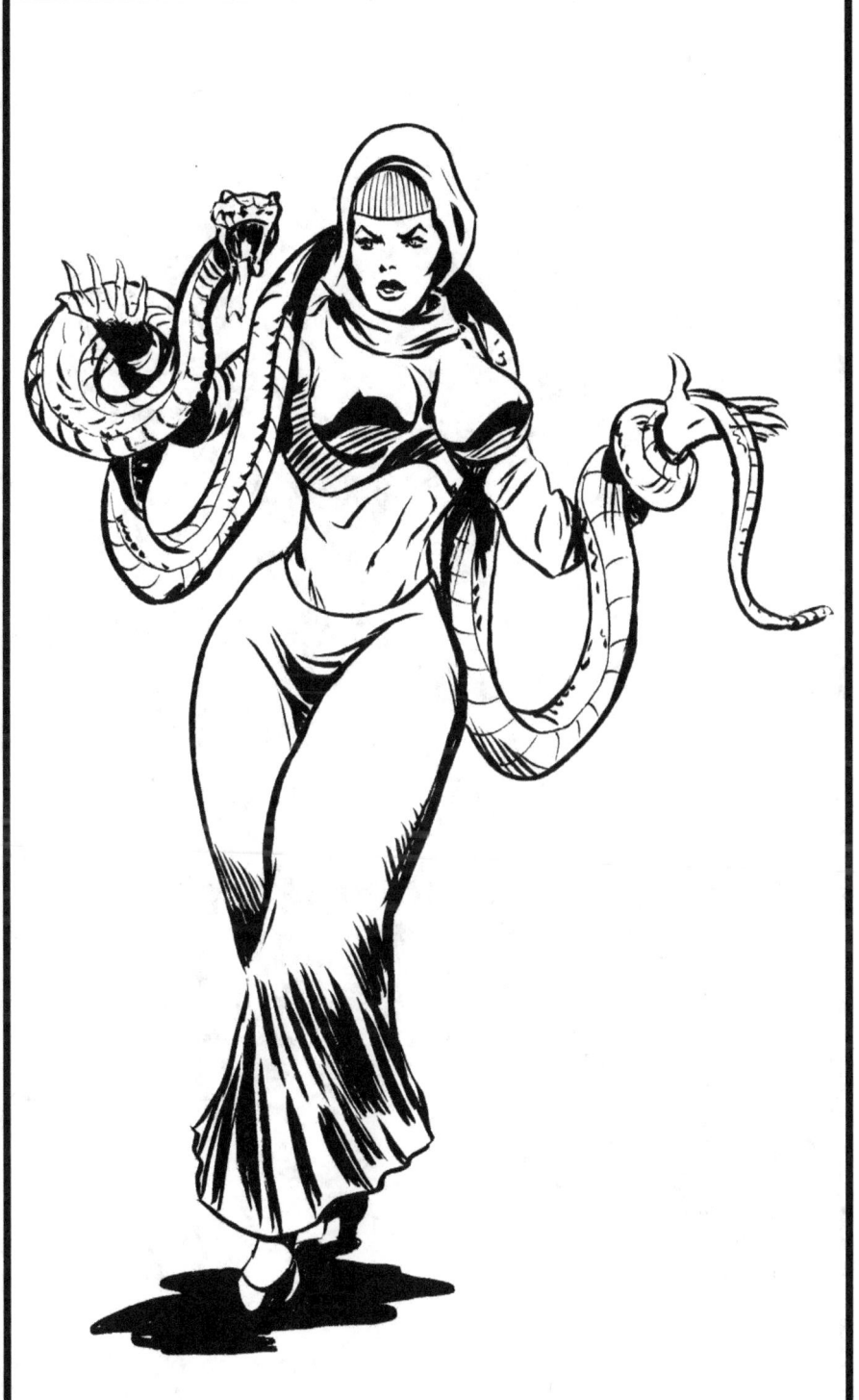

LADY SERPENT – NEDOR

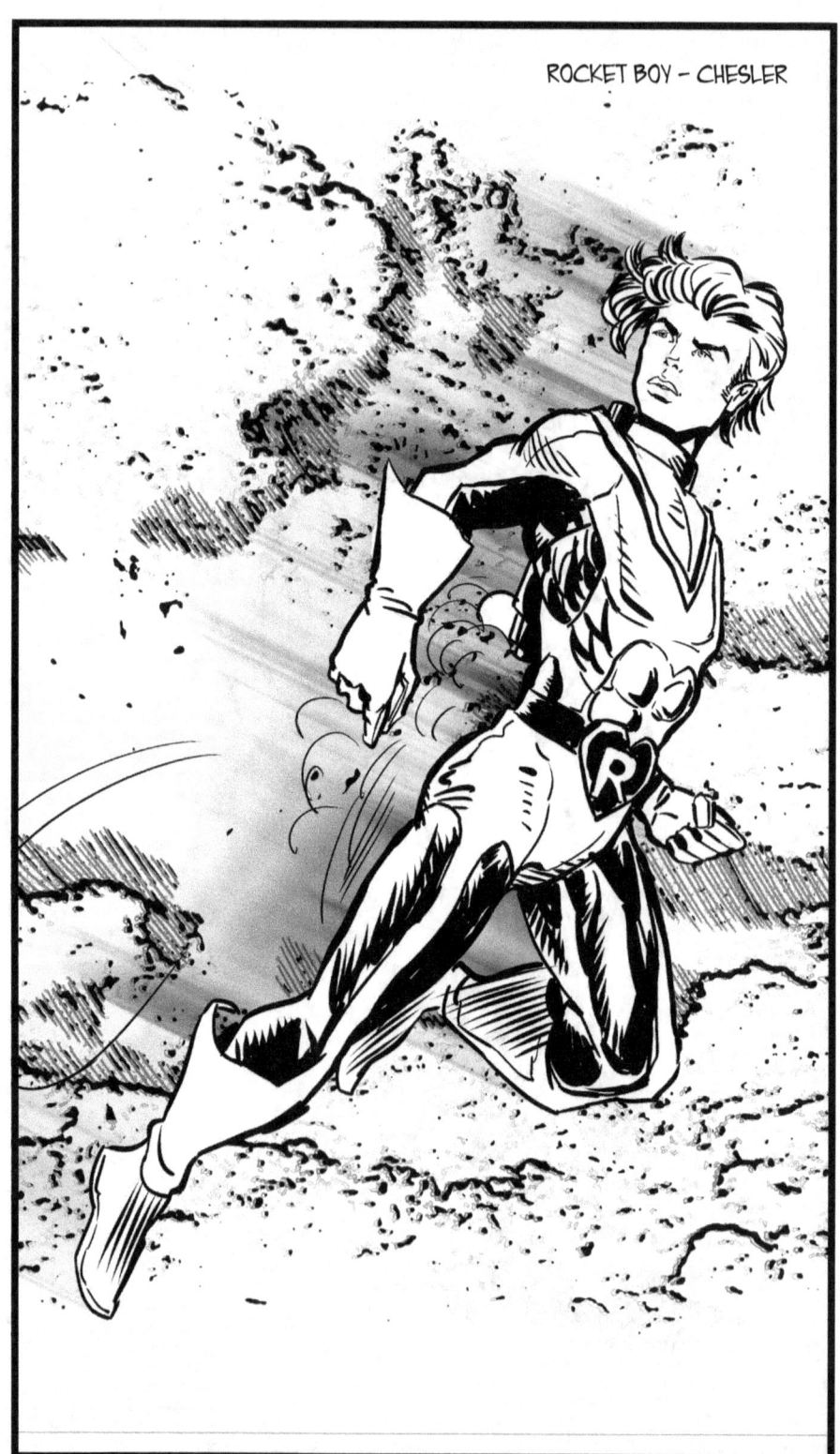

ROCKET BOY - CHESLER

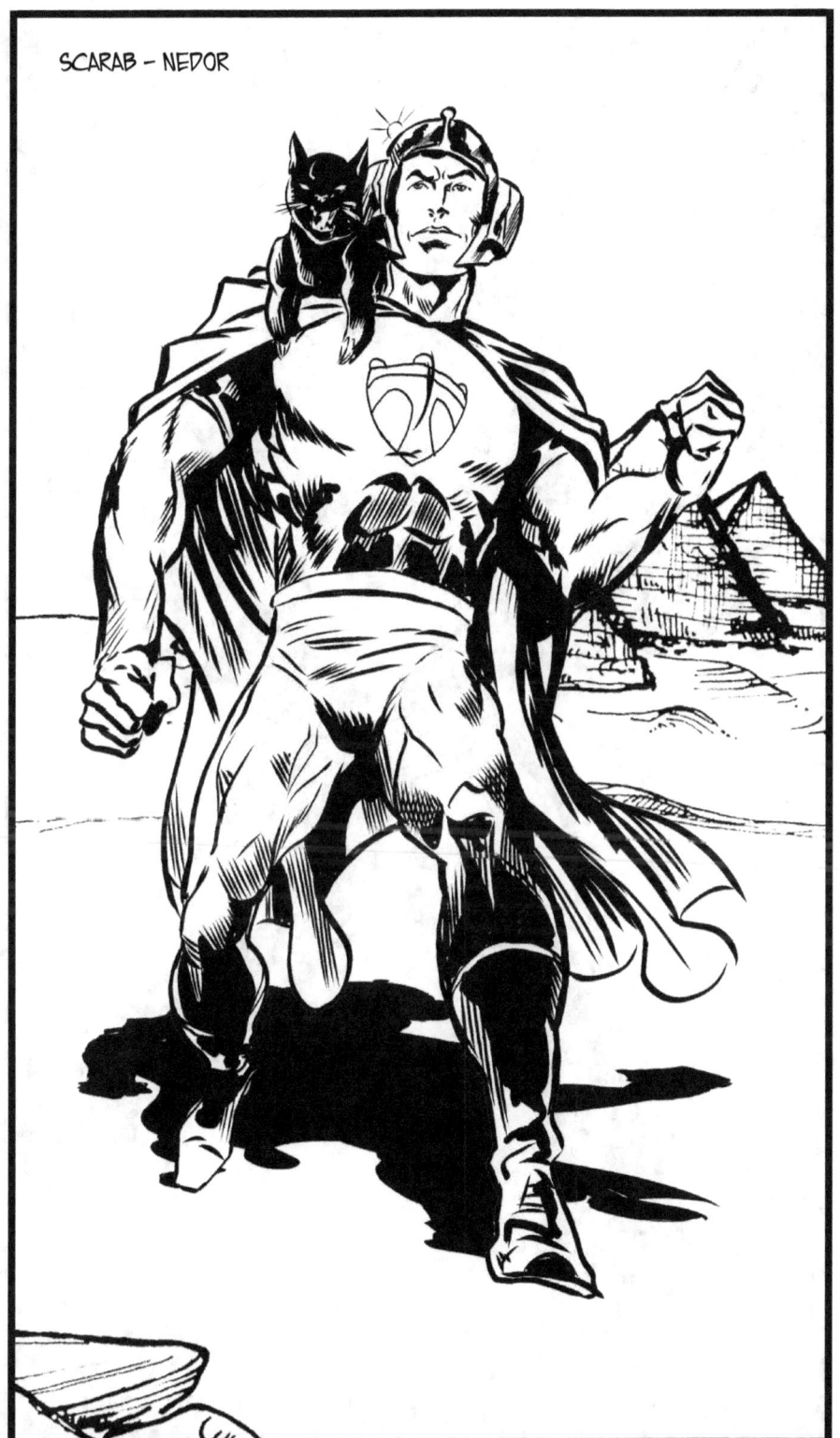

SCARAB - NEDOR

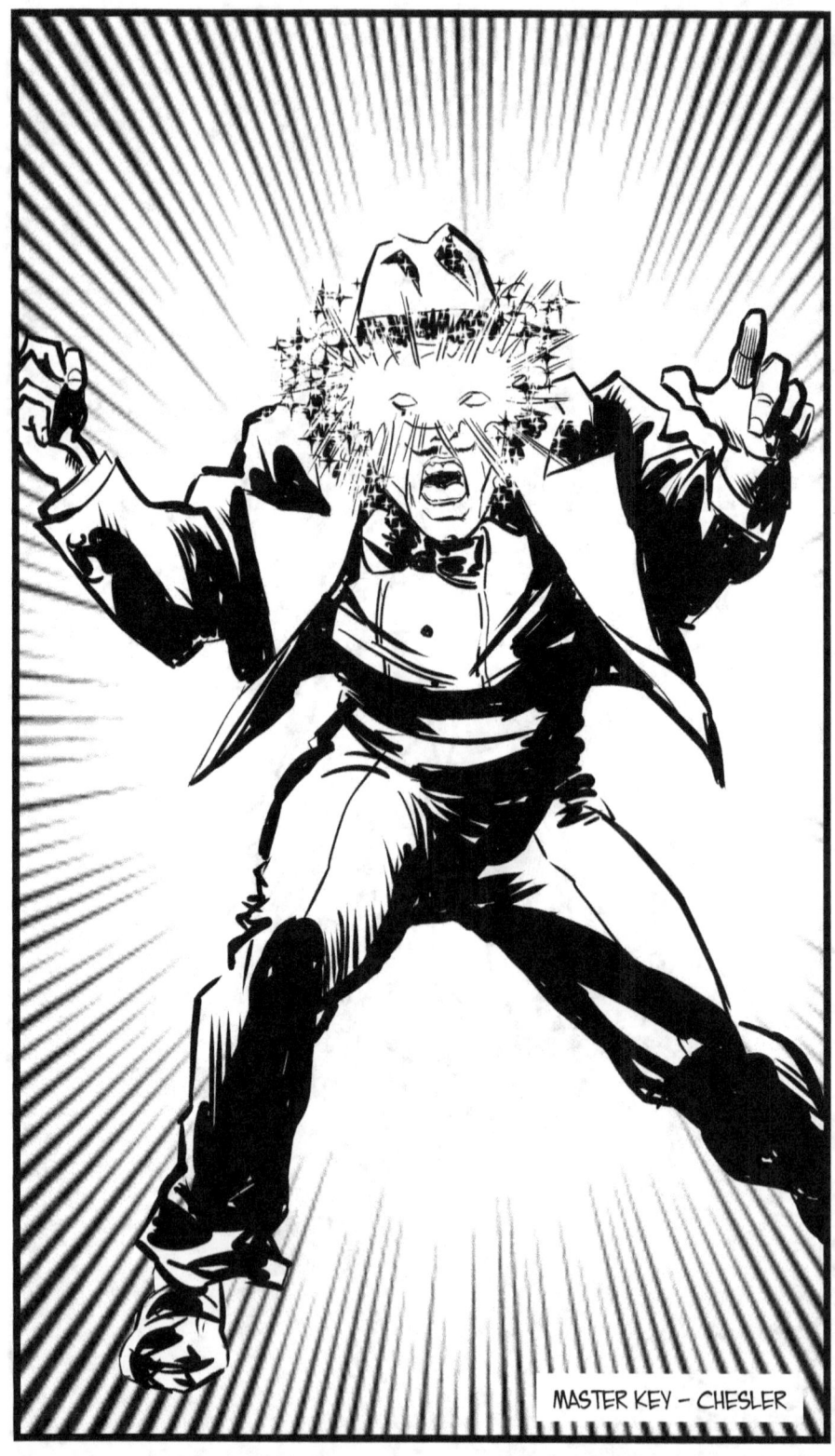

MASTER KEY – CHESLER

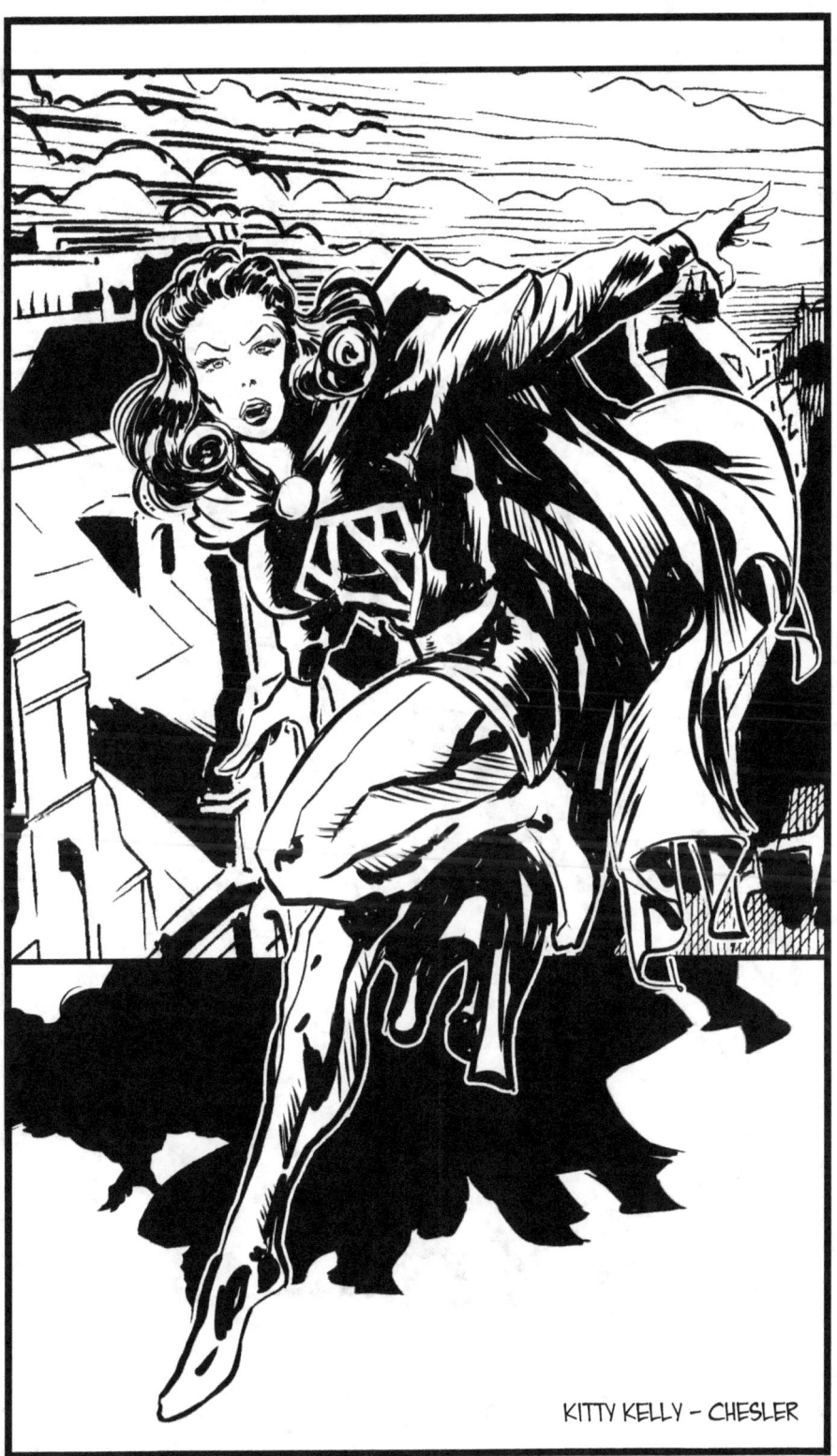

KITTY KELLY - CHESLER

SUB-ZERO MAN –
NOVELTY PRESS

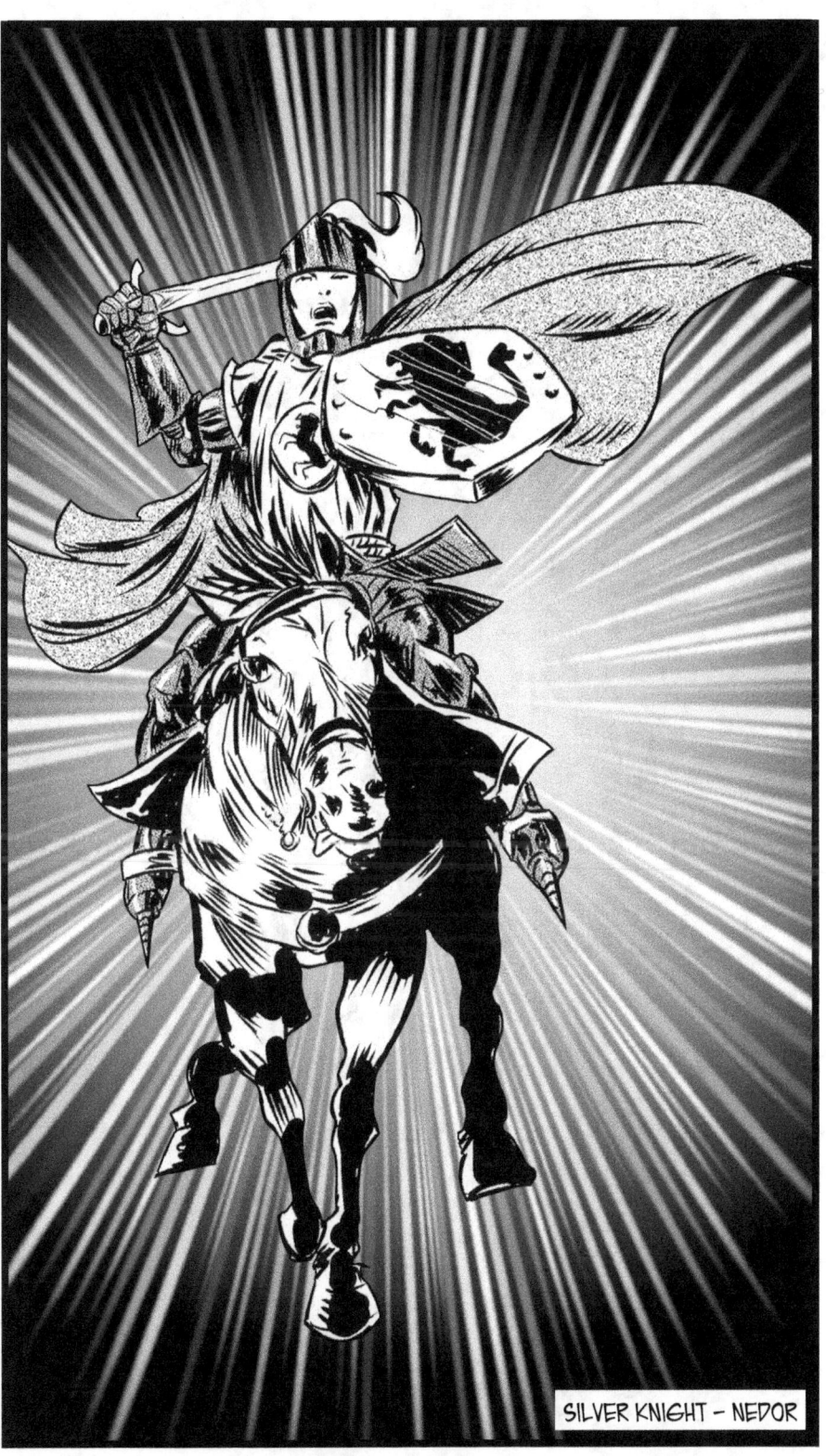

SILVER KNIGHT - NEDOR

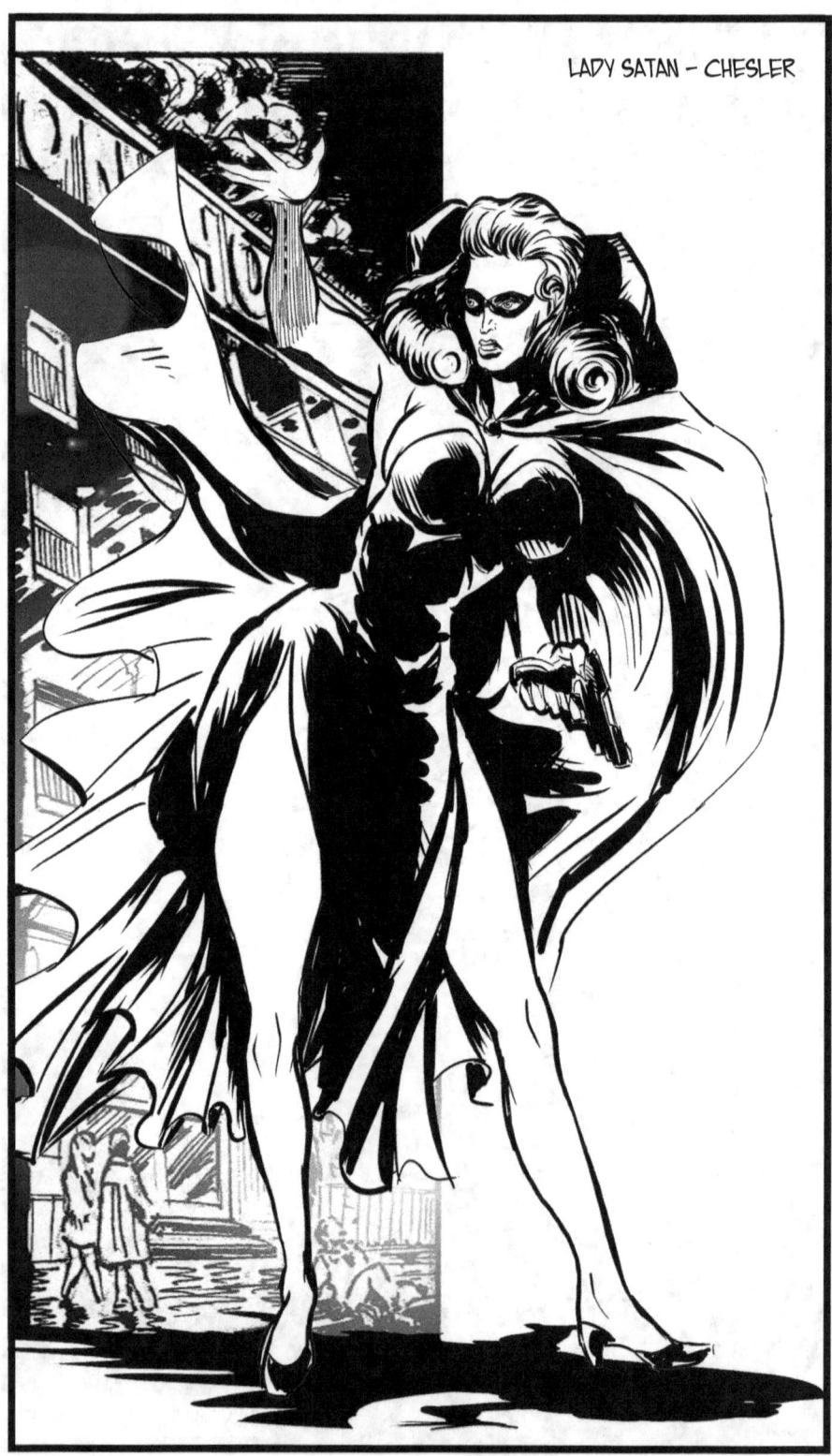

LADY SATAN - CHESLER

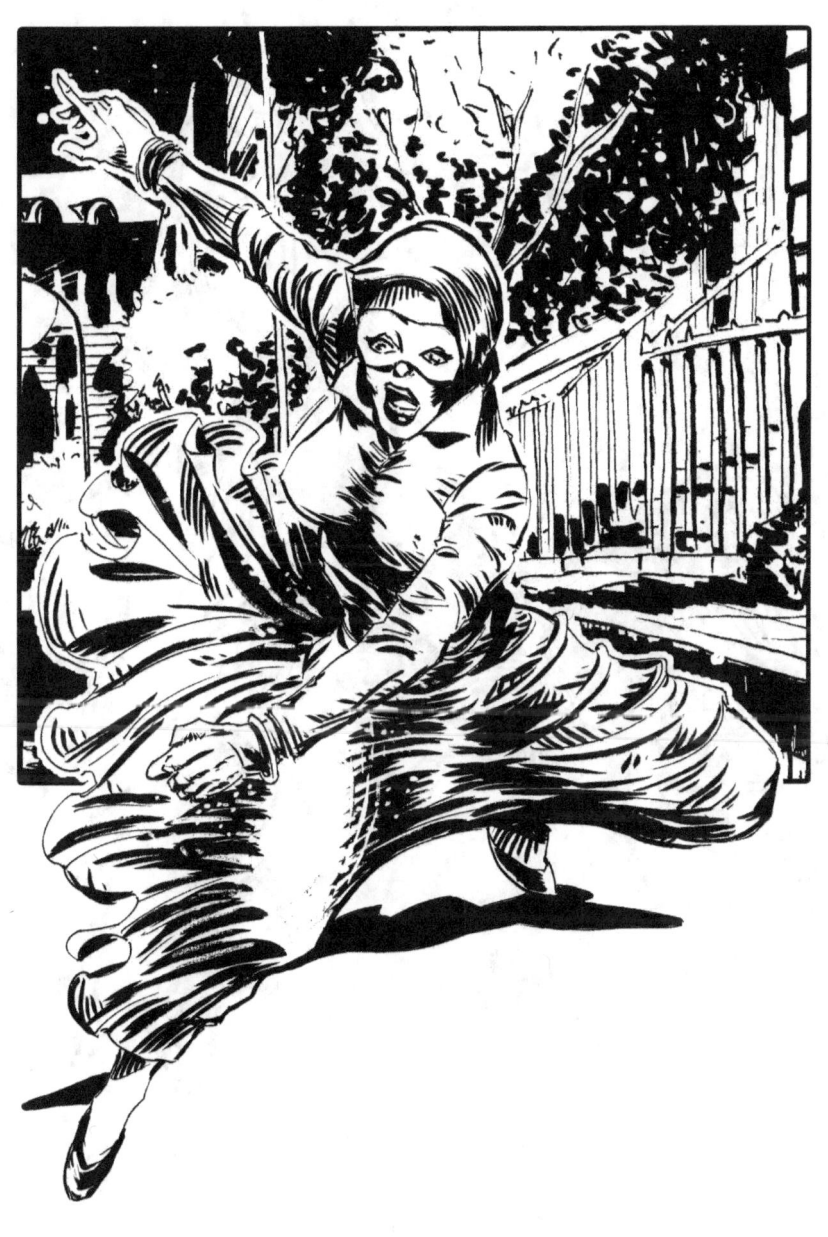

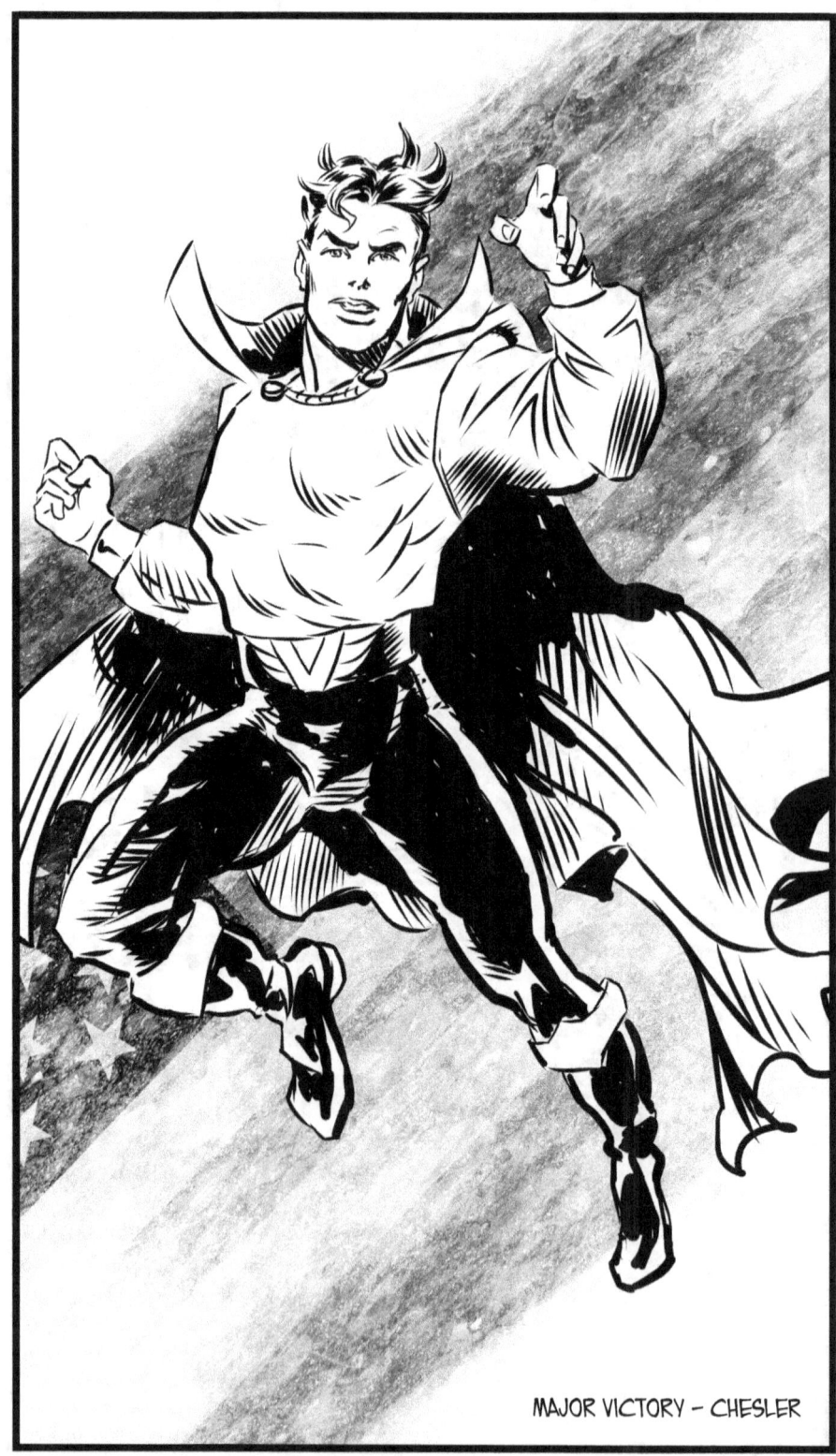

MAJOR VICTORY — CHESLER

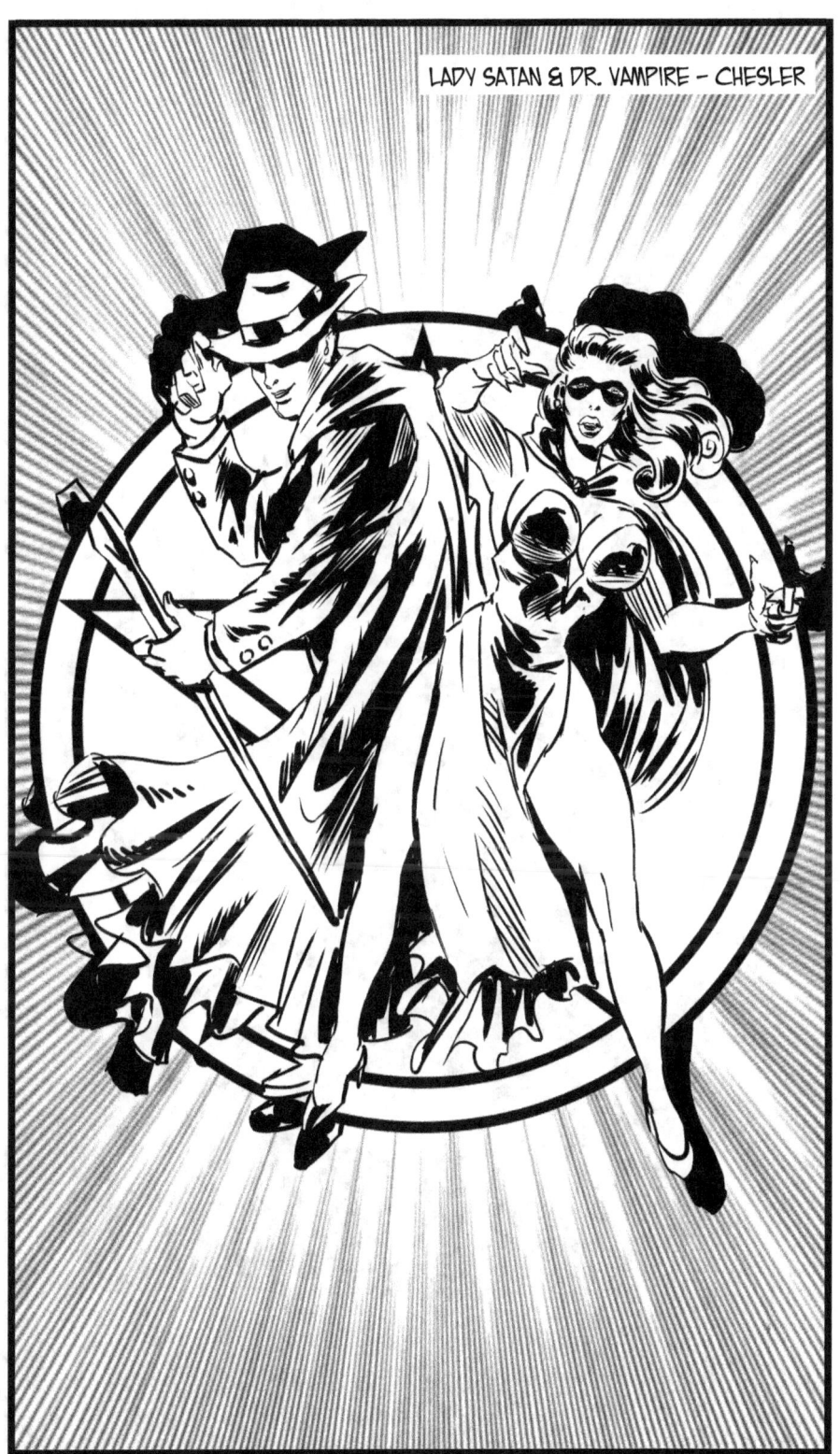

LADY SATAN & DR. VAMPIRE - CHESLER

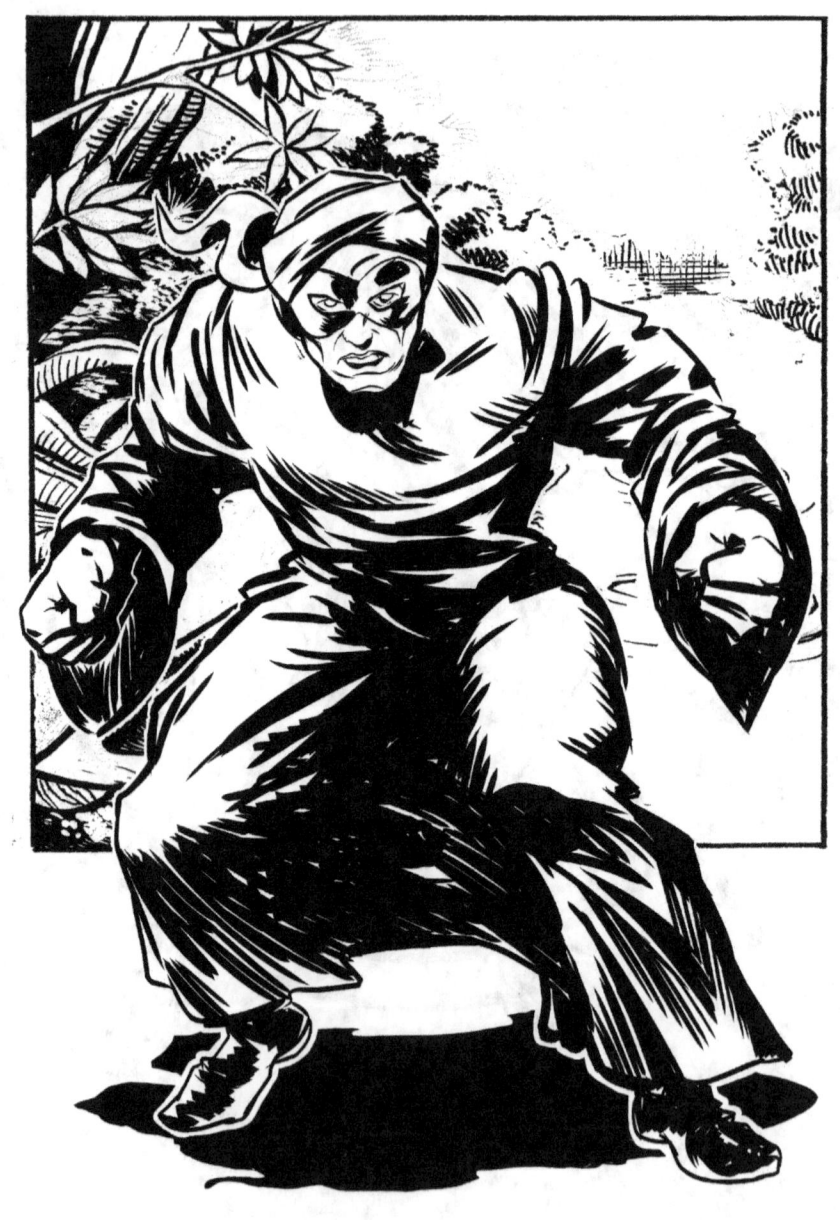

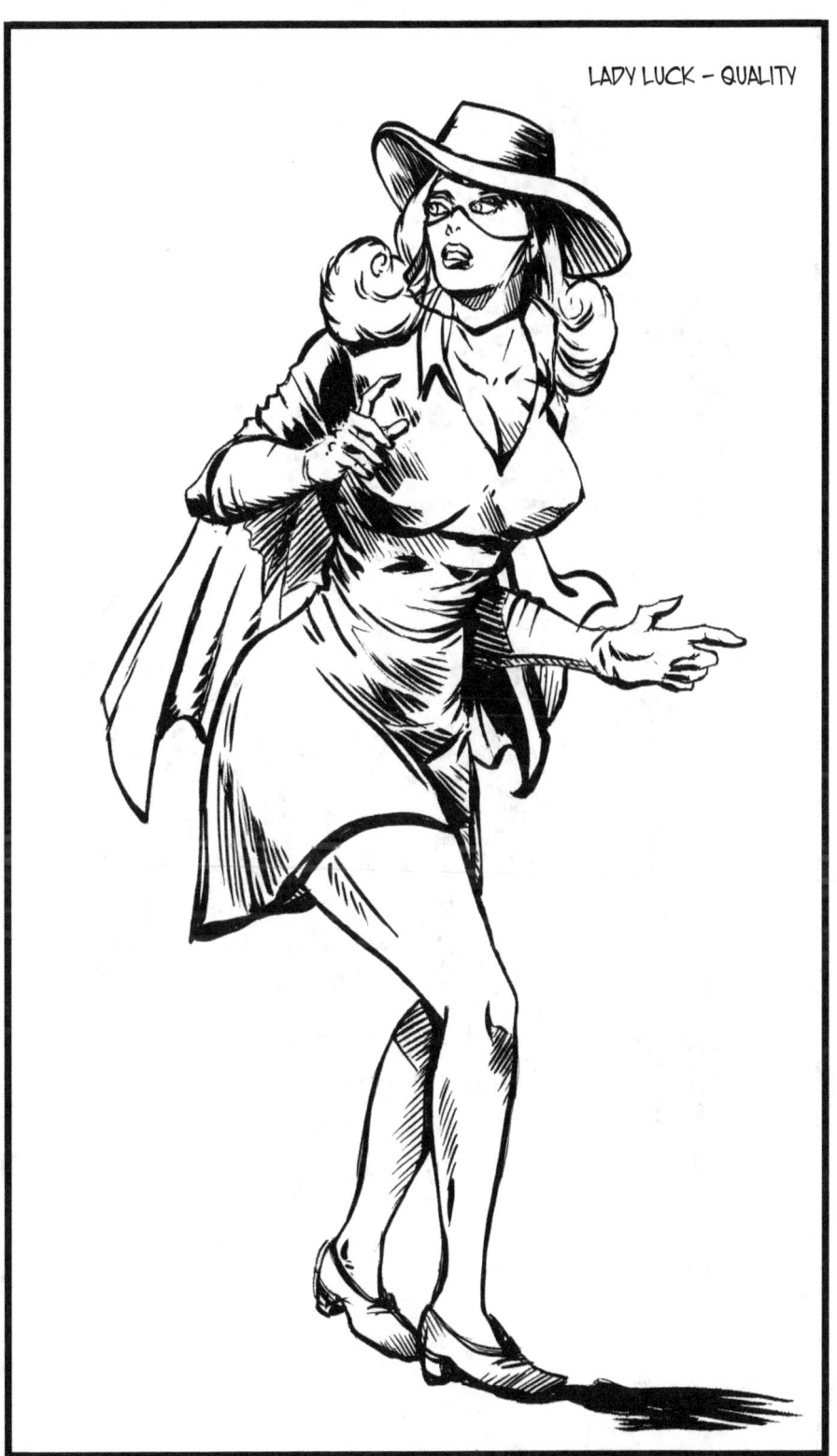

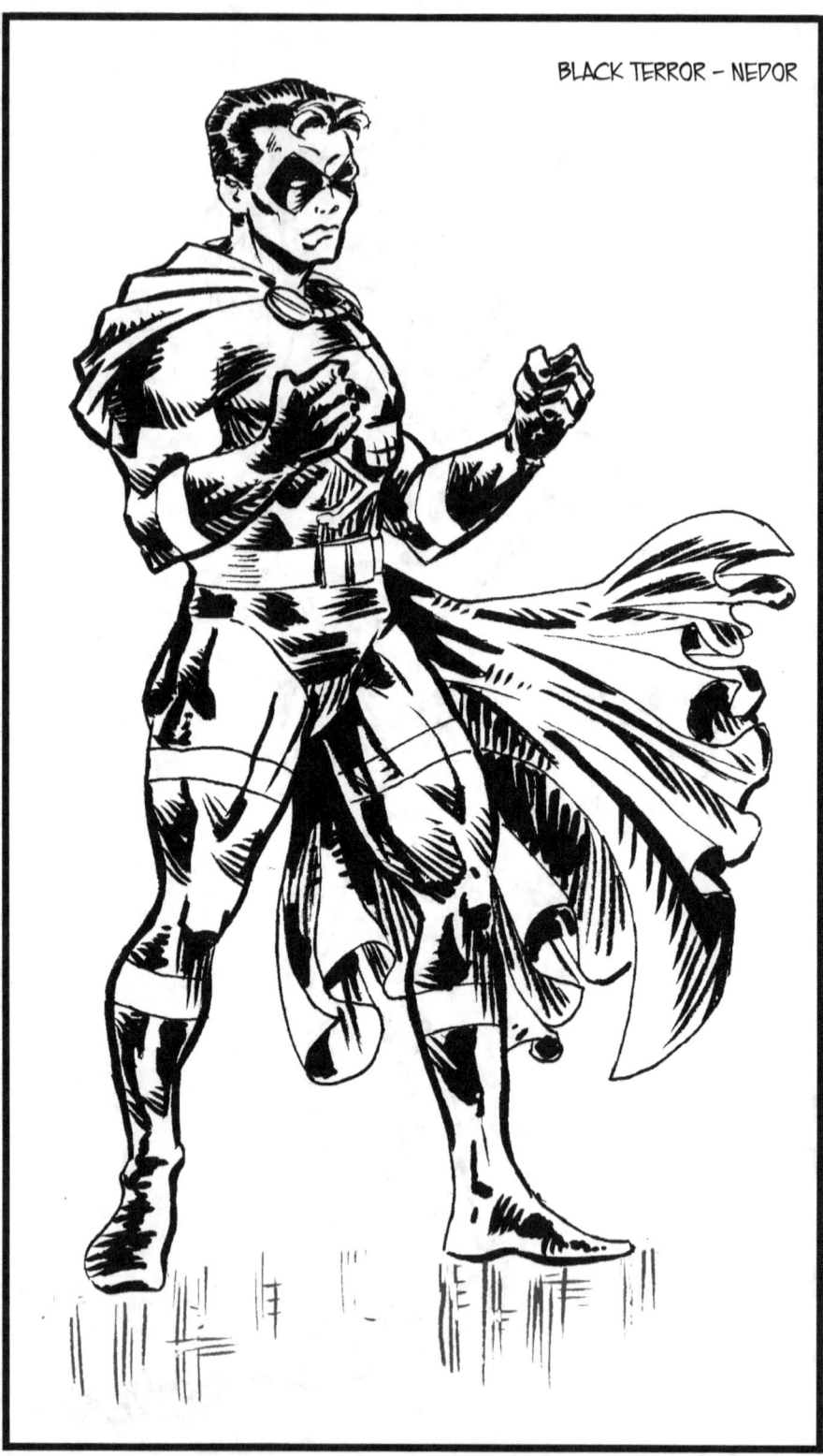

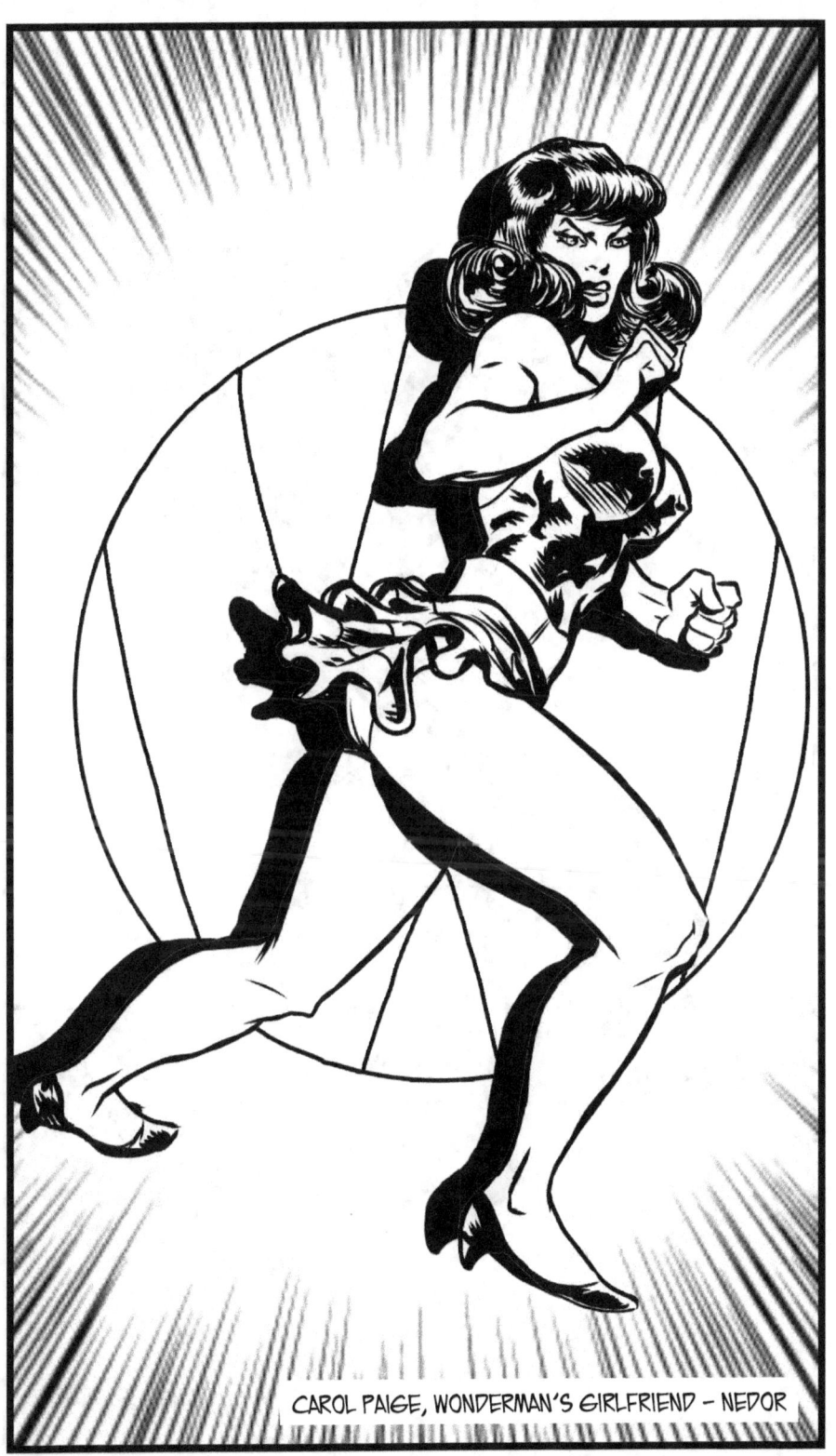

CAROL PAIGE, WONDERMAN'S GIRLFRIEND - NEDOR

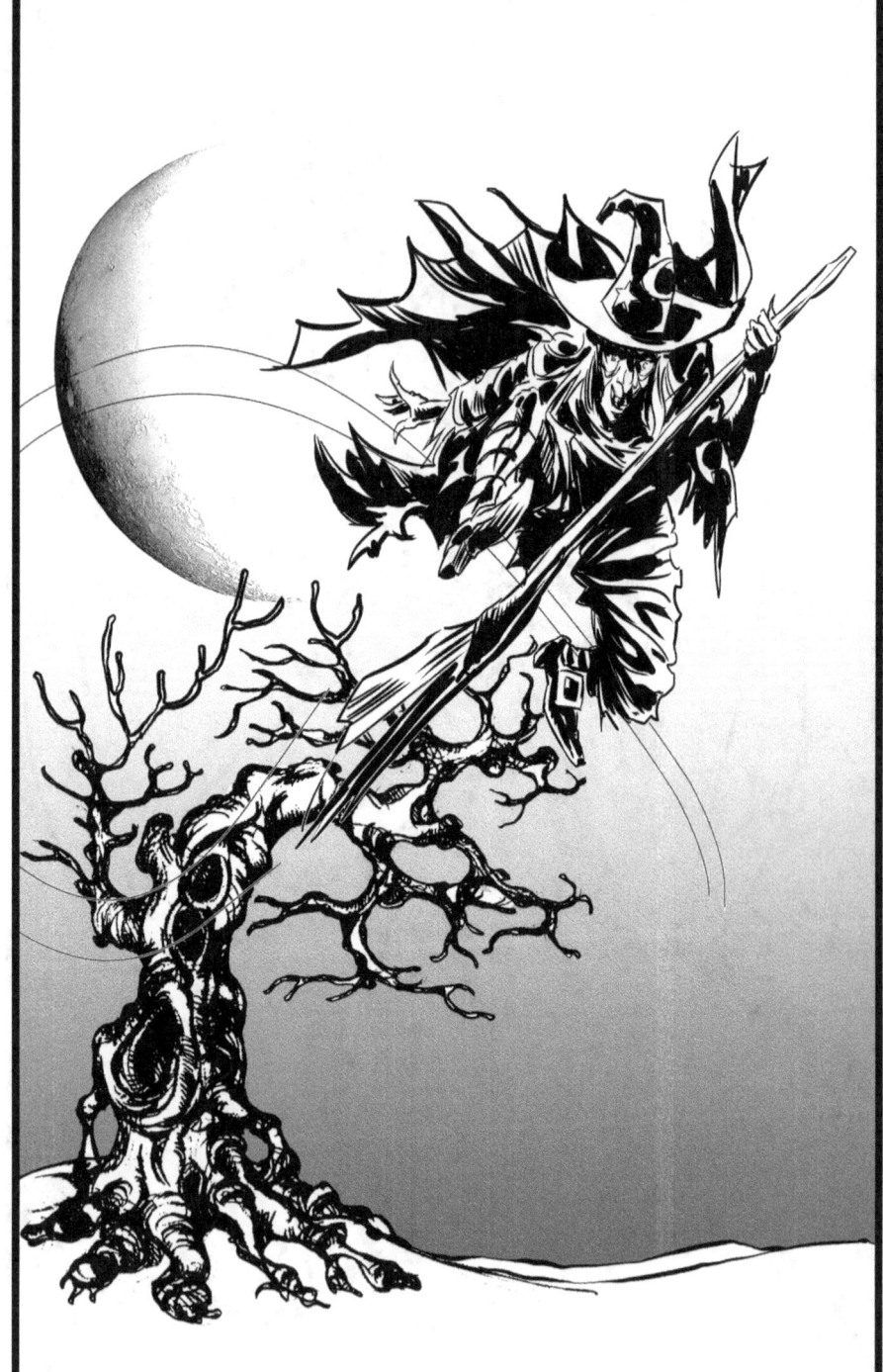

MOTHER HUBBARD - CHESLER

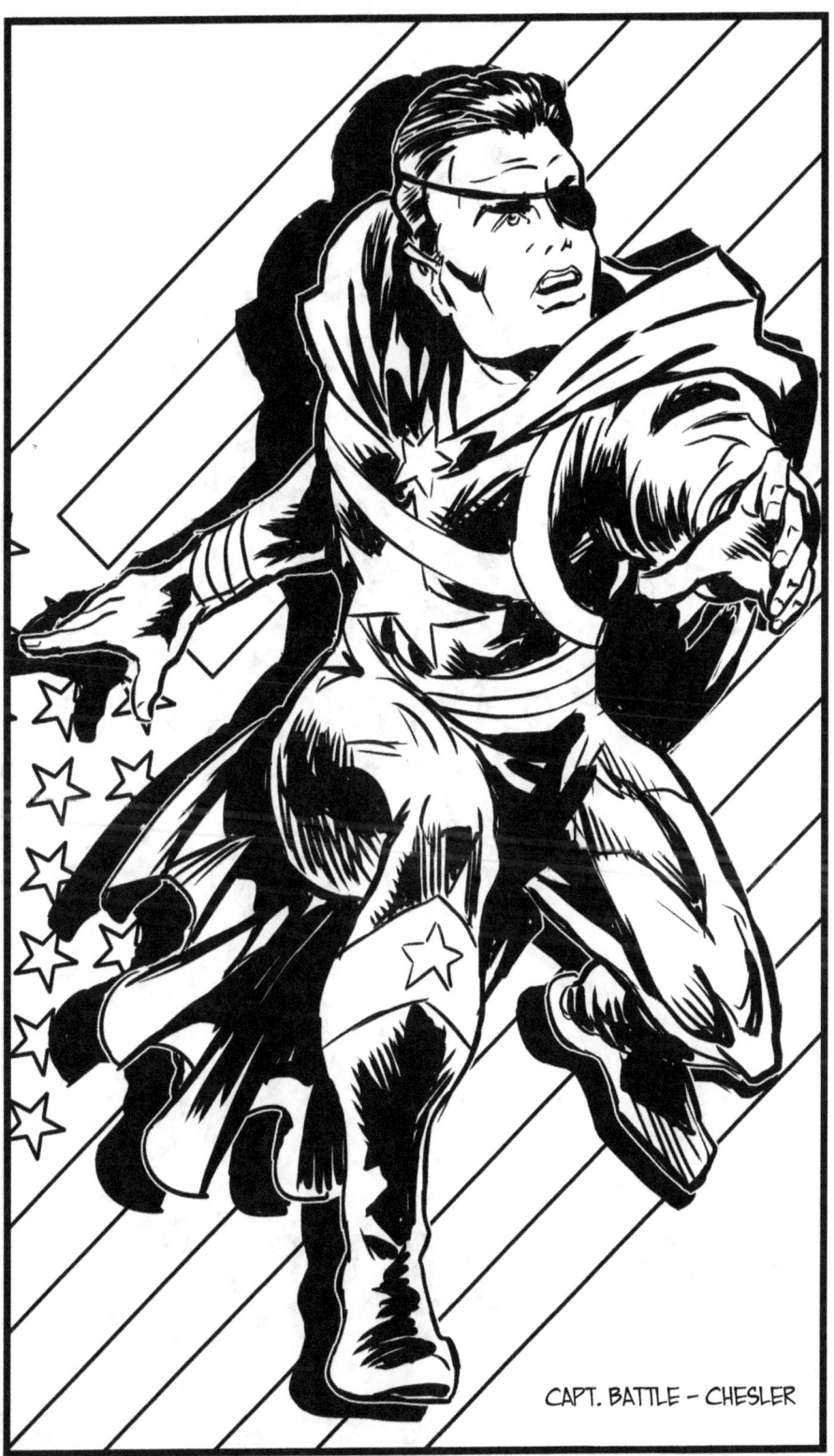

CAPT. BATTLE – CHESLER

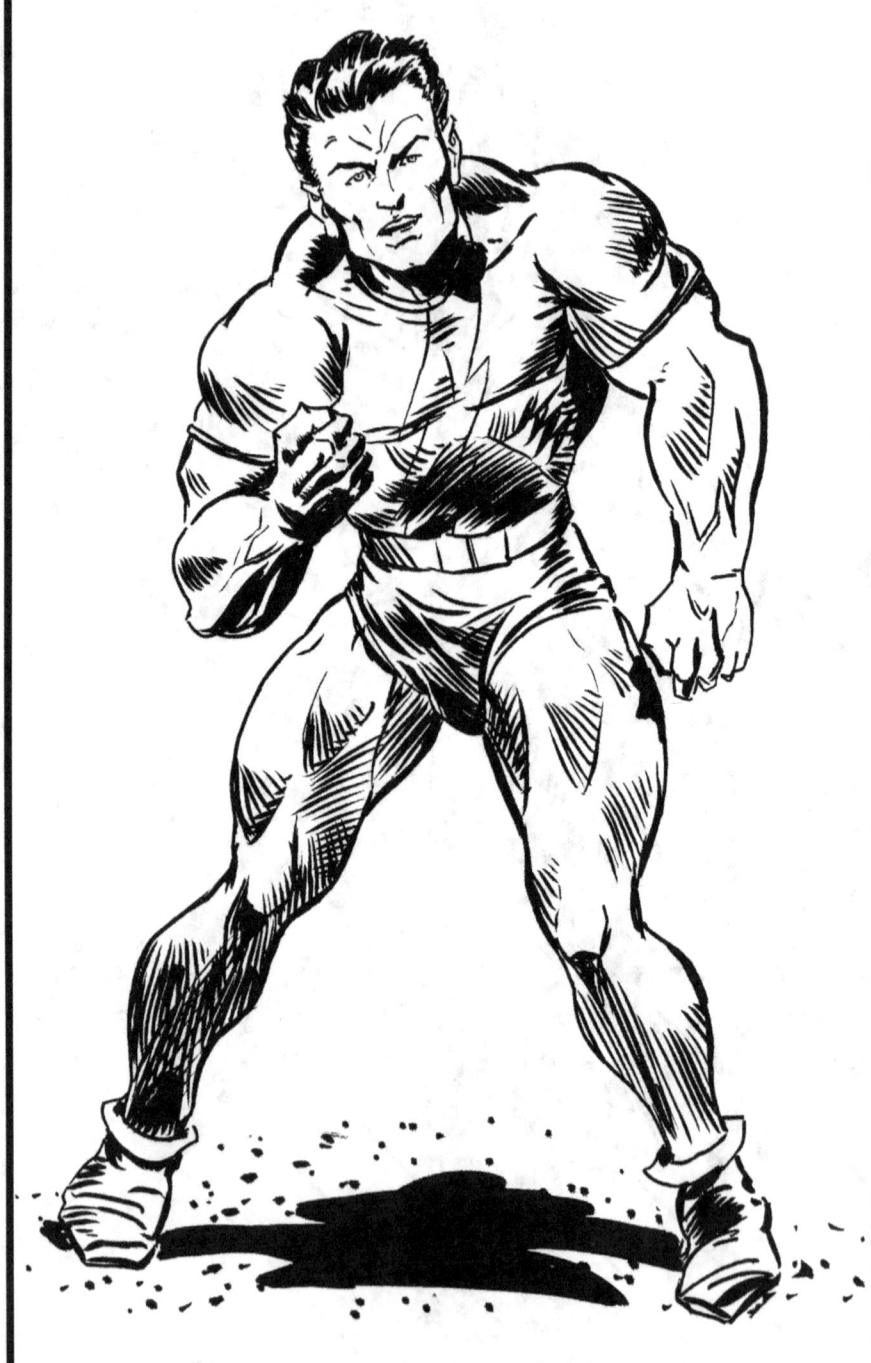

CAPT. FUTURE - NEDOR

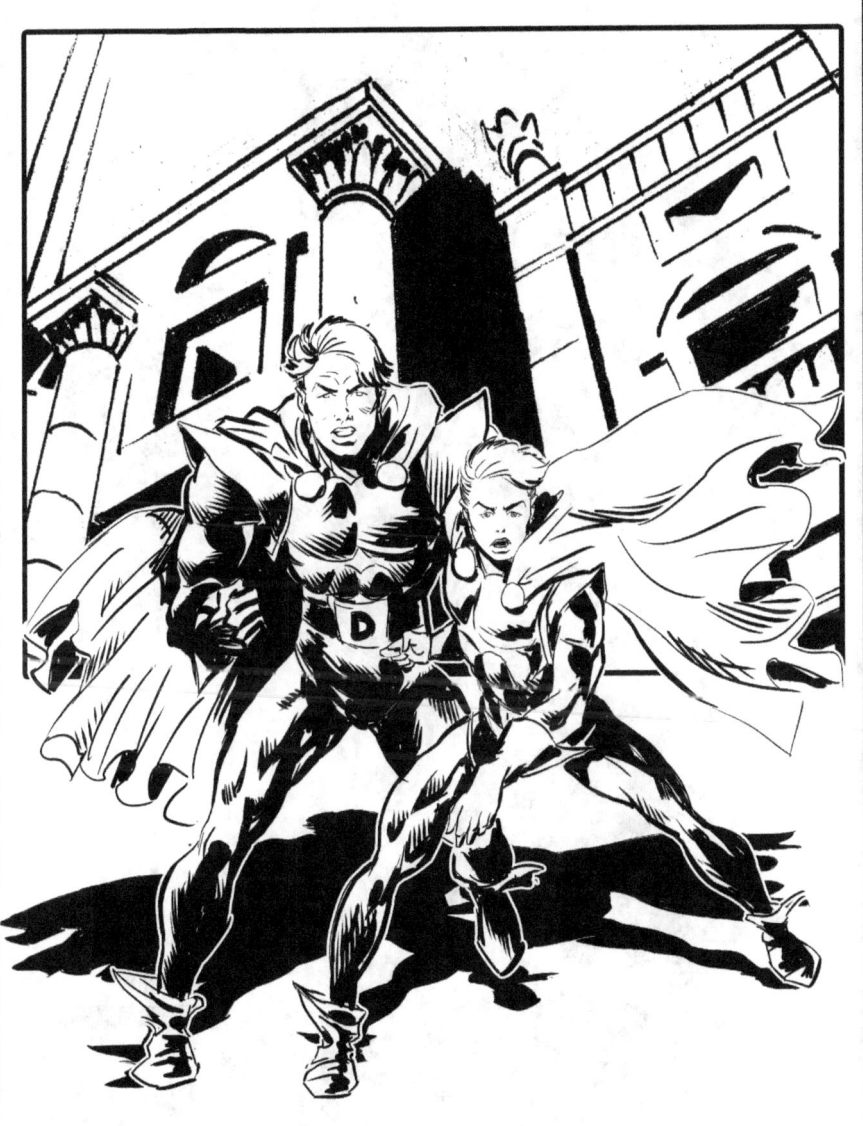

DYNAMIC MAN & DYNAMIC BOY - CHESLER

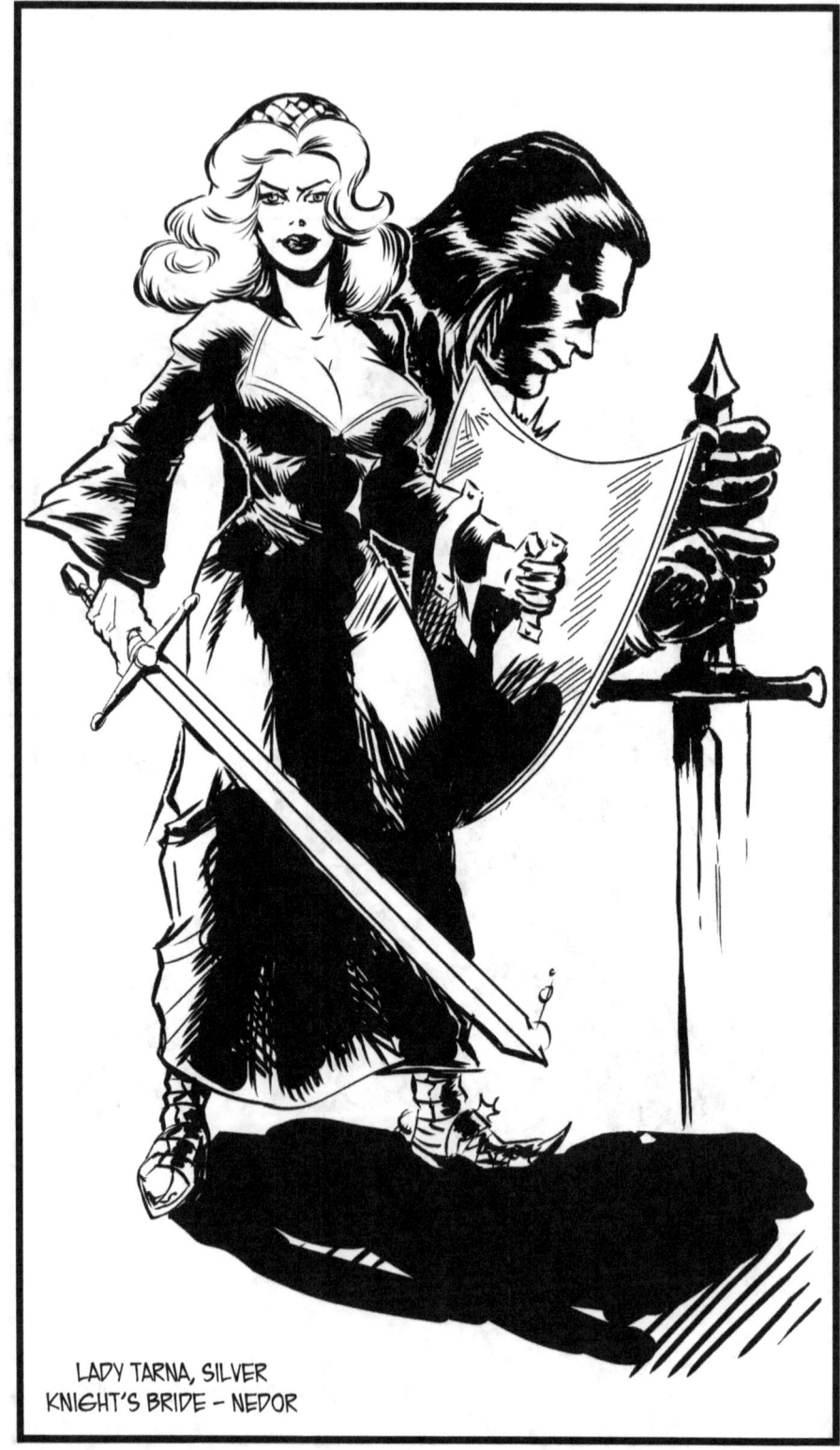

LADY TARNA, SILVER
KNIGHT'S BRIDE – NEDOR

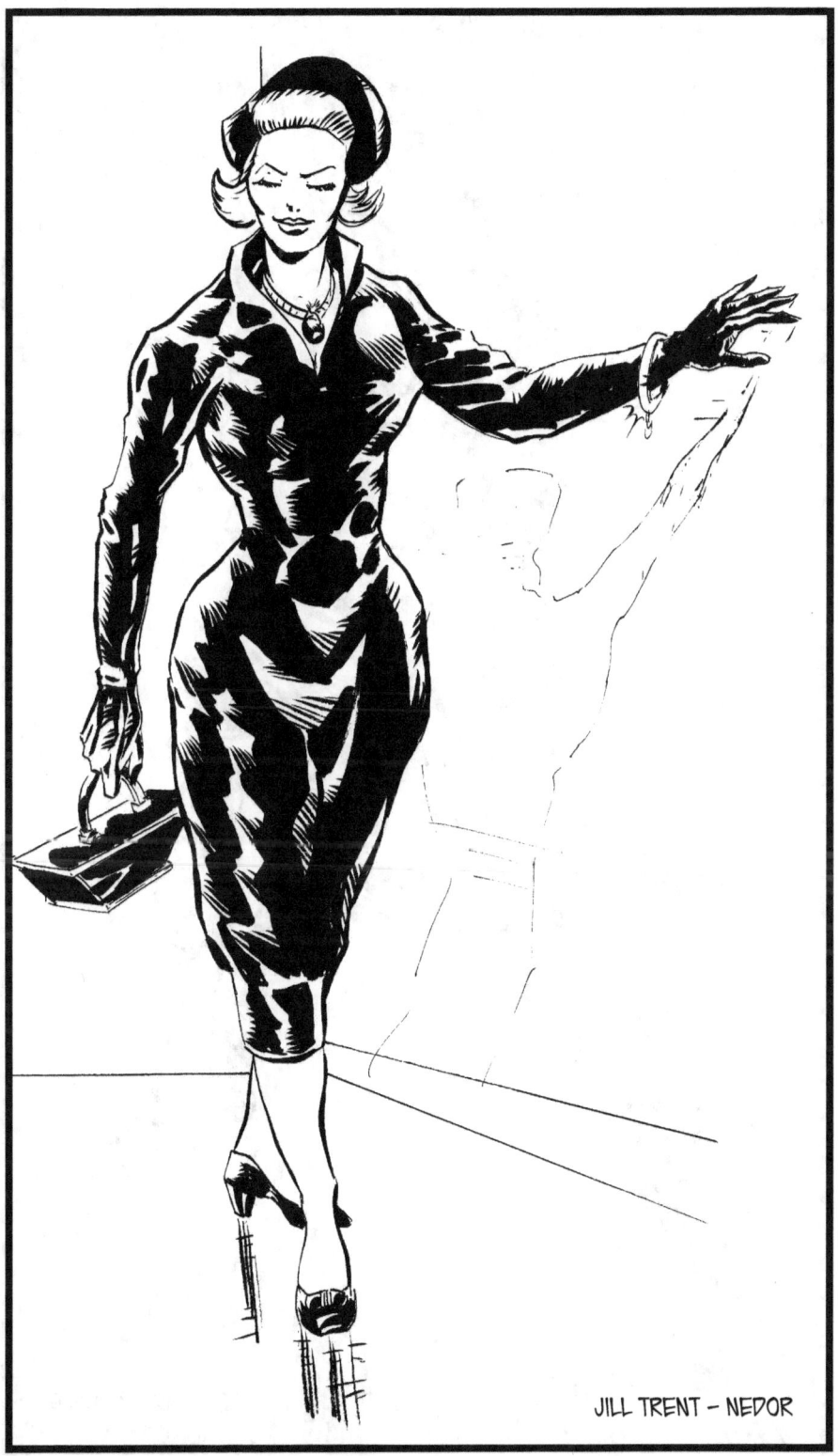

JILL TRENT — NEDOR

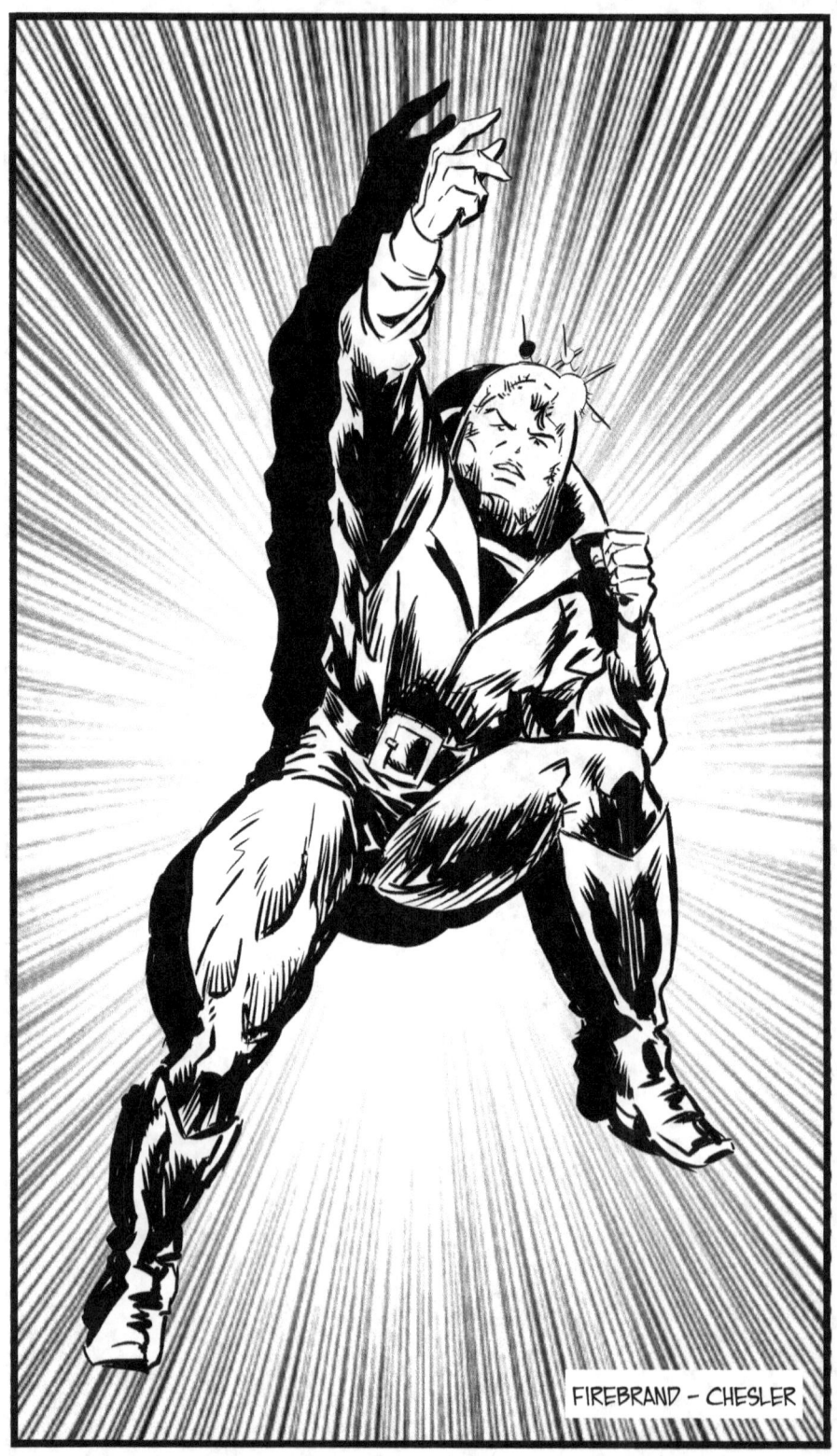

FIREBRAND - CHESLER

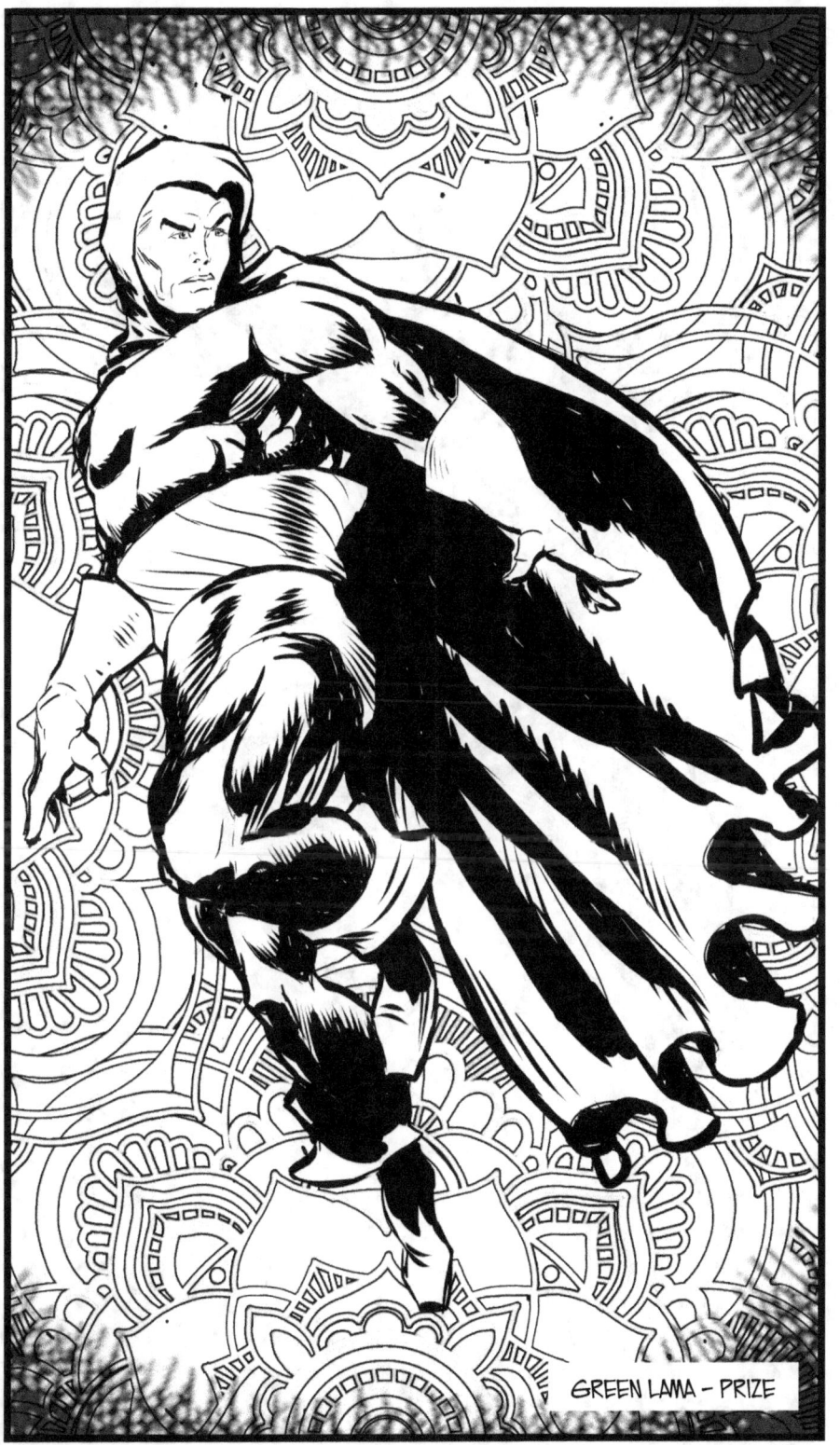

GREEN LAMA - PRIZE

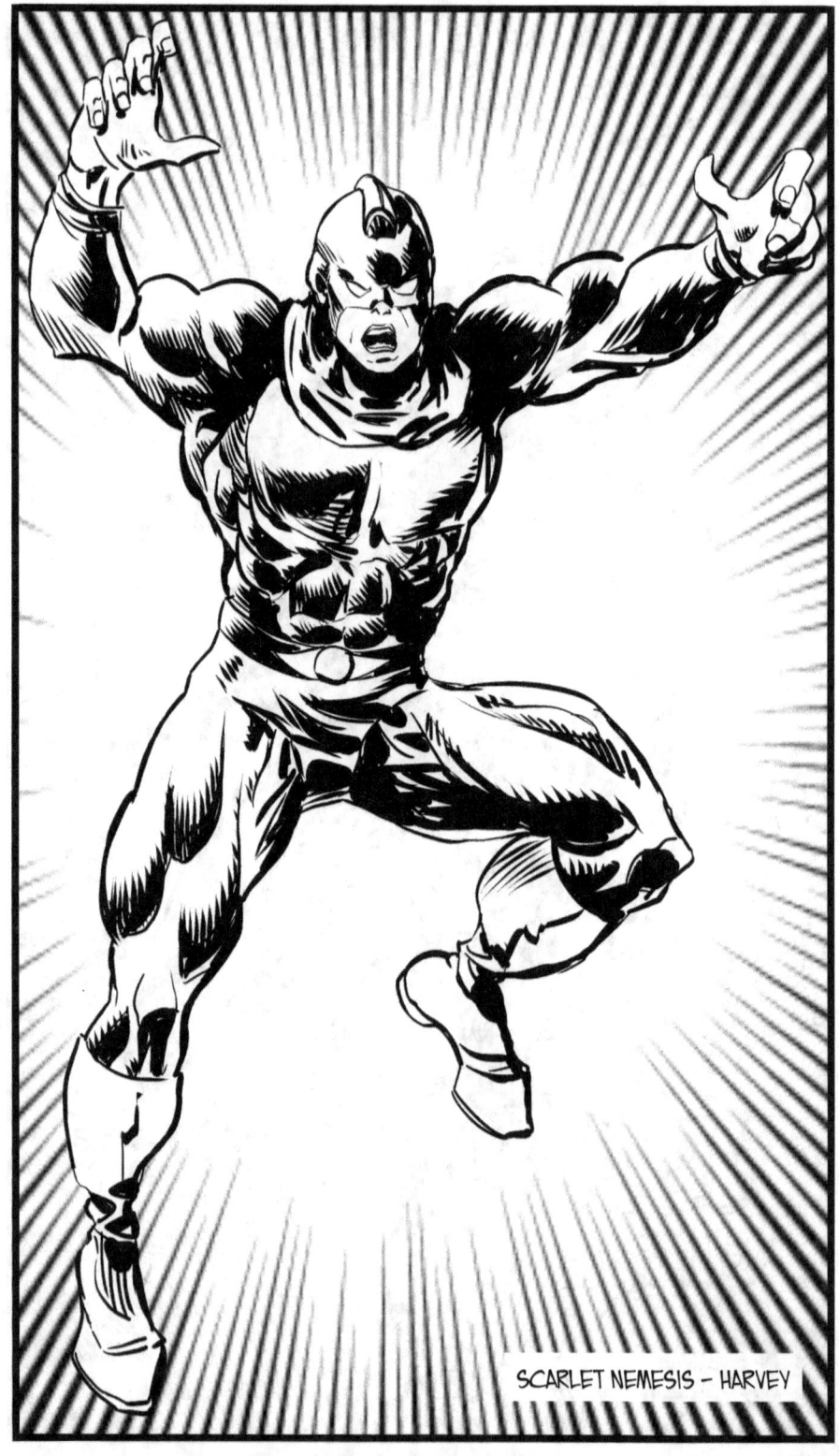

SCARLET NEMESIS — HARVEY

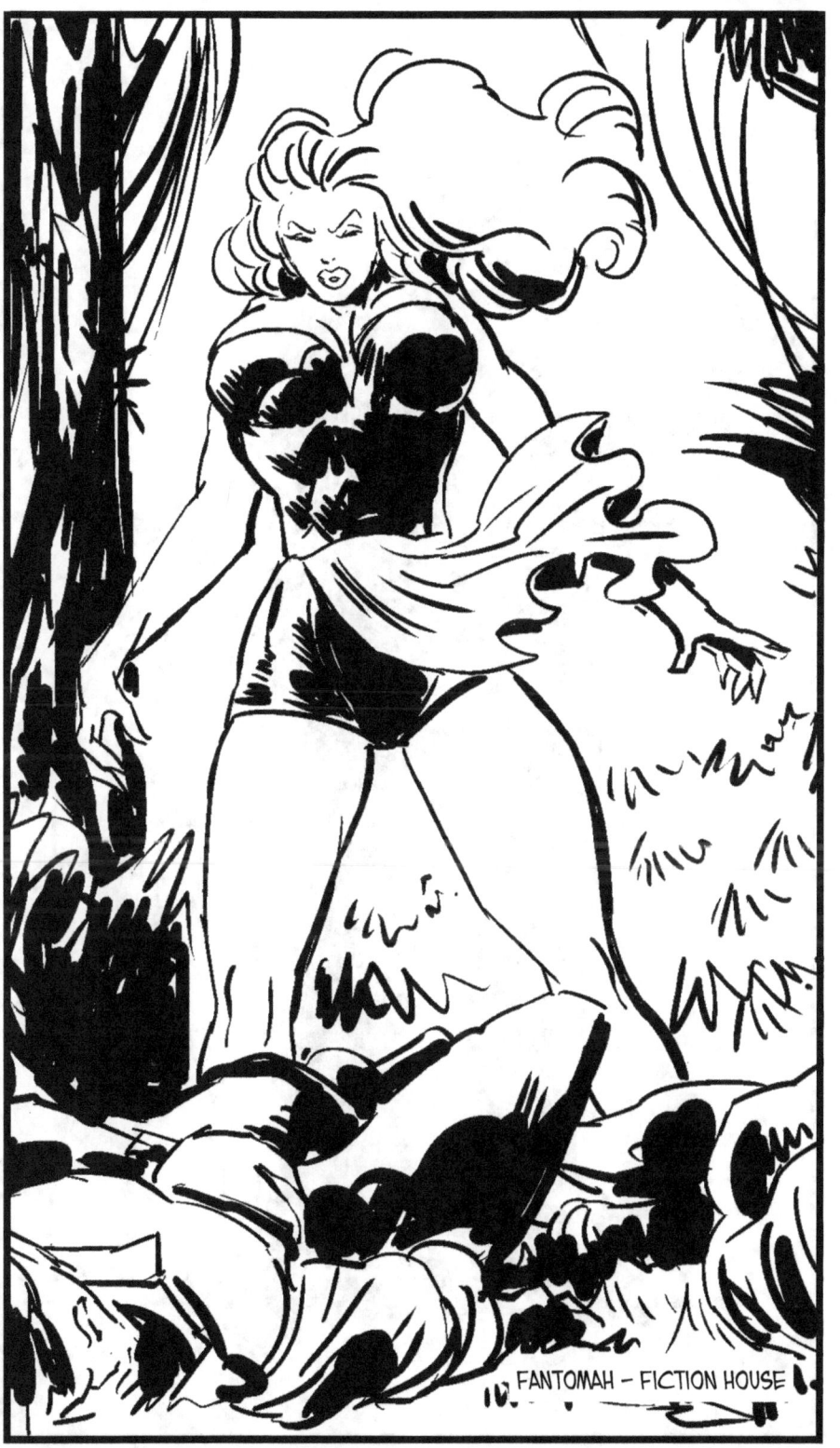

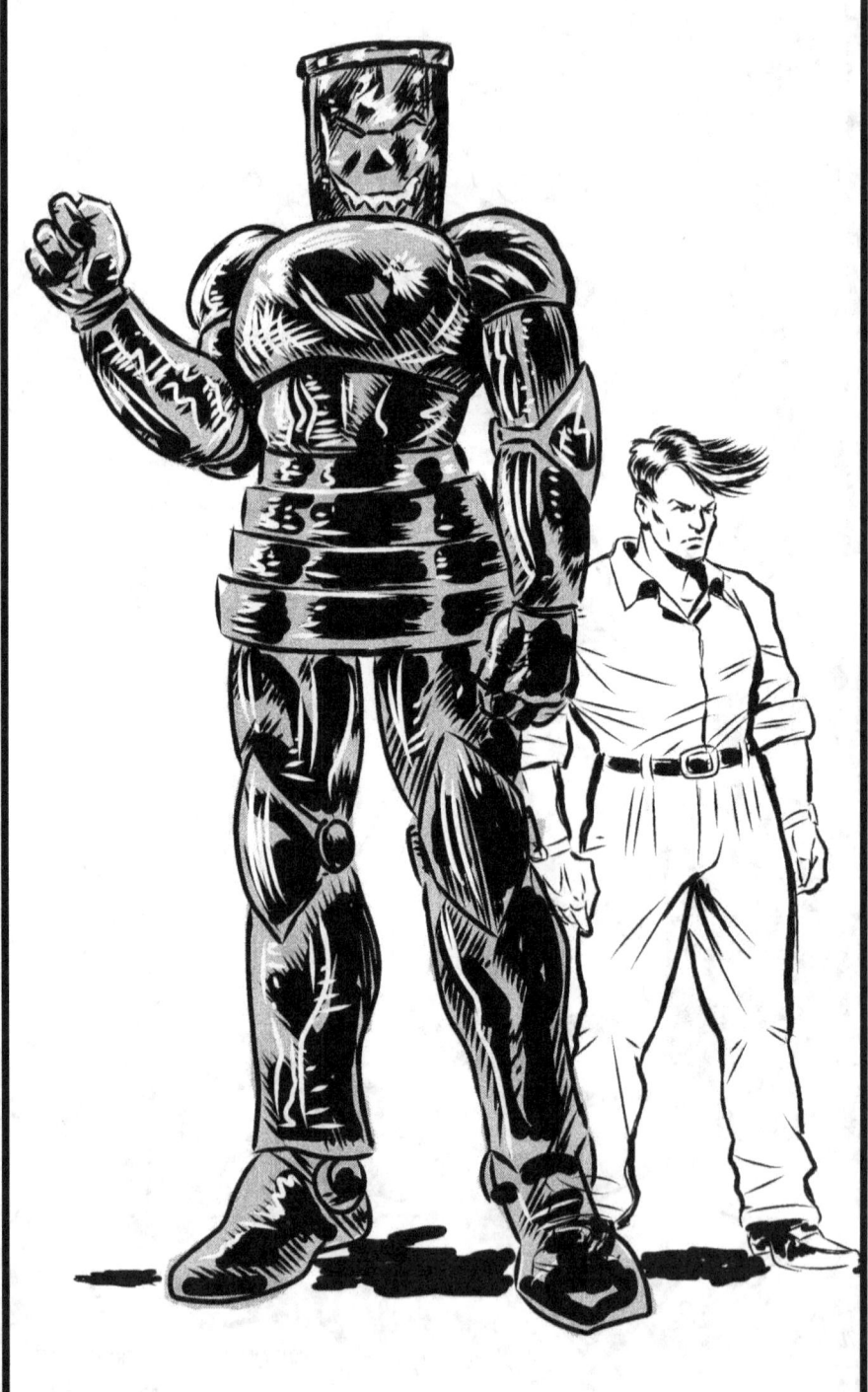

MEKANO & BILL FOSTER - NEDOR

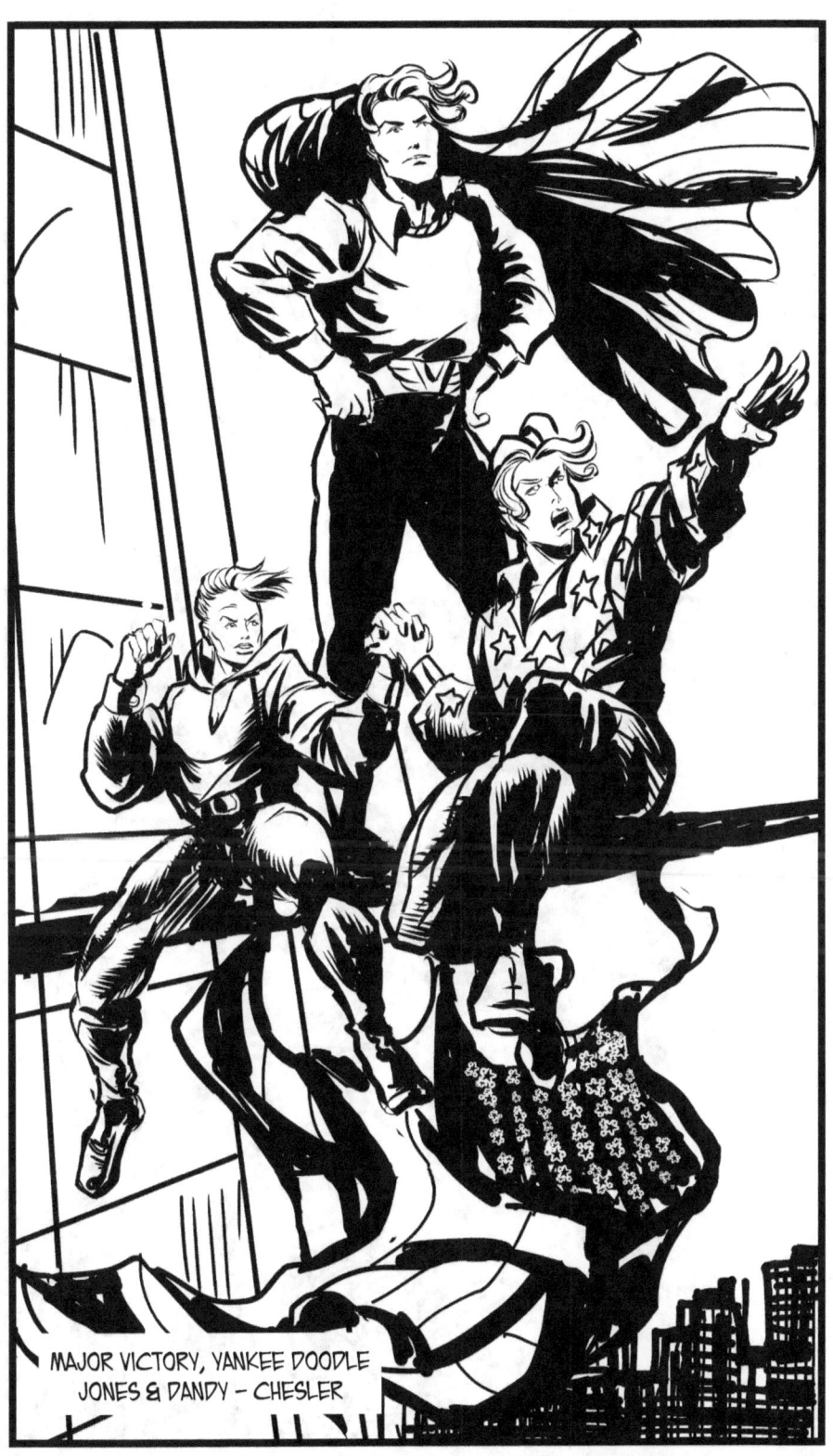

MAJOR VICTORY, YANKEE DOODLE
JONES & DANDY – CHESLER

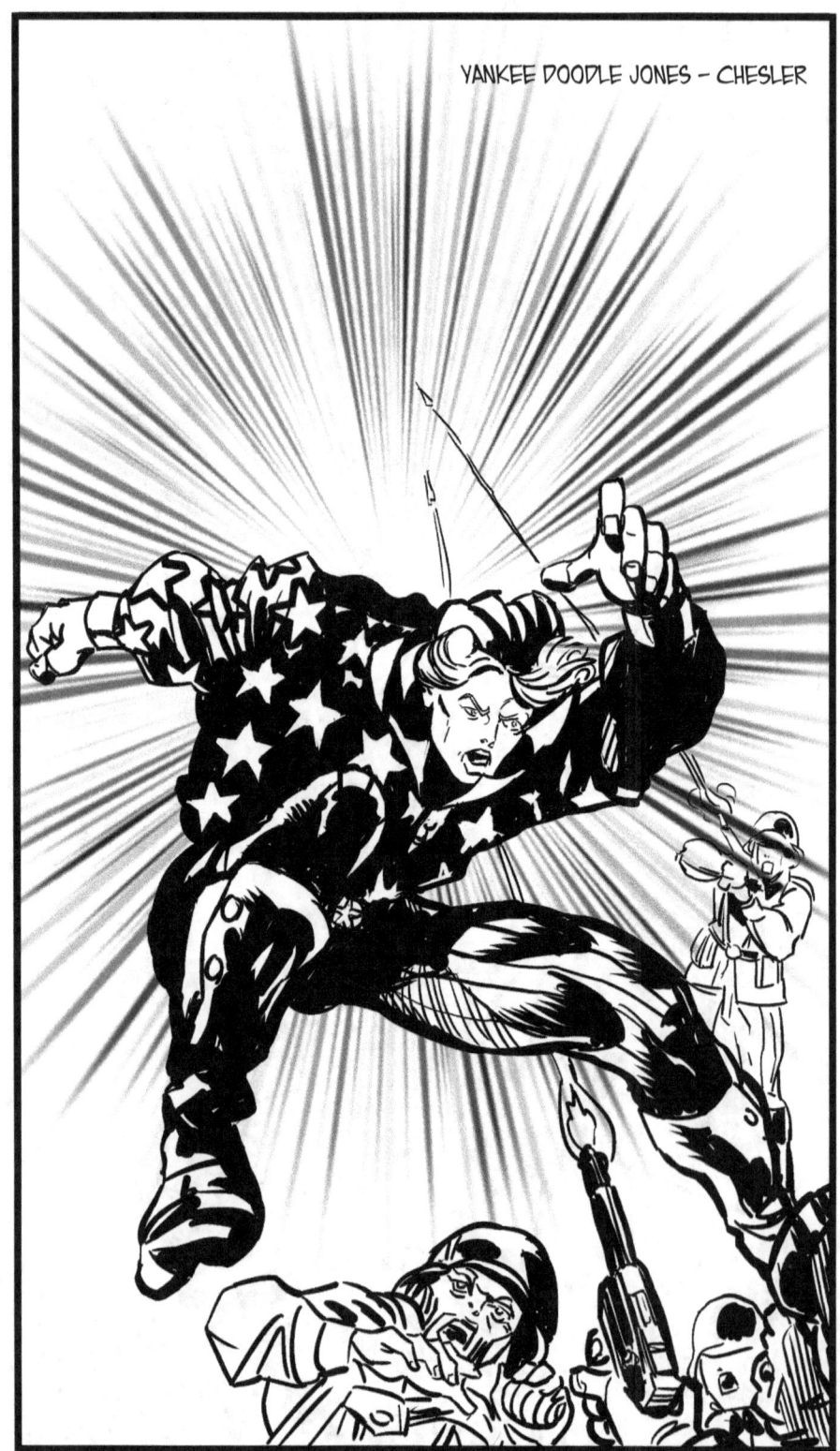

YANKEE DOODLE JONES - CHESLER

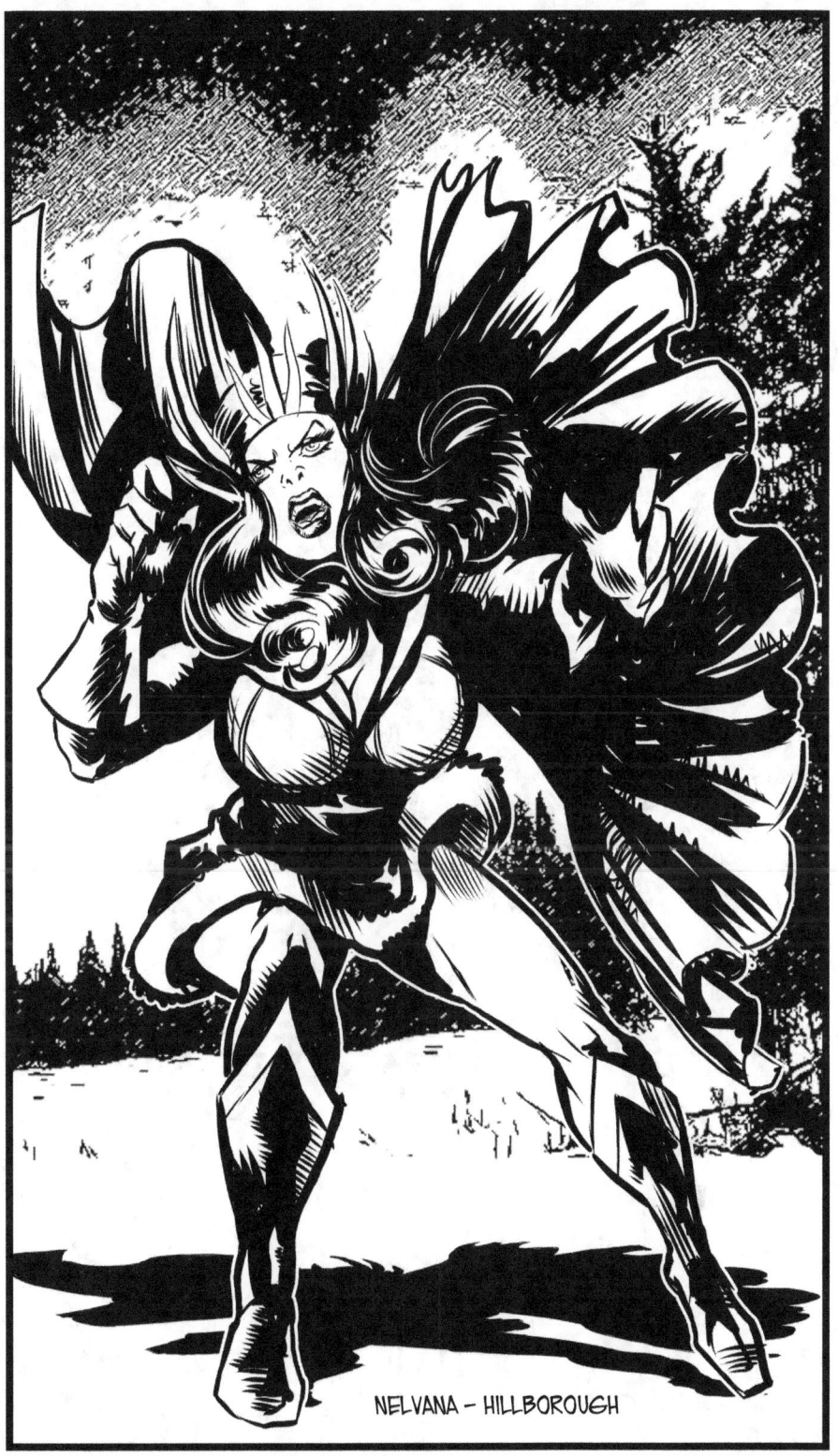

NELVANA - HILLBOROUGH

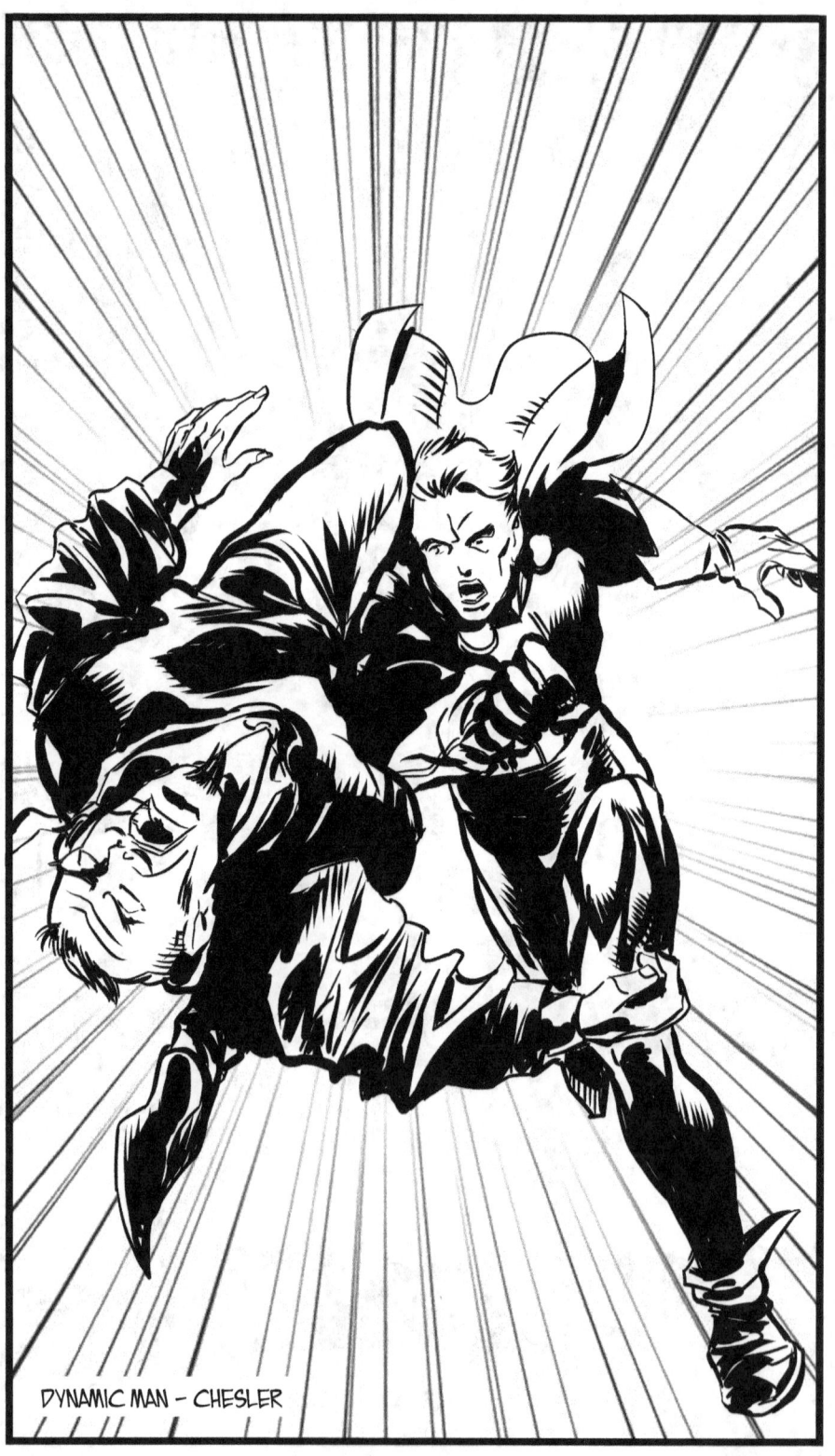

DYNAMIC MAN – CHESLER

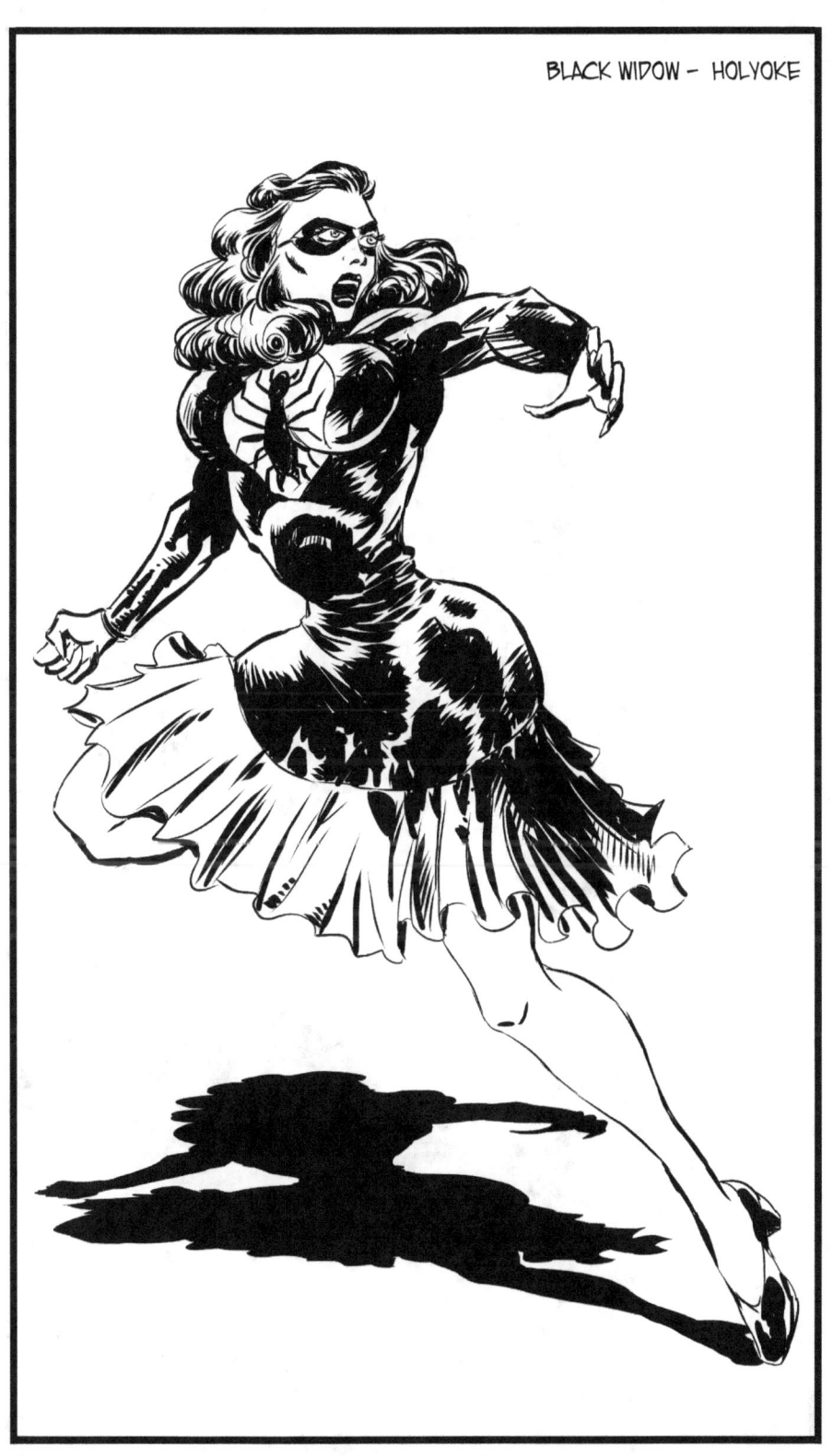

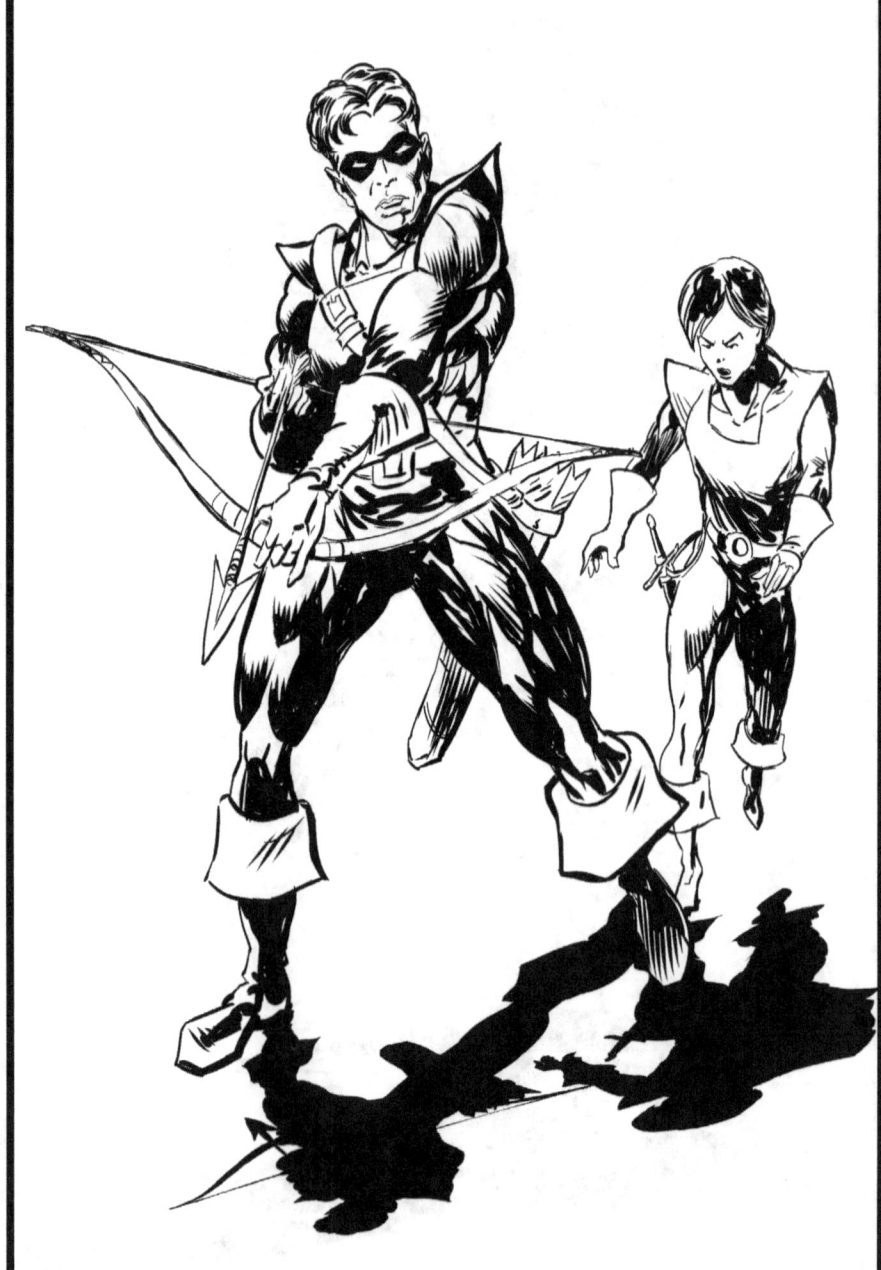

GREEN KNIGHT & LANCE -
CHESLER

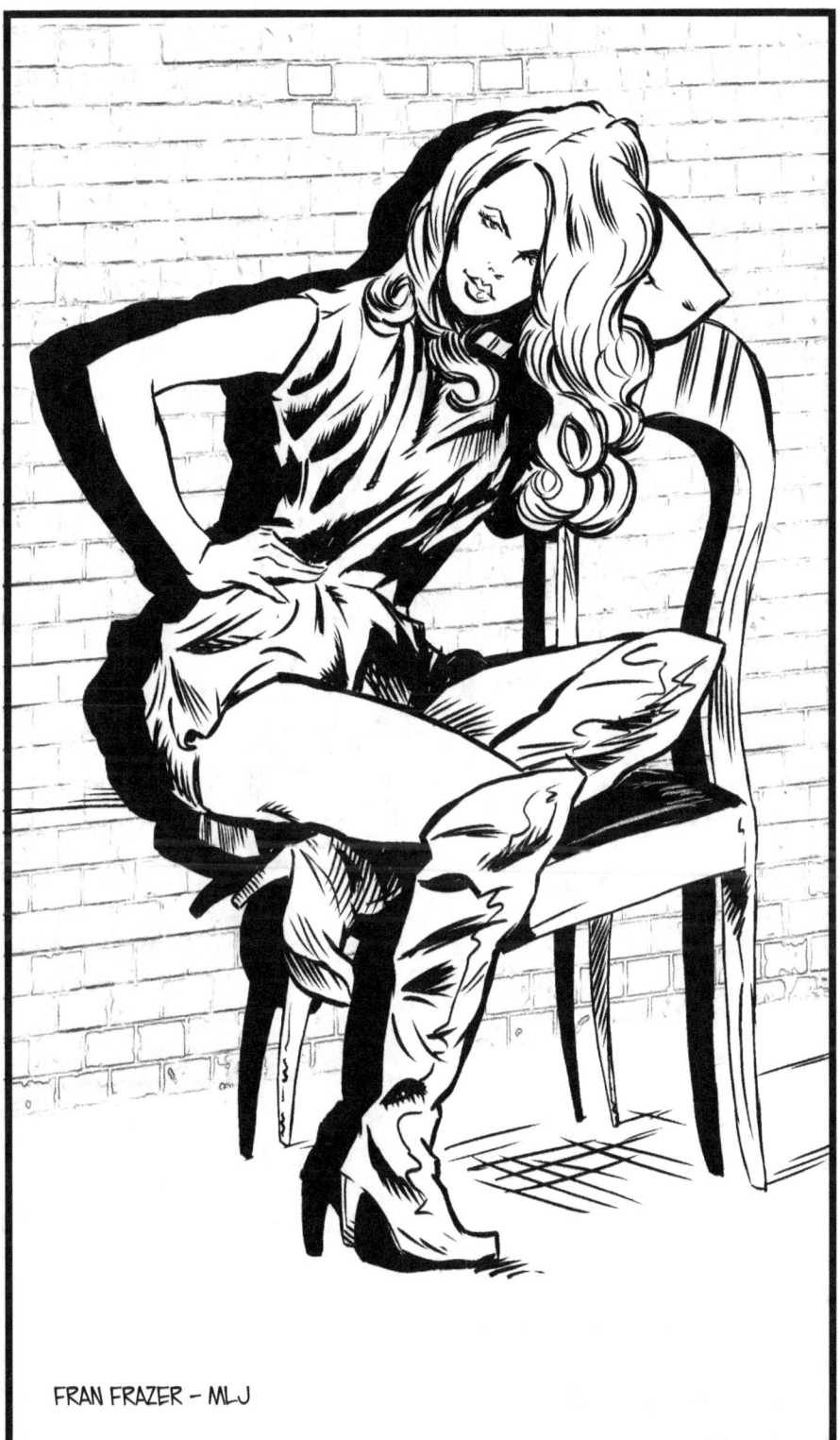

FRAN FRAZER – MLJ

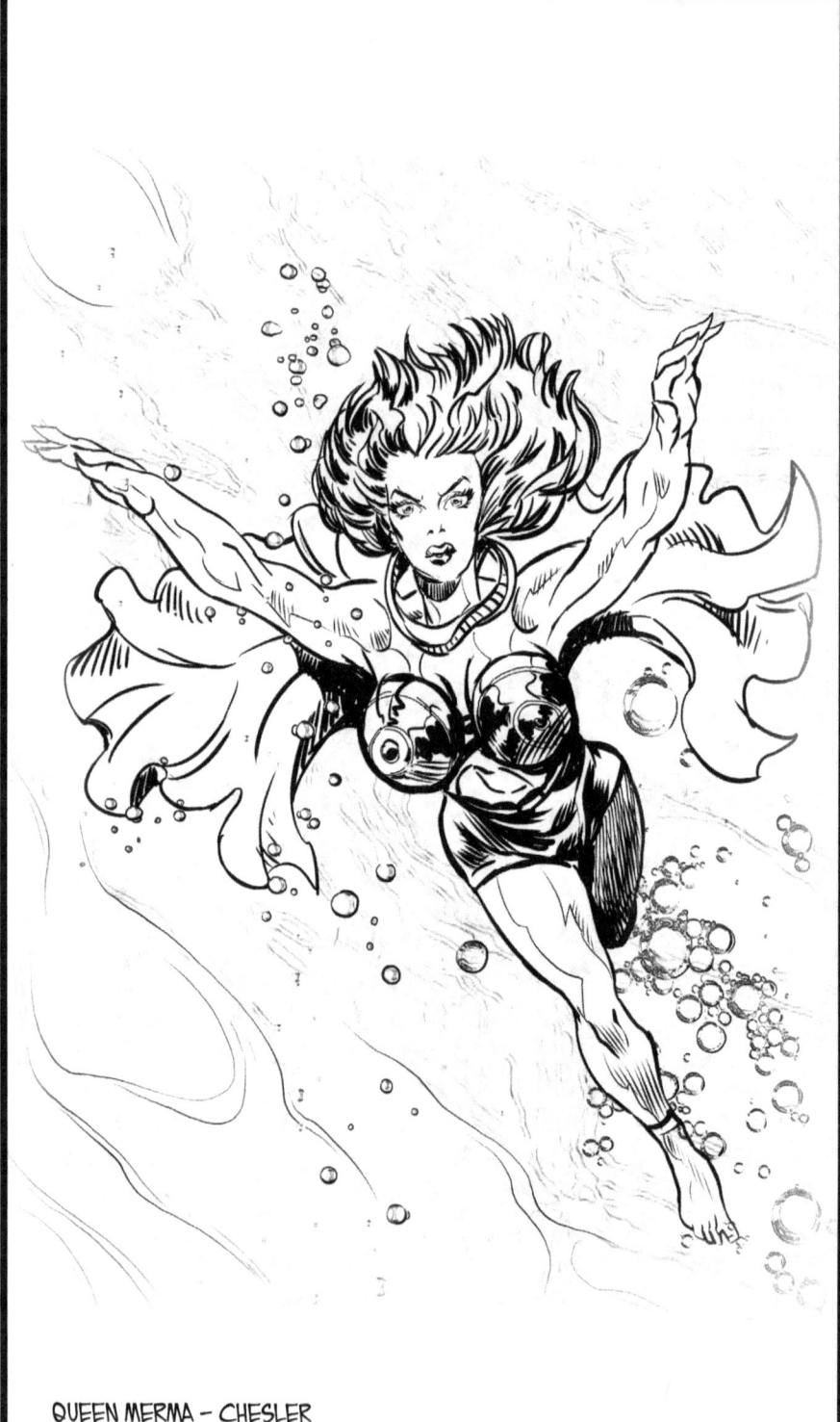

QUEEN MERMA – CHESLER

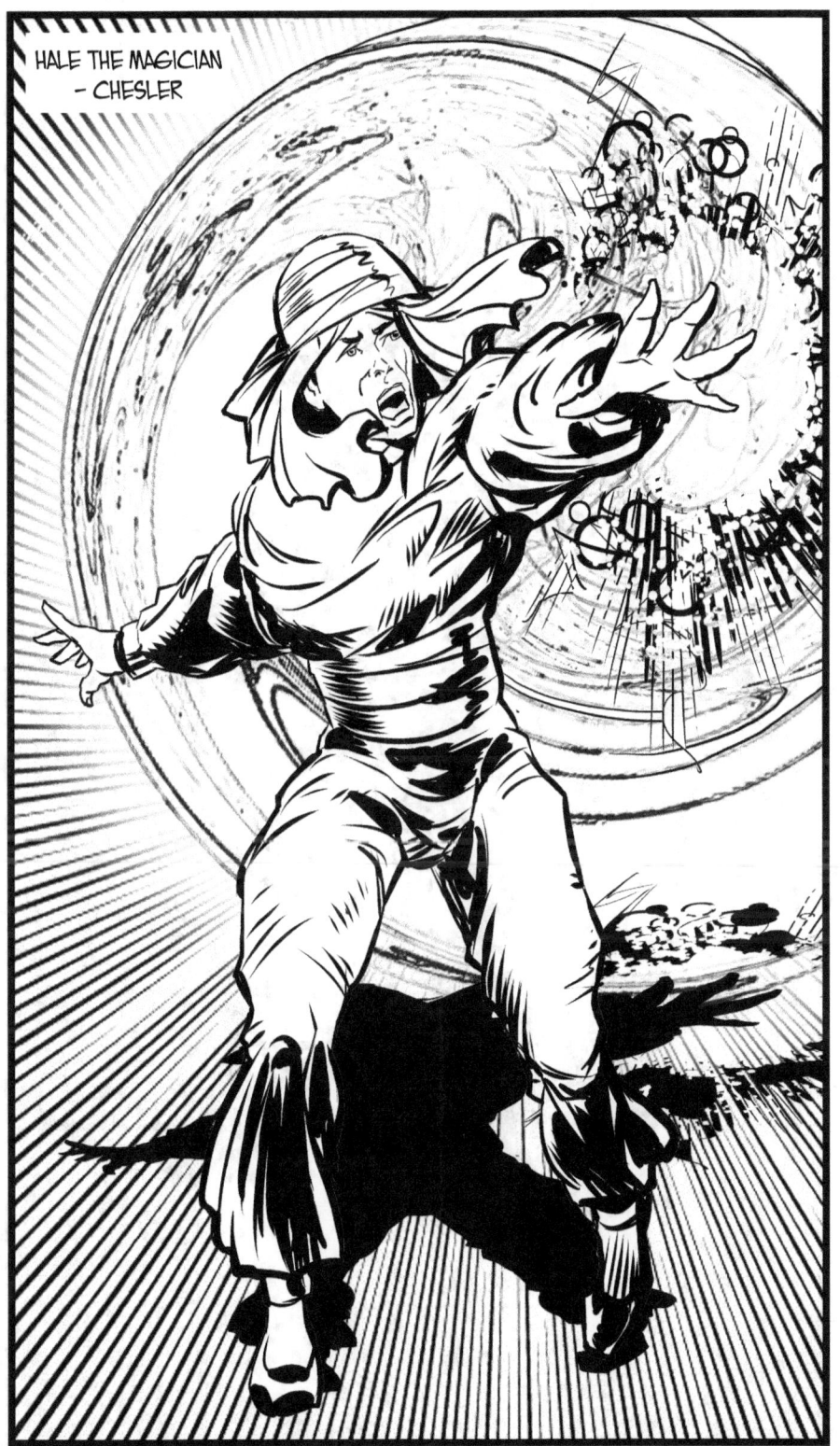

HALE THE MAGICIAN
– CHESLER

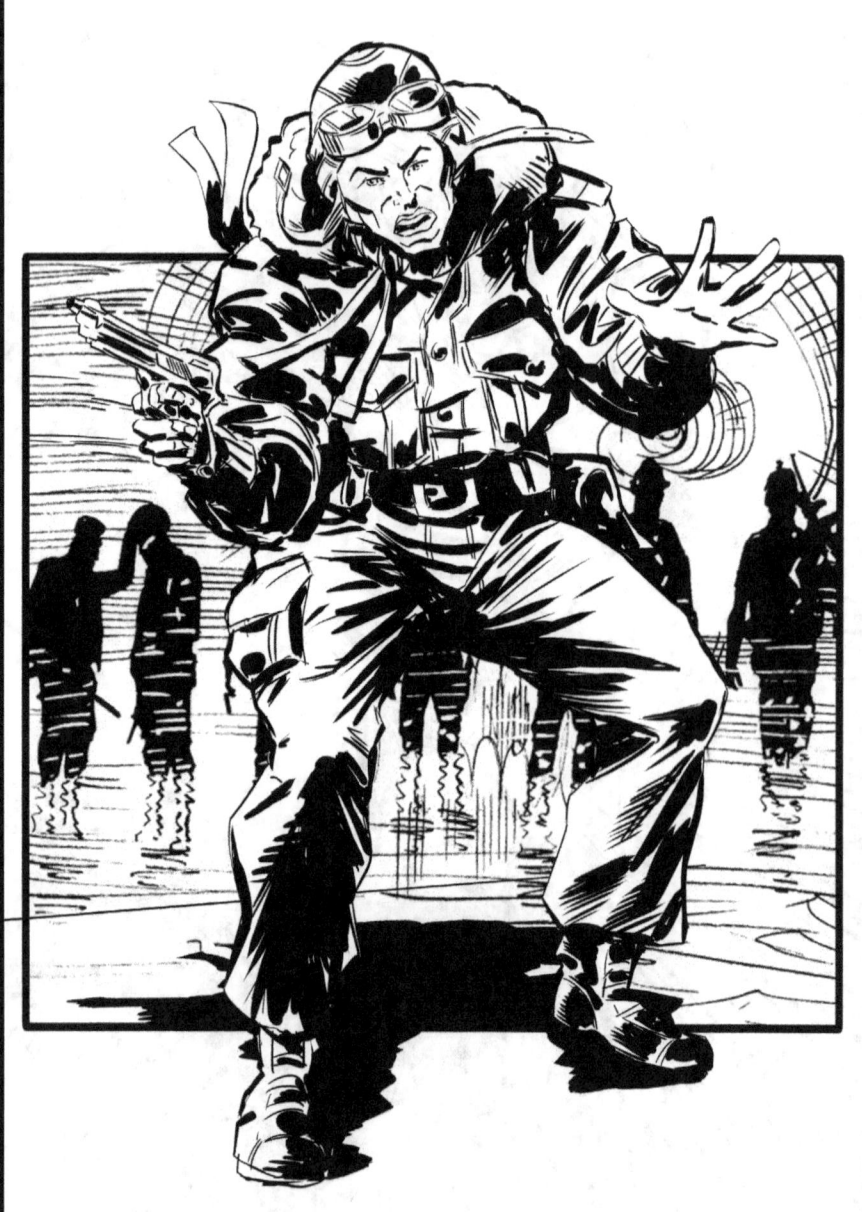

LARRY NORTH - NEDOR

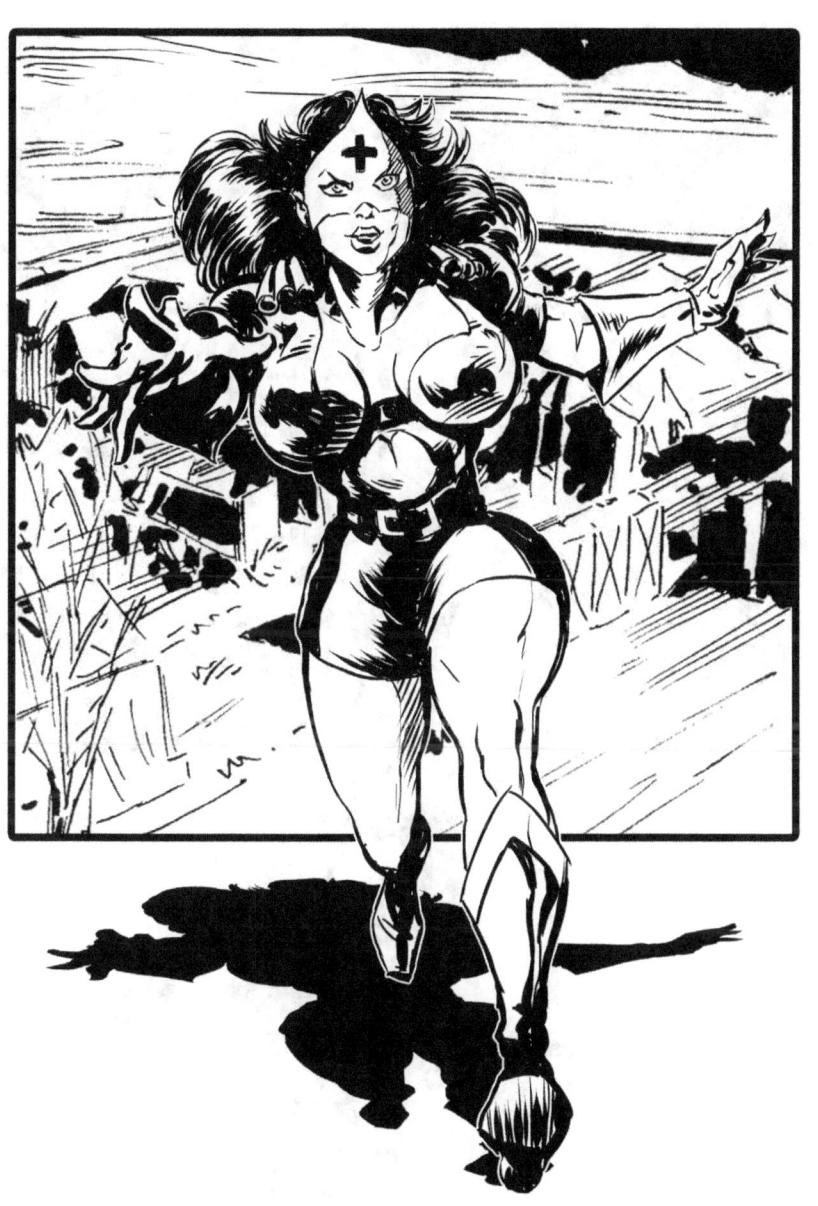

WAR NURSE — HARVEY

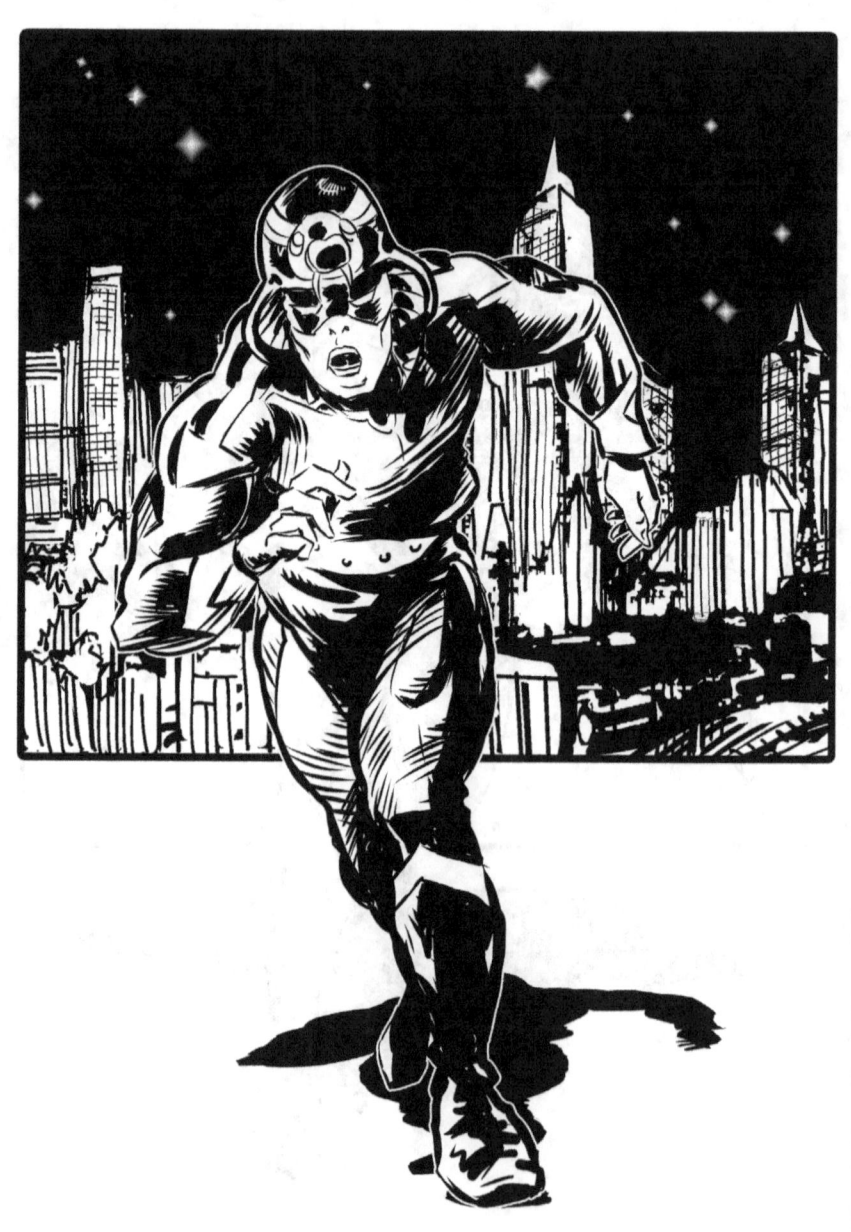

BLACK COBRA – CHESLER

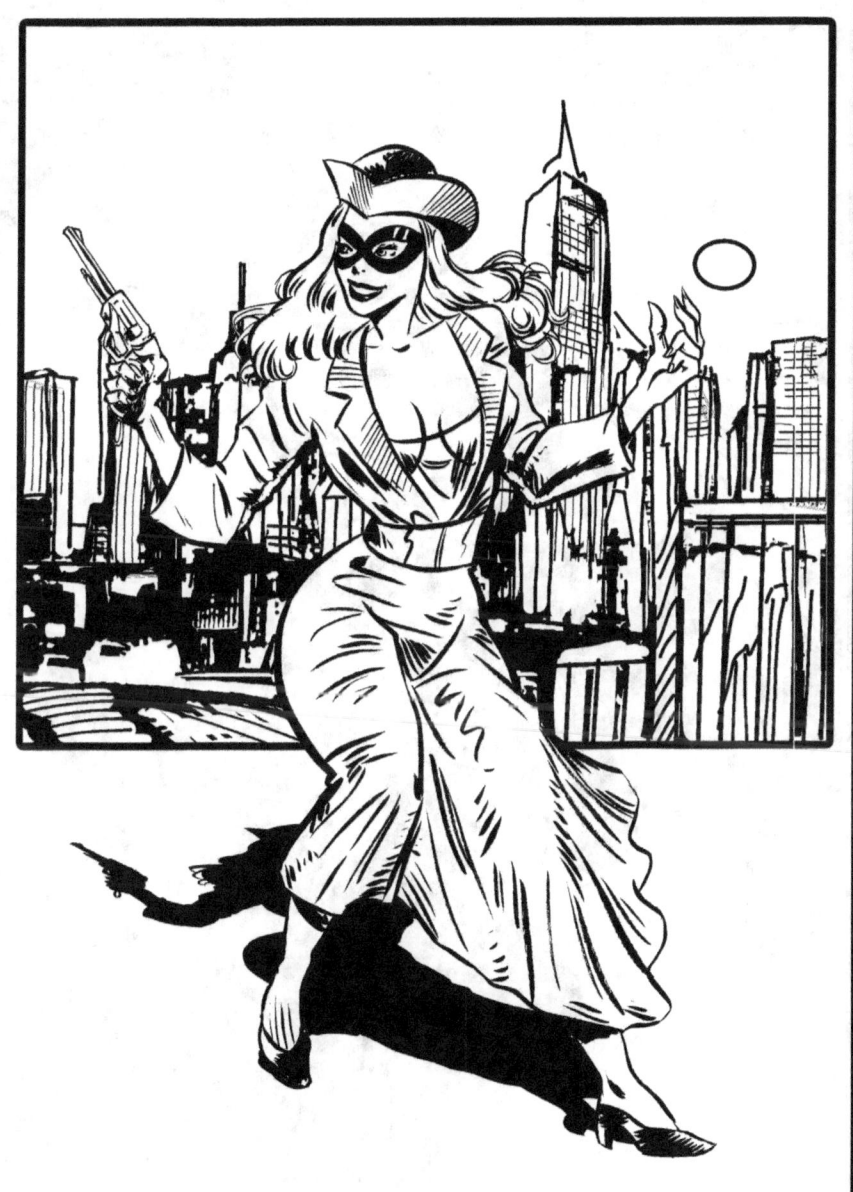

RED ANN - NEDOR

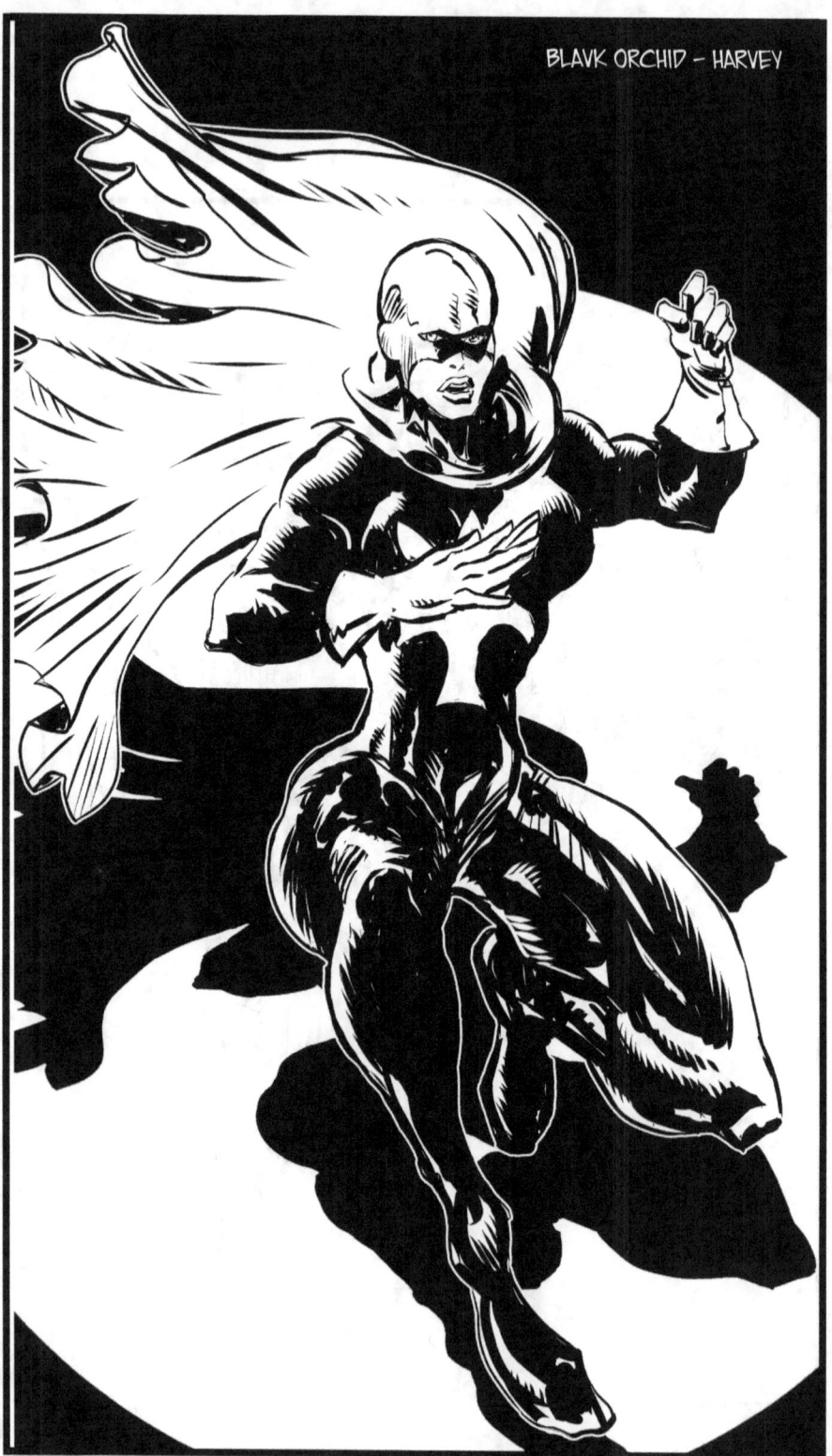

BLAVK ORCHID - HARVEY

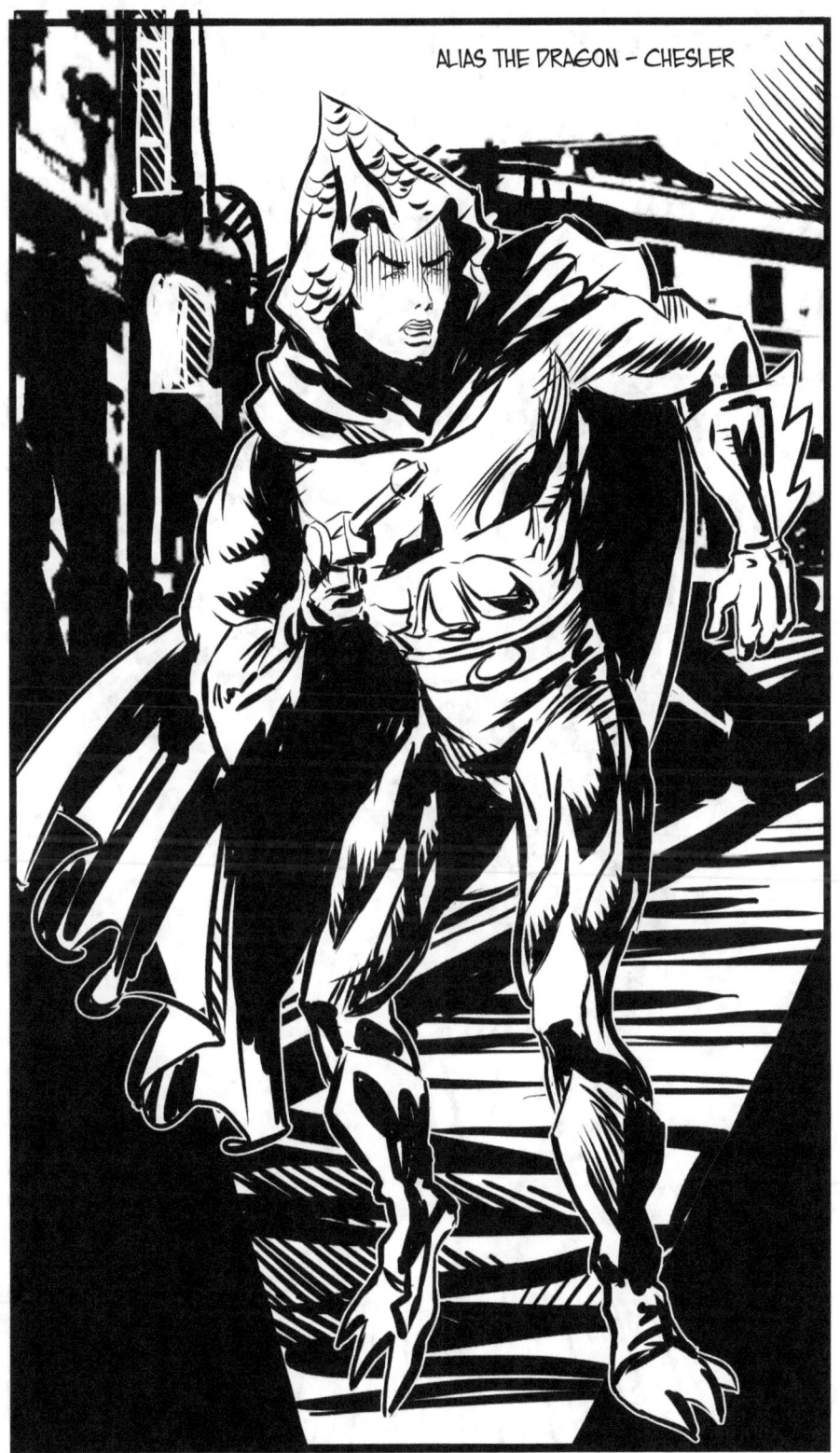

ALIAS THE DRAGON - CHESLER

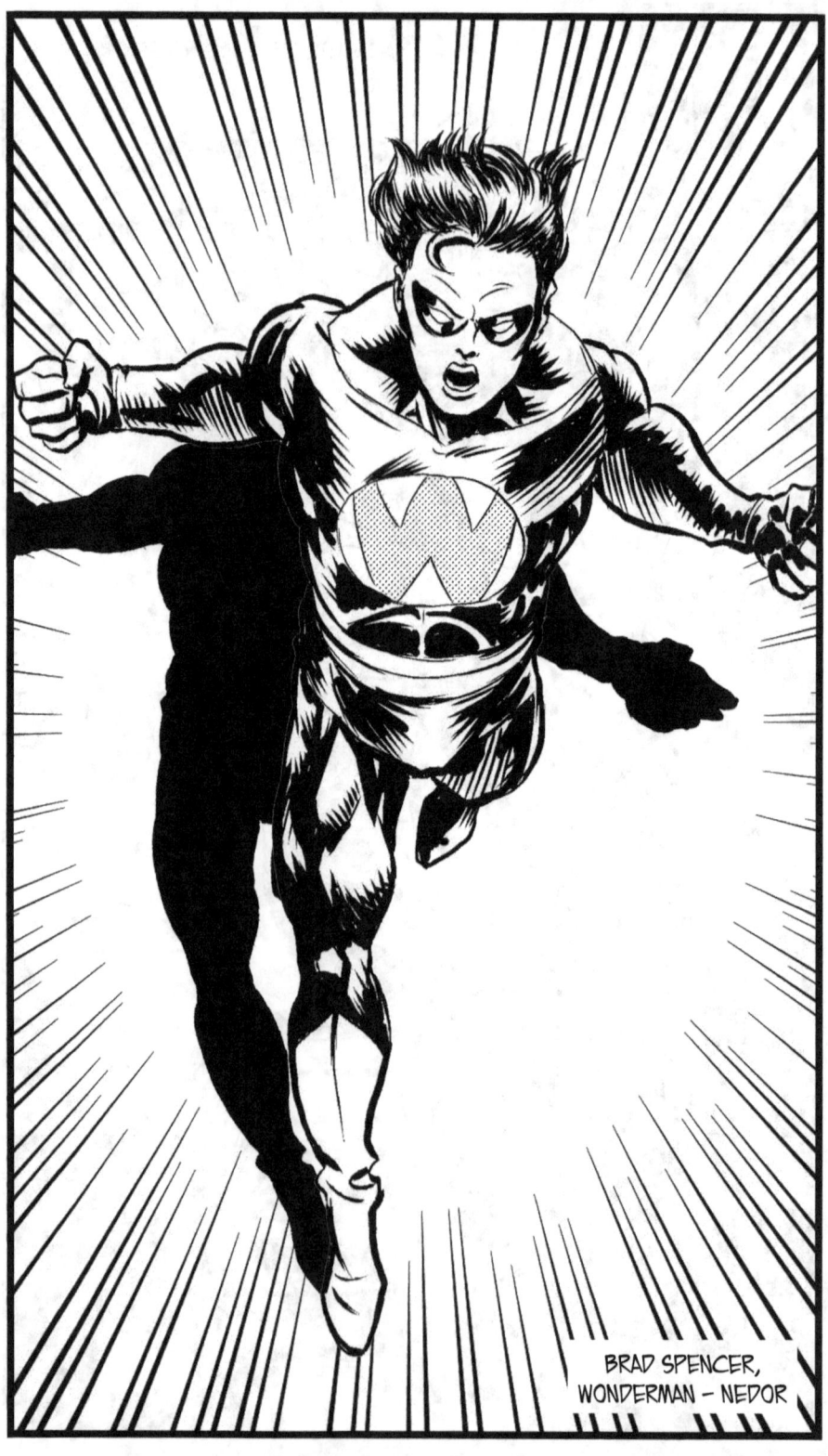

BRAD SPENCER,
WONDERMAN – NEDOR

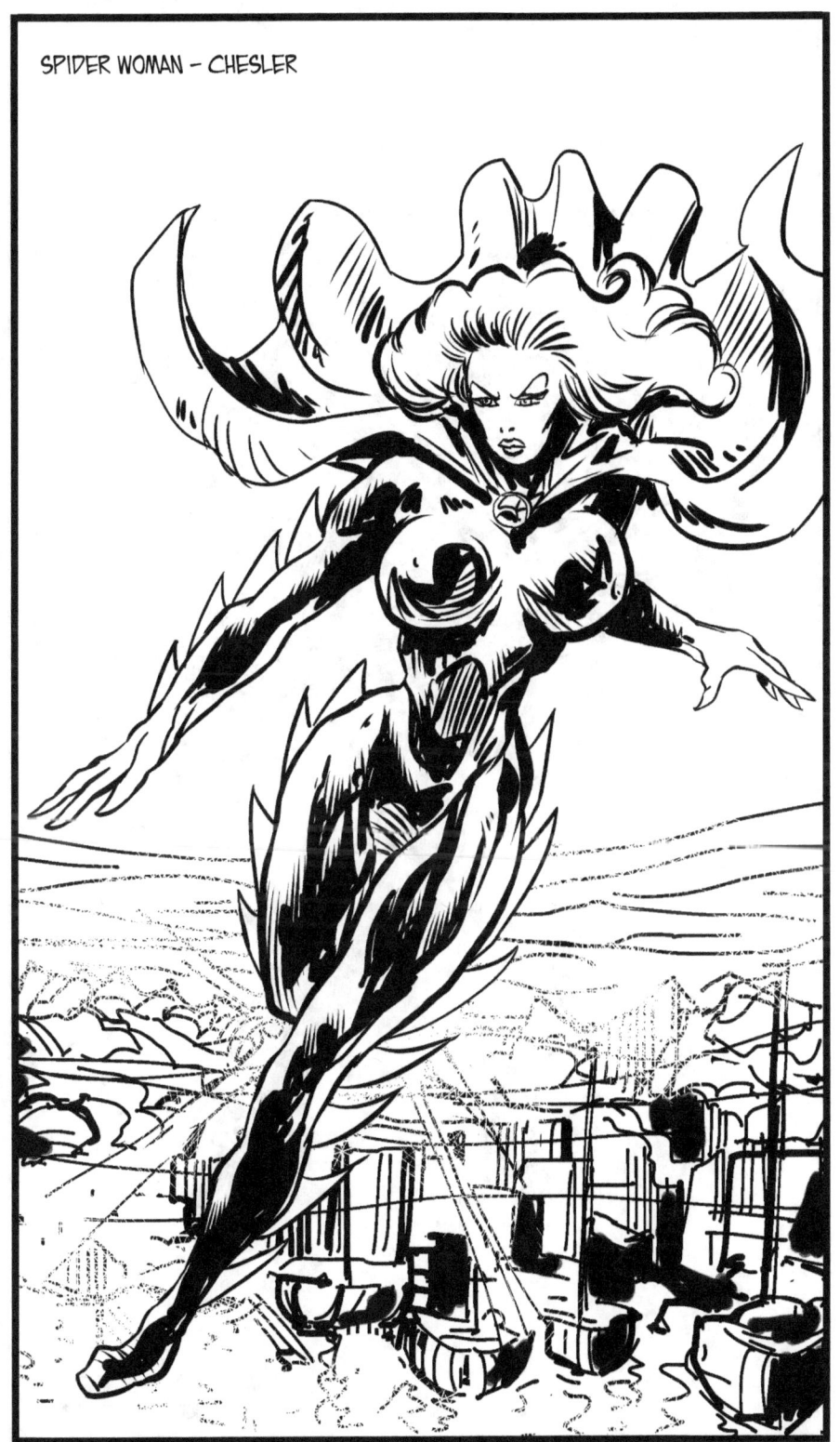

SPIDER WOMAN - CHESLER

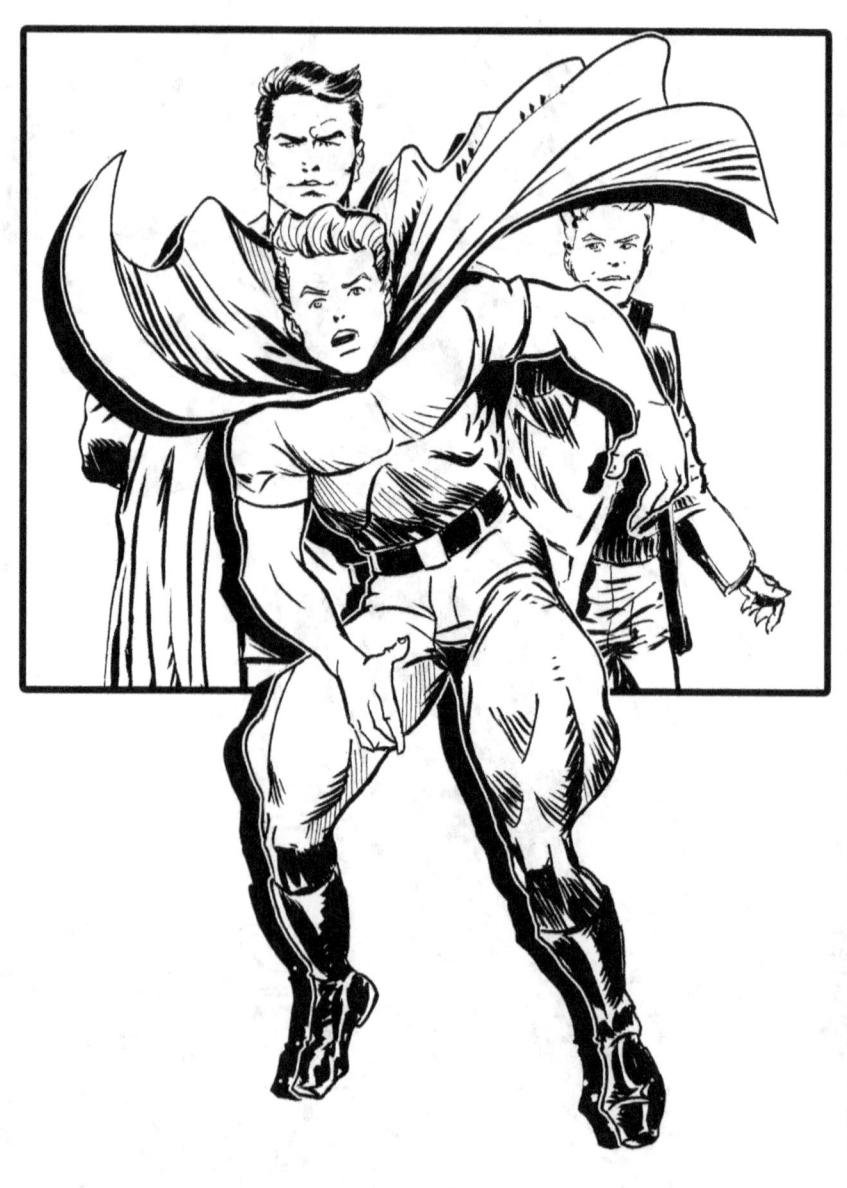

MIKE, DOC STRANGE'S
SIDEKICK – NEDOR

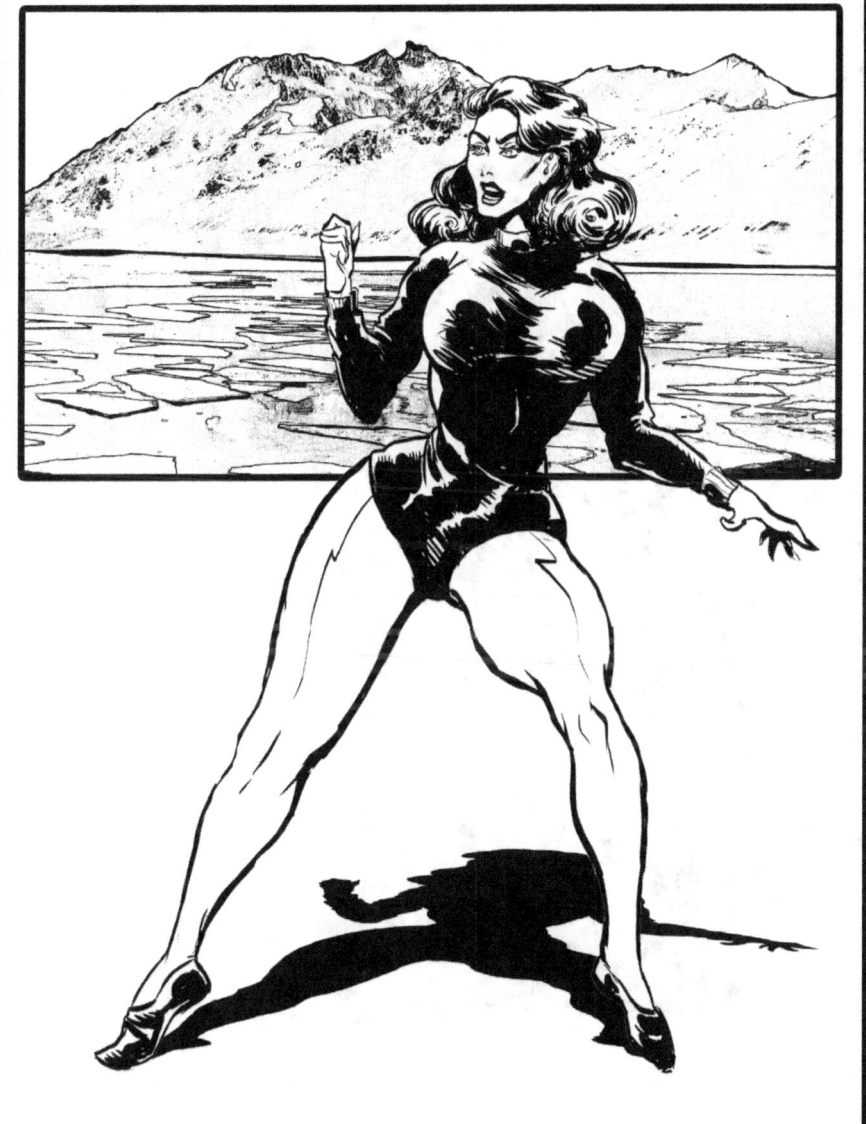

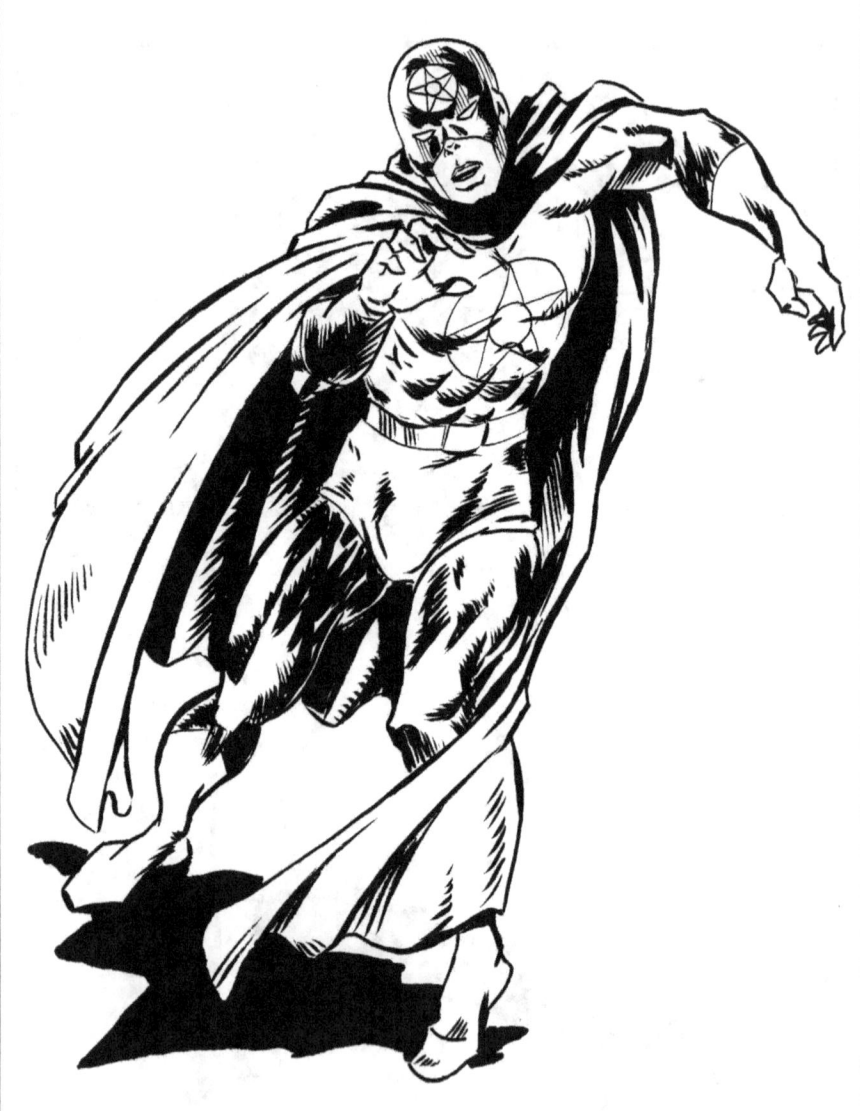

AMERICA CRUSADER - NEDOR

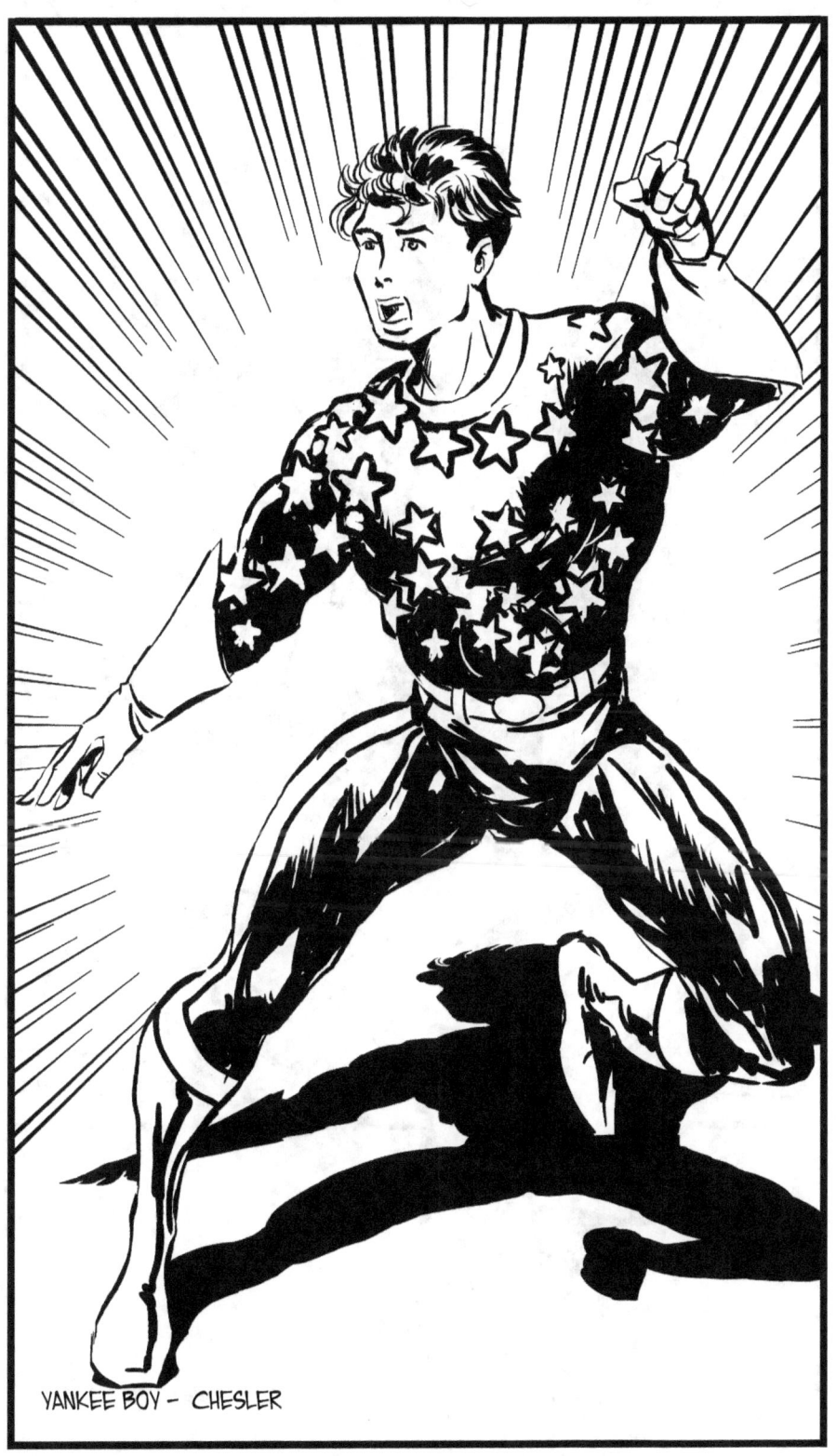

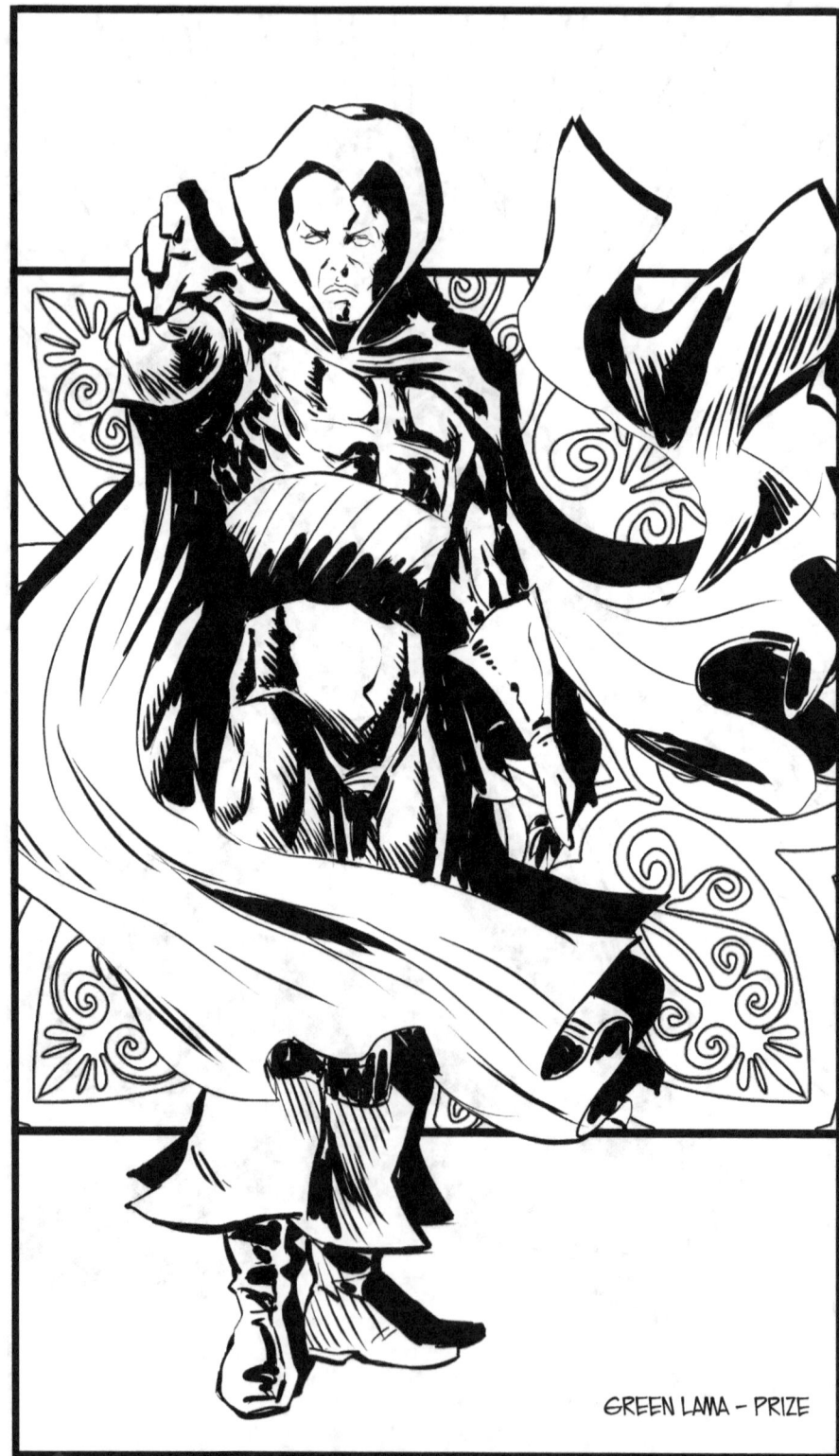

GREEN LAMA - PRIZE

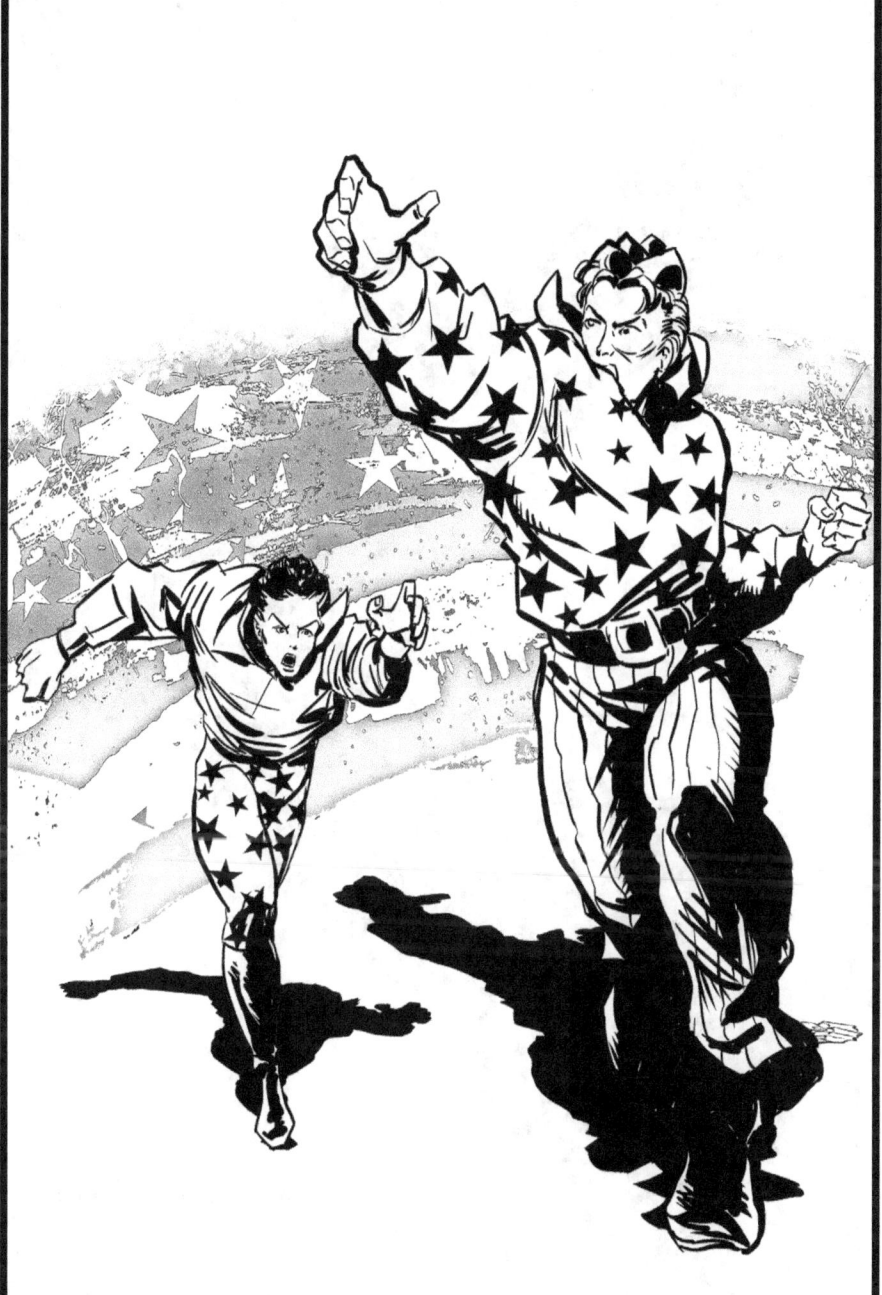

YANKEE DOODLE JONES &
DANDY - CHESLER

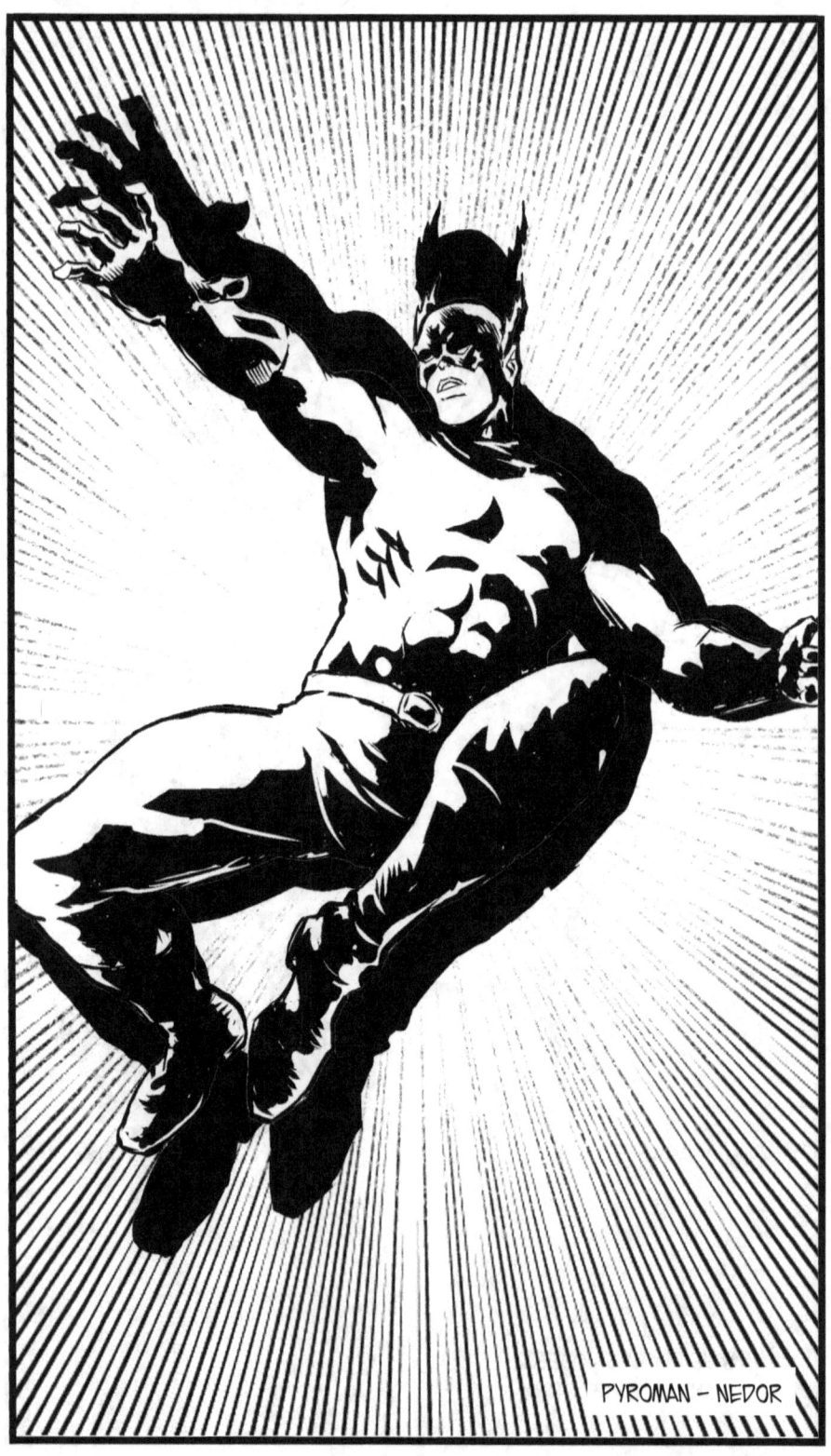

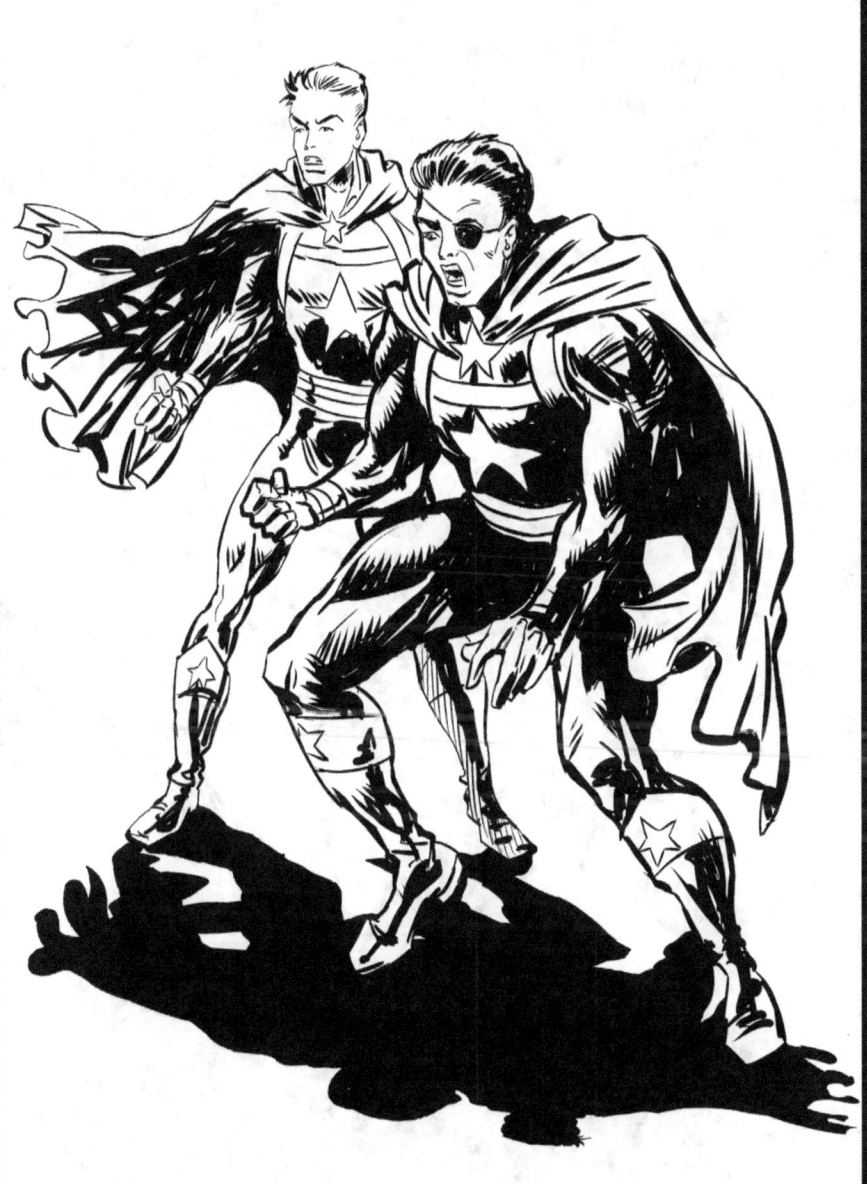

CAPT. BATTLE &
KANE - CHESLER

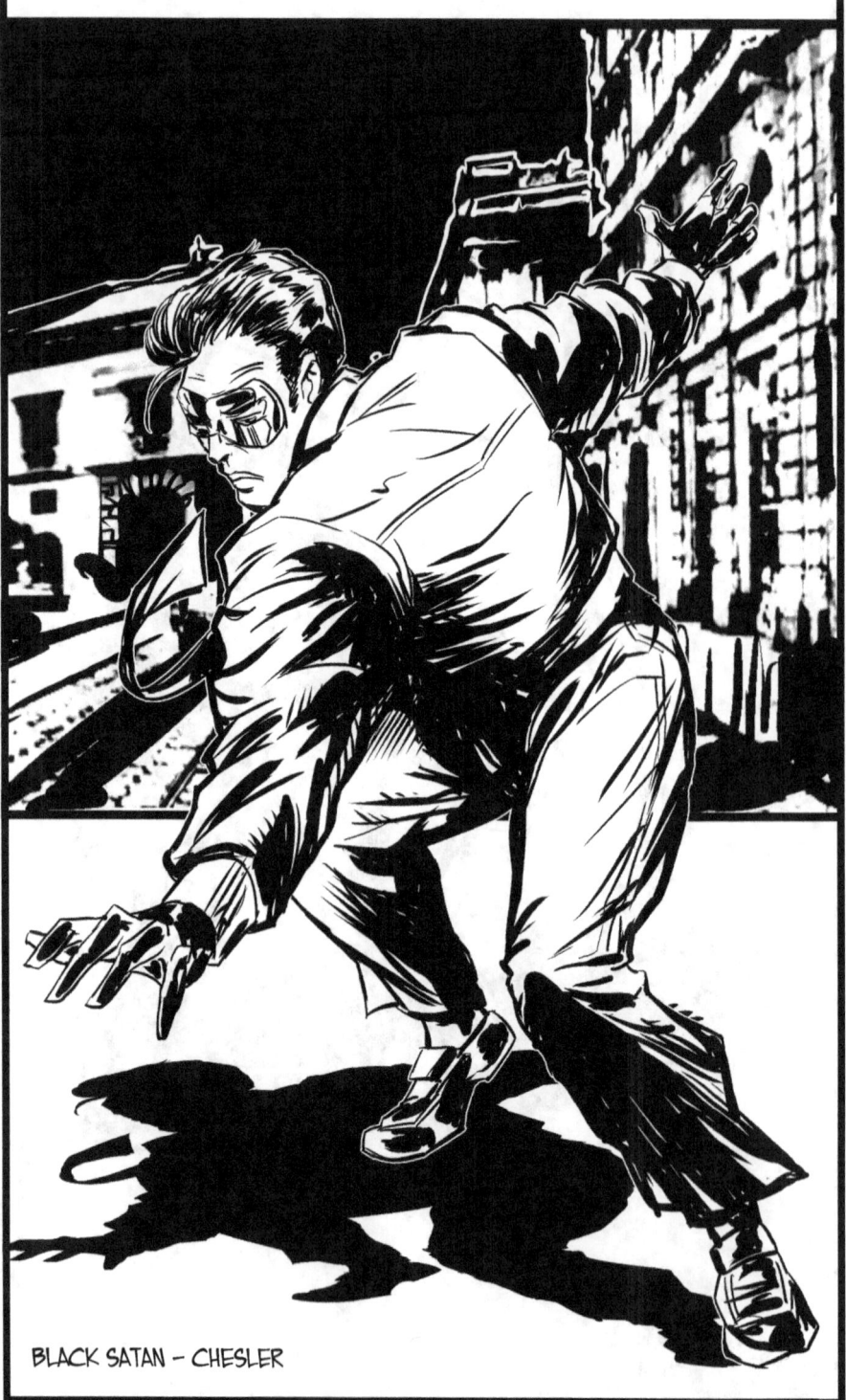

BLACK SATAN - CHESLER

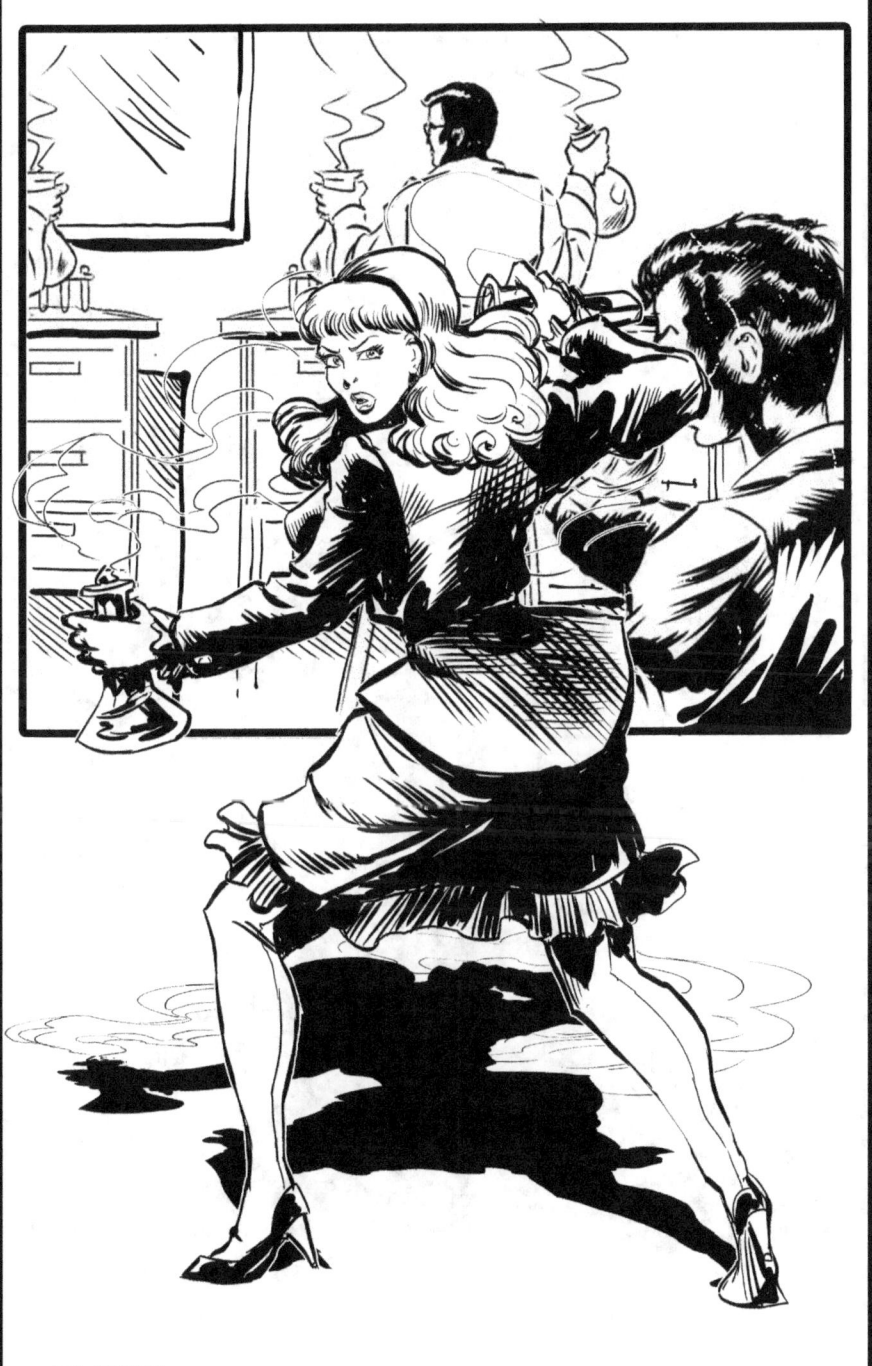

JILL TRENT –
NEDOR

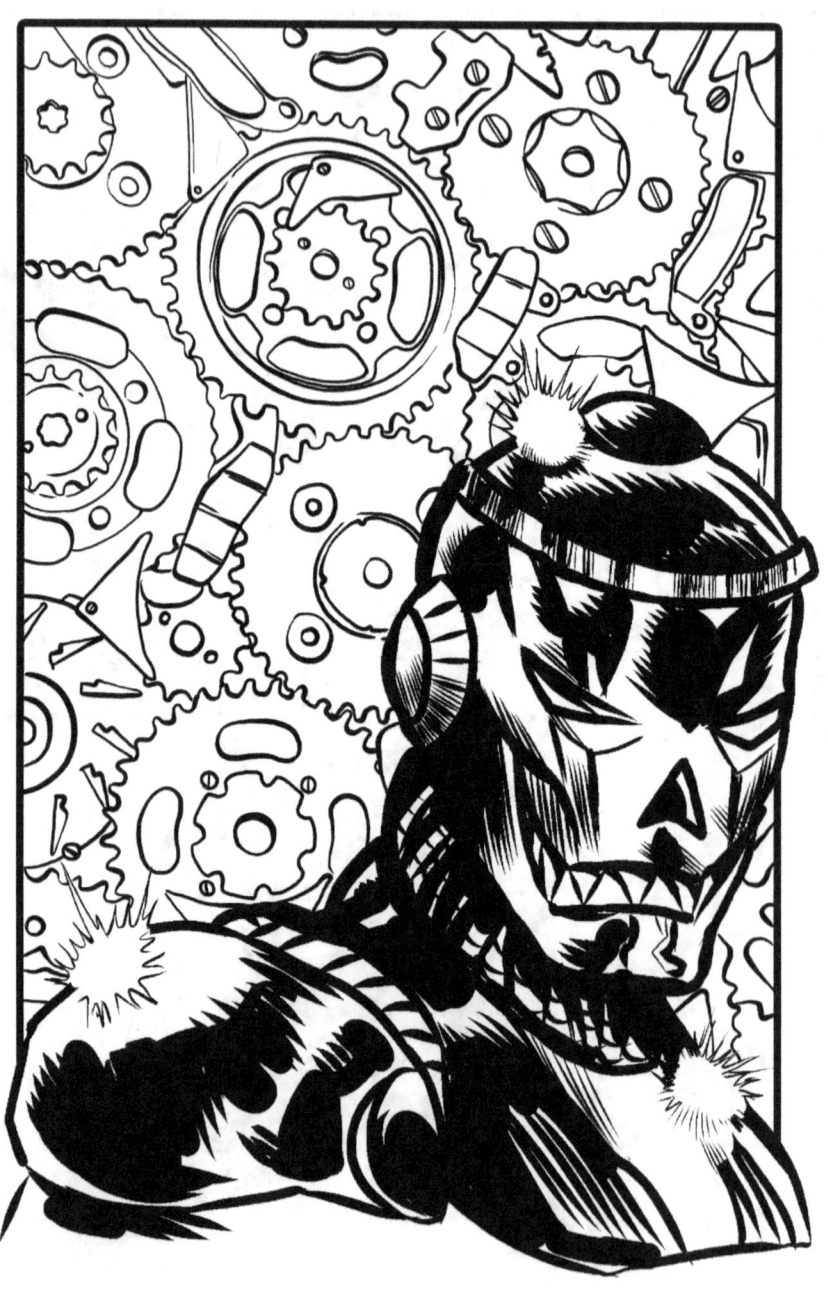

MEKANO - NEDOR

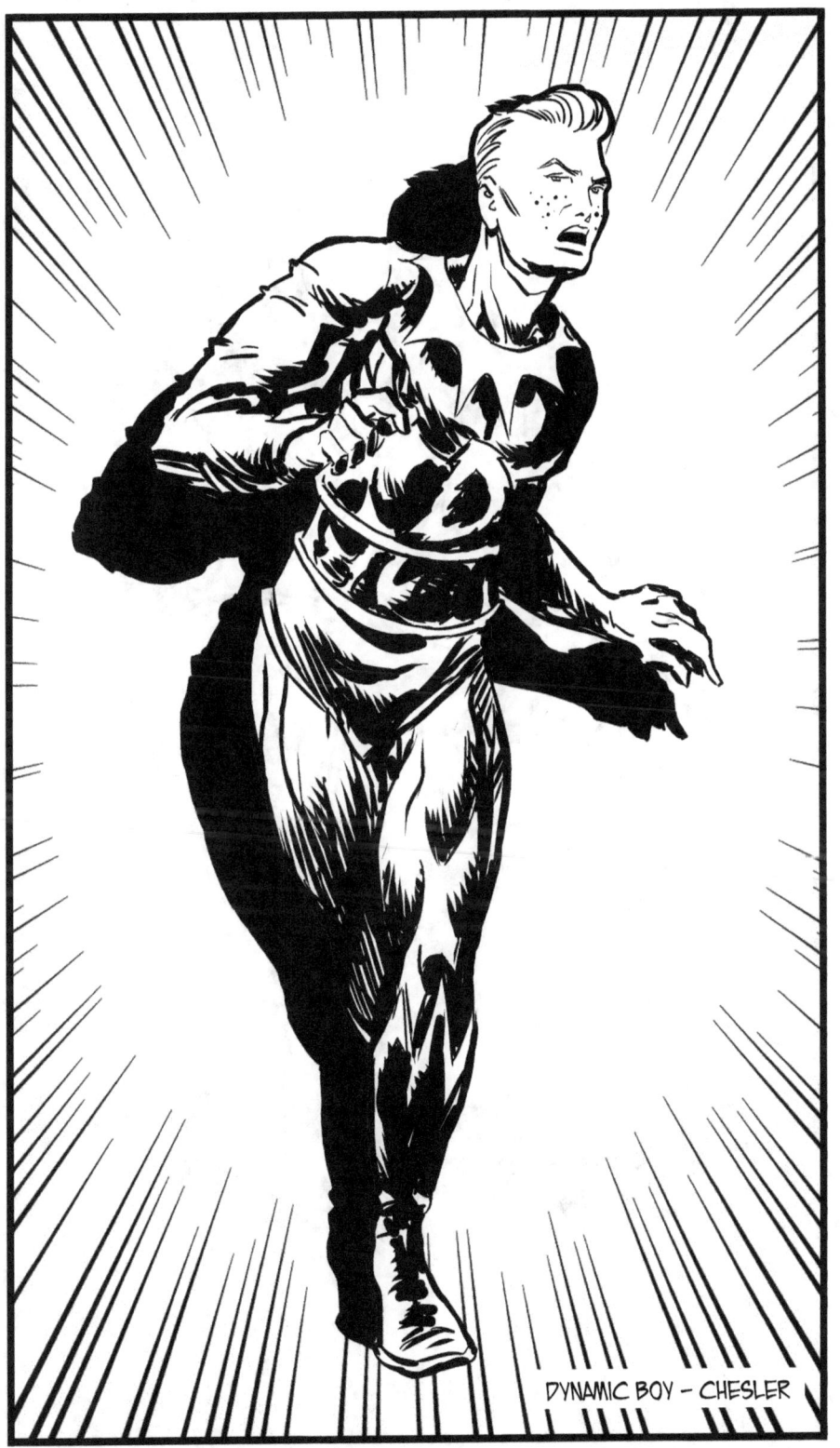

DYNAMIC BOY - CHESLER

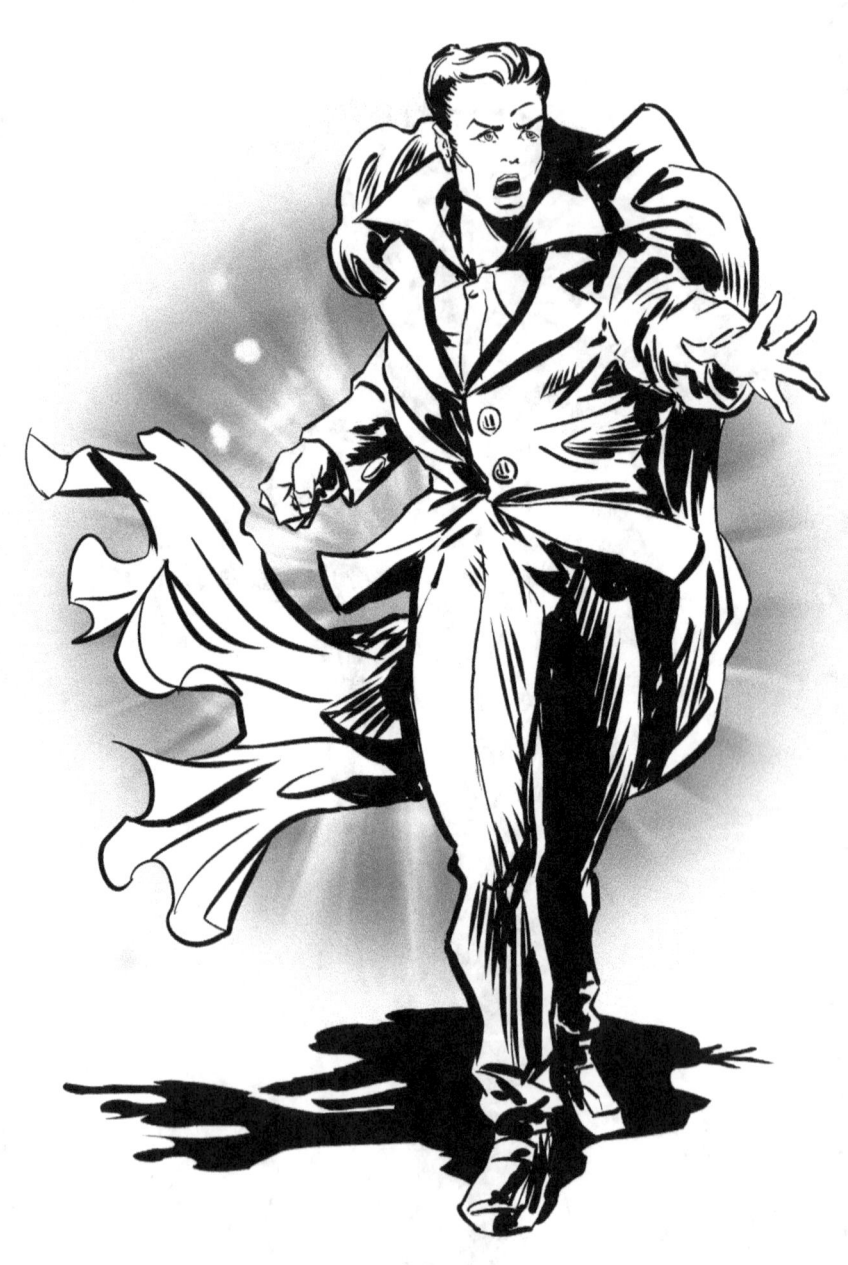

ECHO - CHESLER

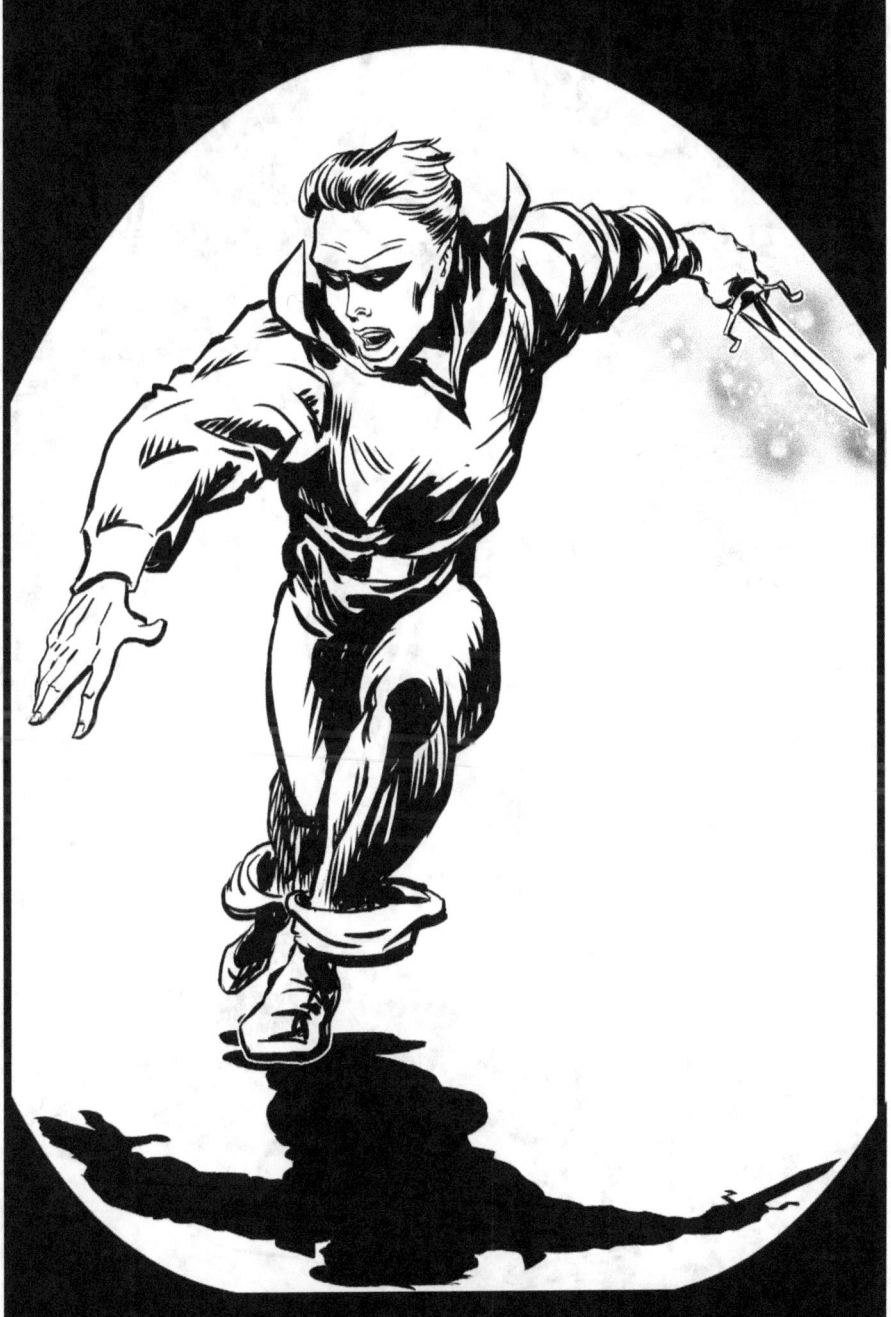

ENCHANTED DAGGER –
CHESLER

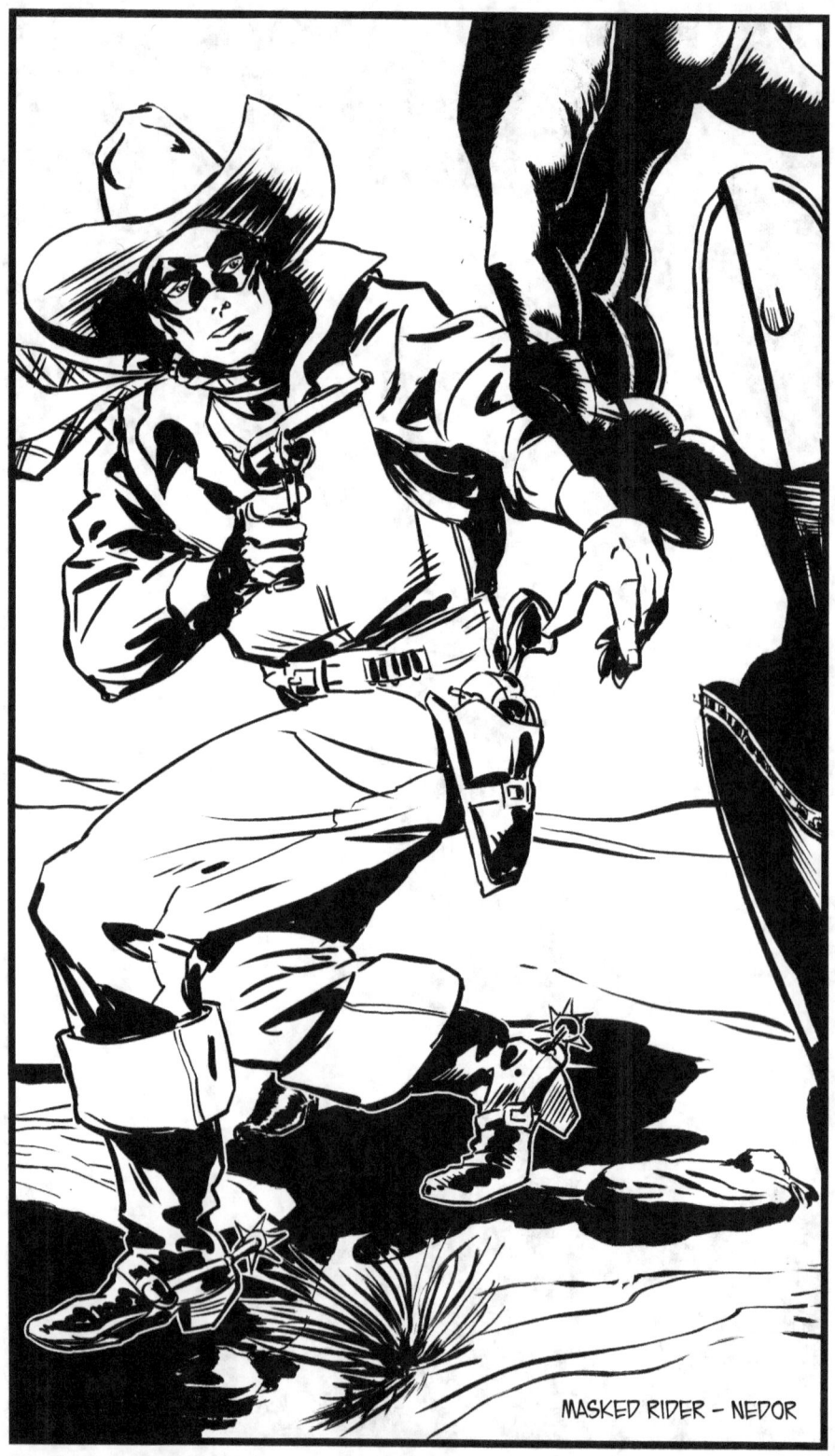

MASKED RIDER - NEDOR

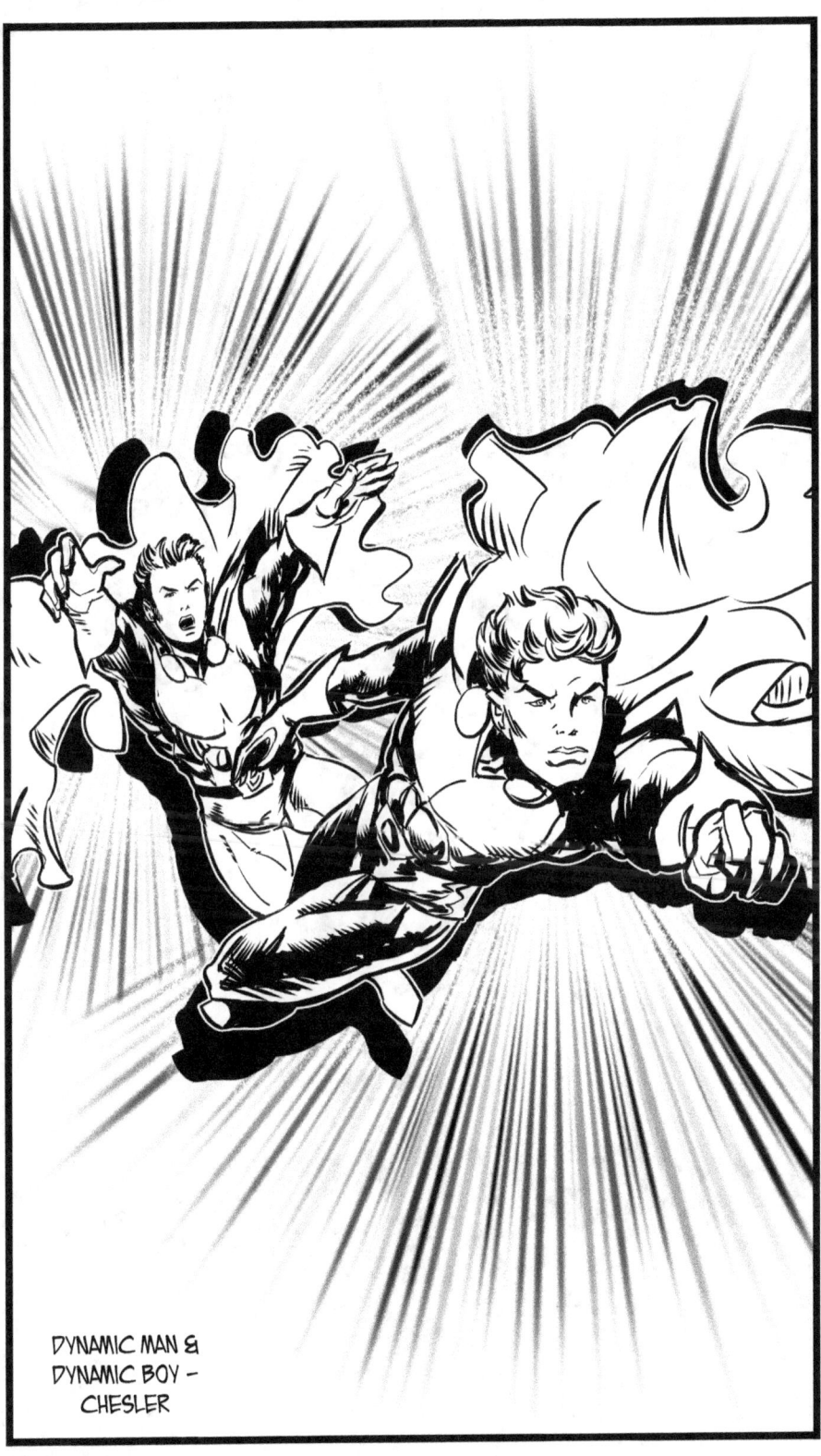

DYNAMIC MAN &
DYNAMIC BOY –
CHESLER

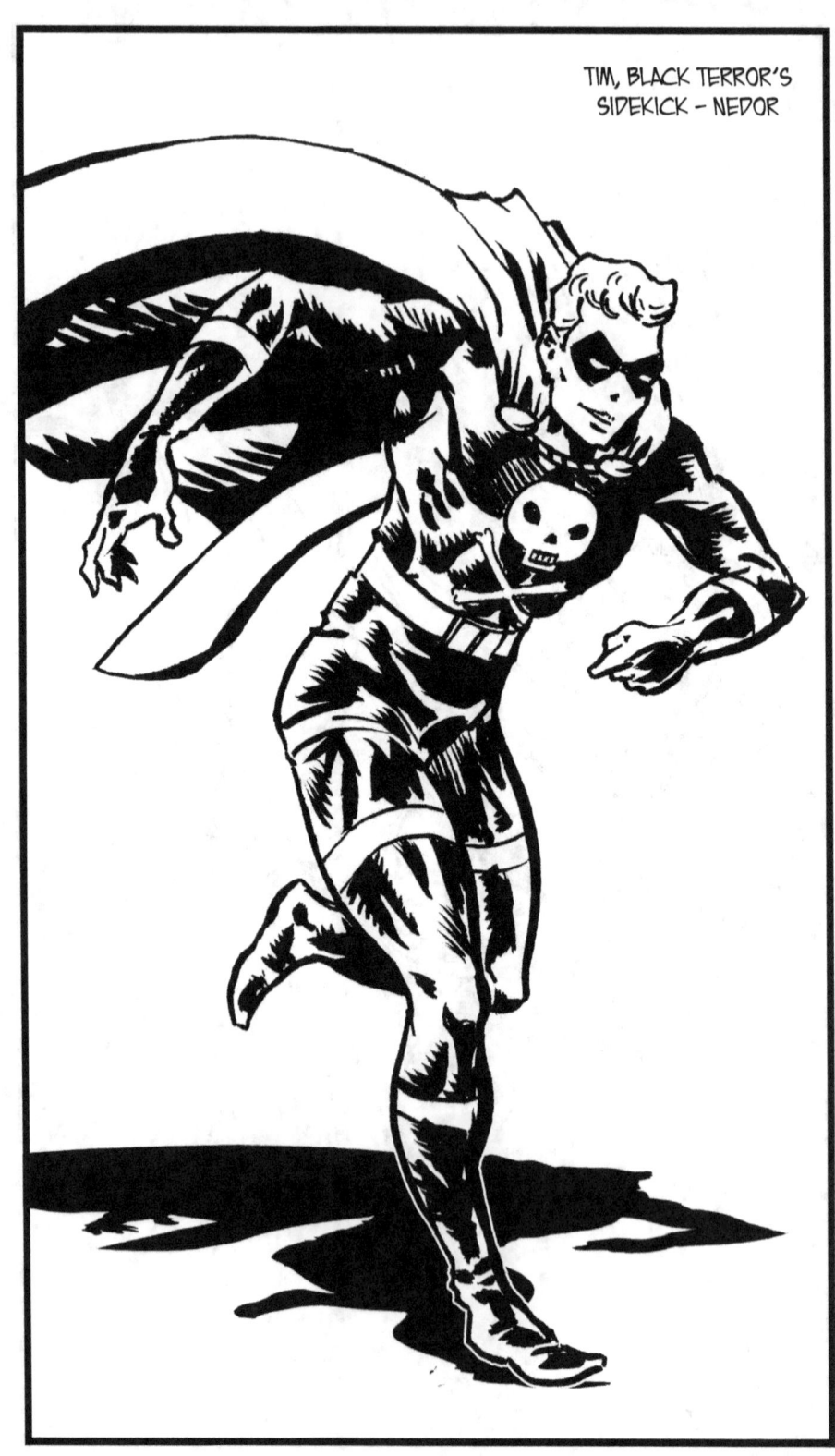

TIM, BLACK TERROR'S
SIDEKICK – NEDOR

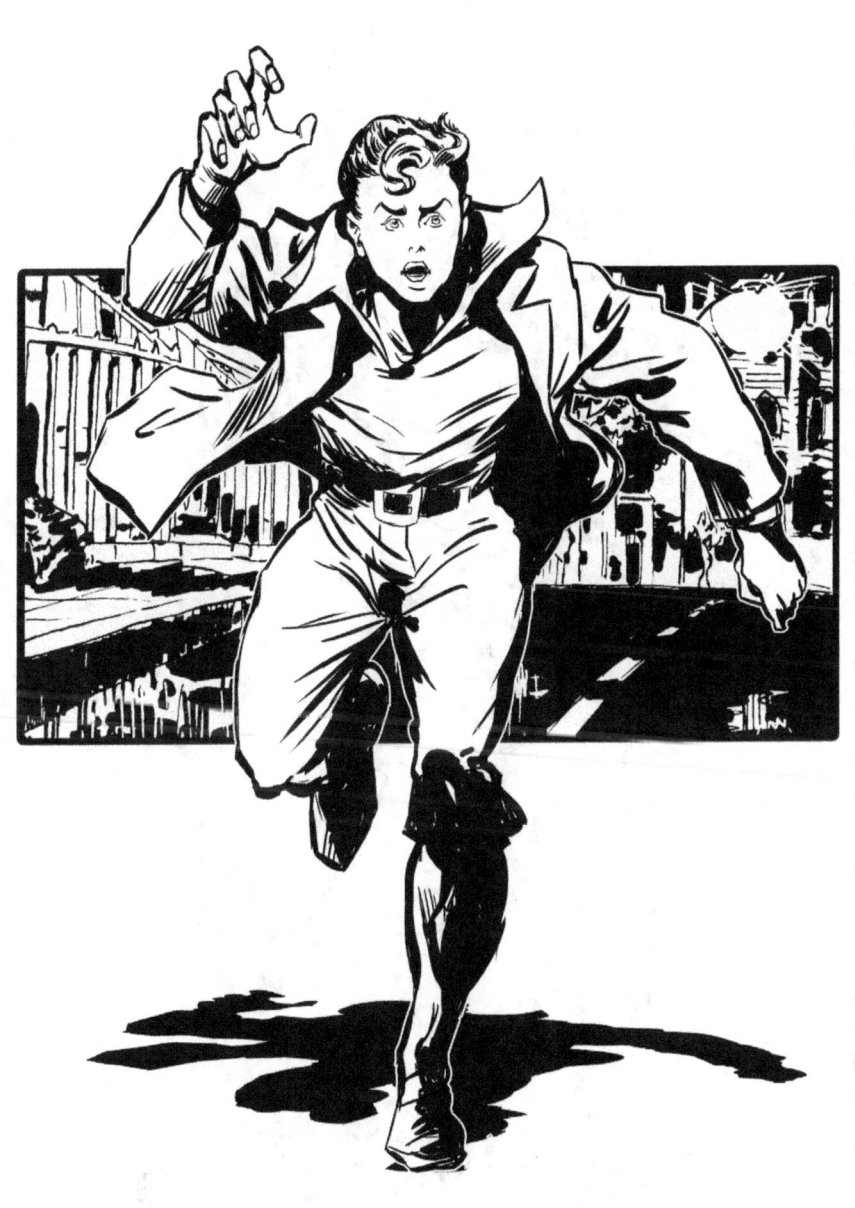

JIMMY COLE - NEDOR

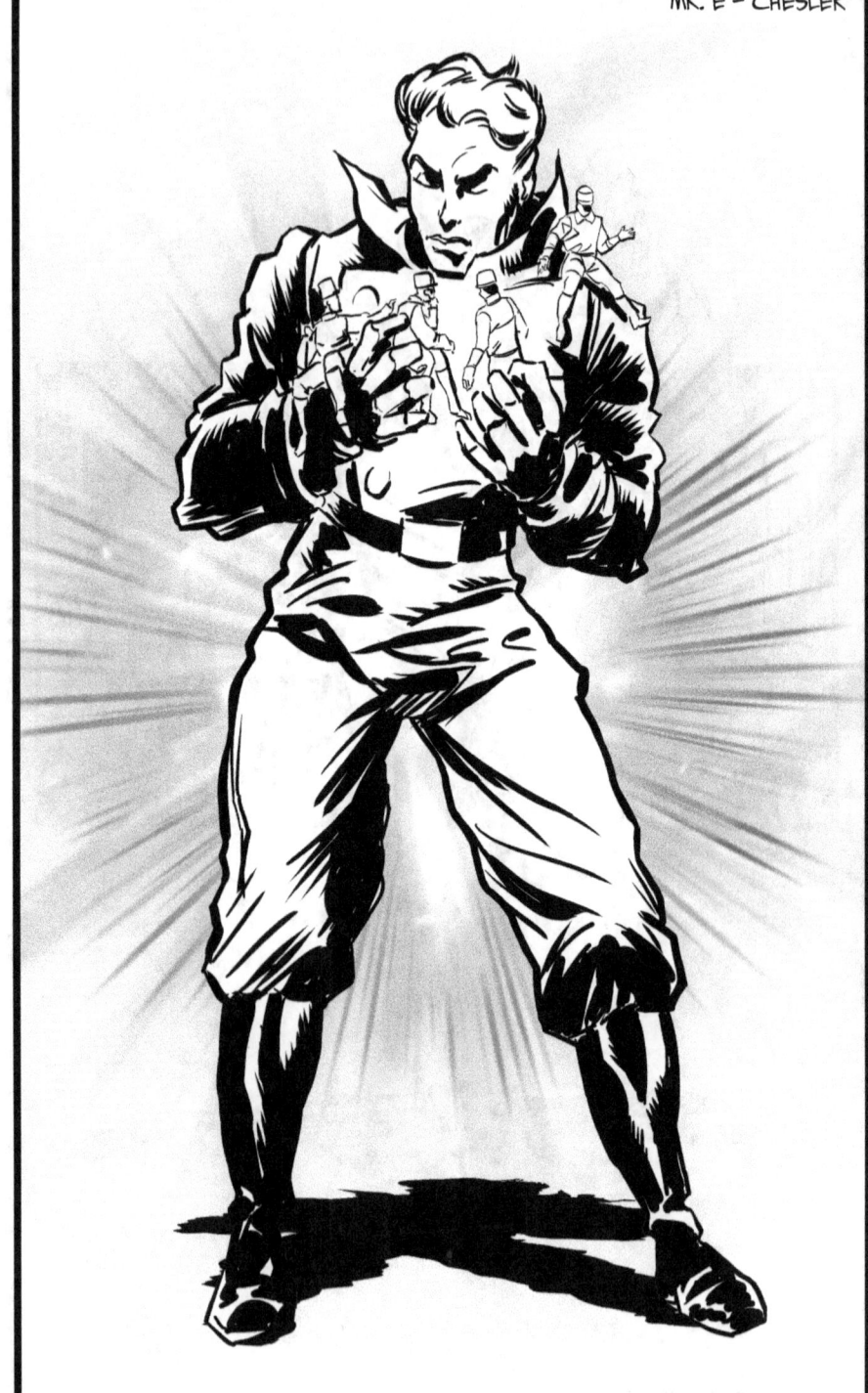

MR. E – CHESLER

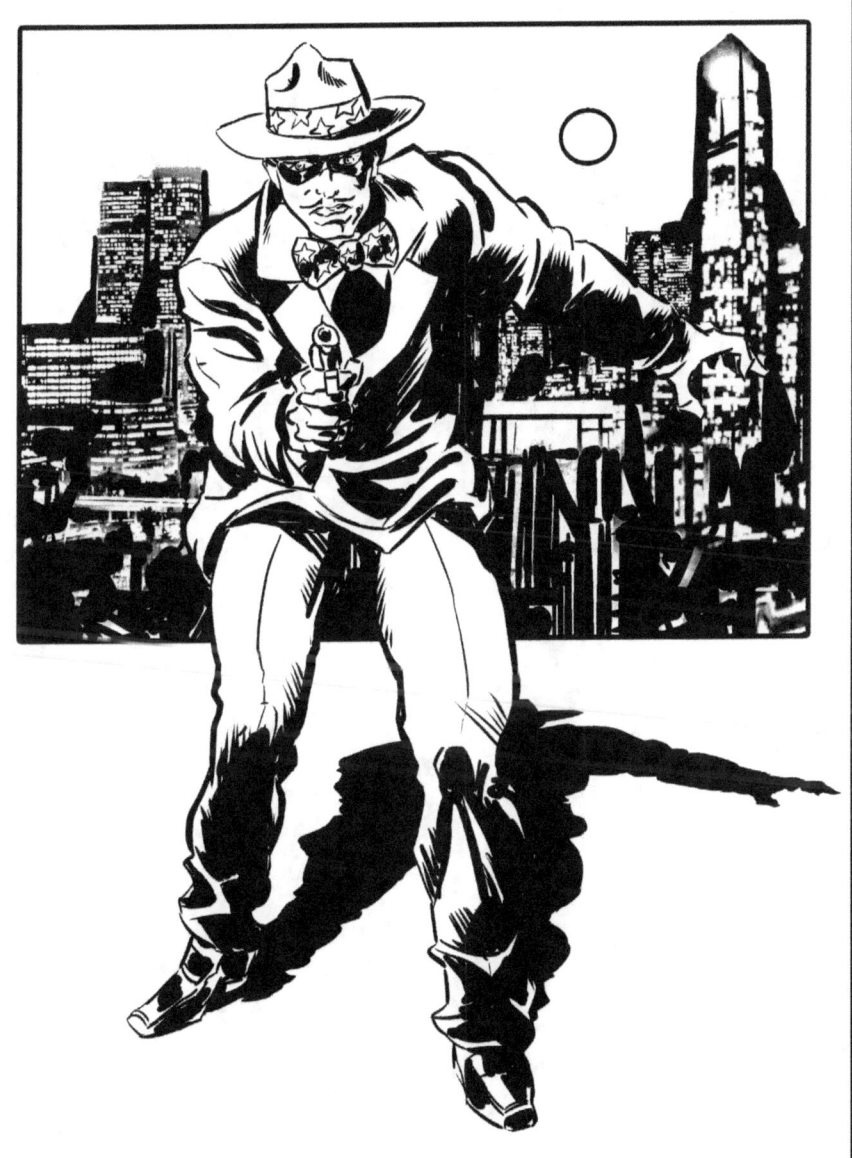

CAPTAIN GLORY – CHESLER

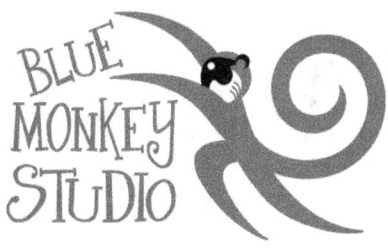
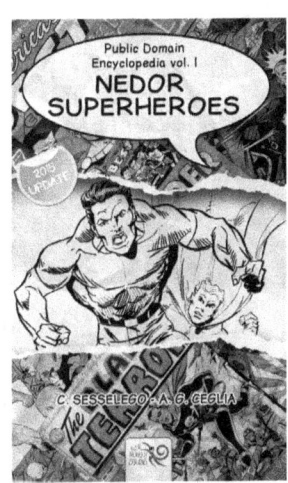
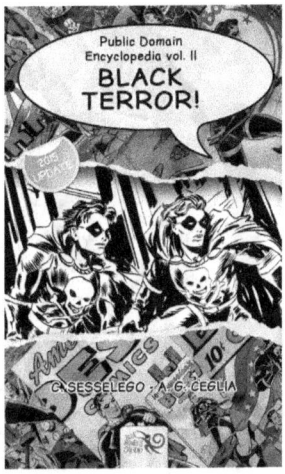
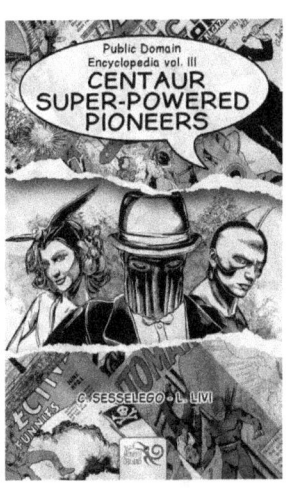
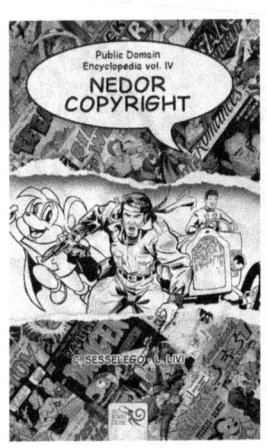
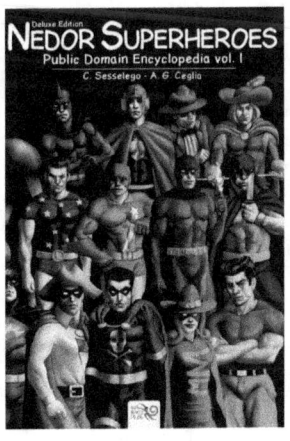

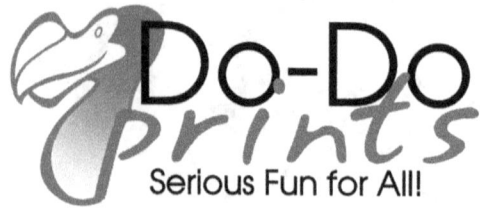
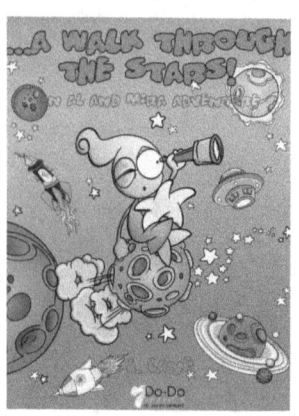
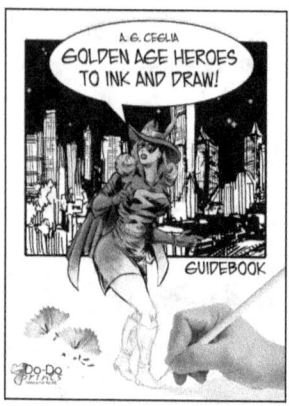
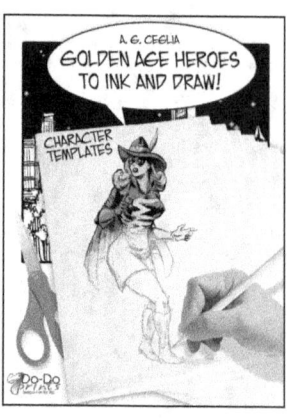
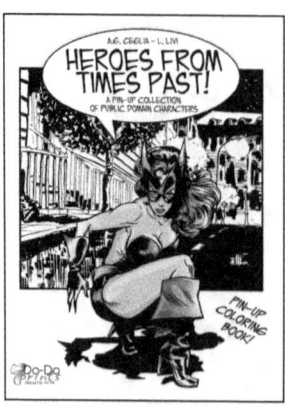
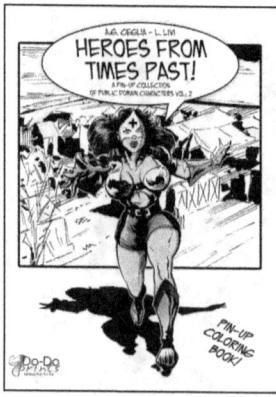
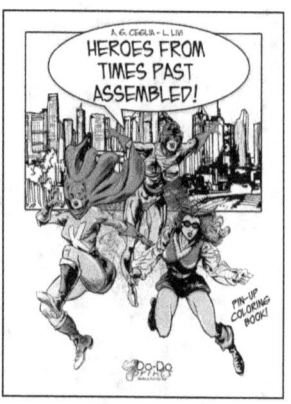

DÉCOUVREZ CES LIVRES DE

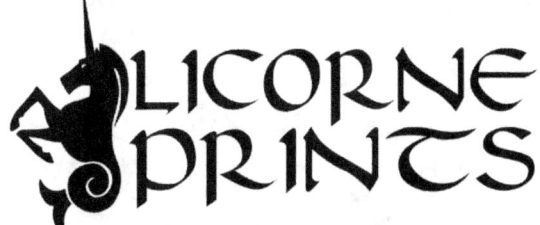

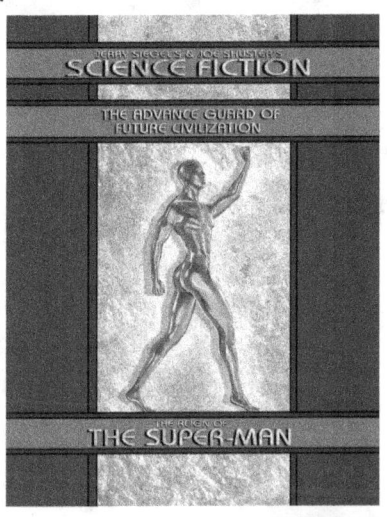

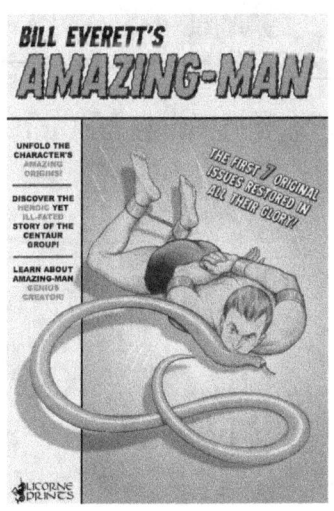

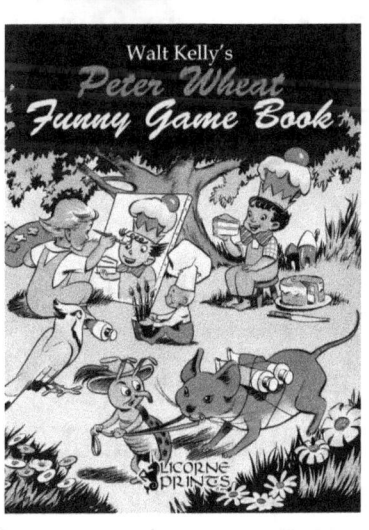

DISPONIBLE SUR LES PLUS POPULAIRES
PLATEFORMES EN LIGNE
EN VERSION IMPRIMÉE ET NUMÉRIQUE!

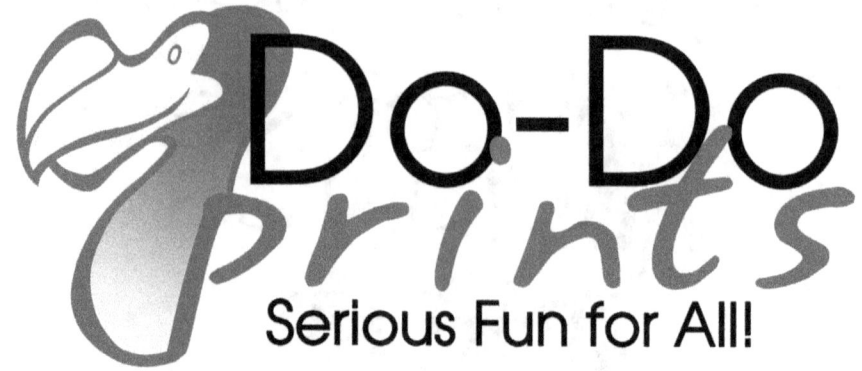

DO-DO PRINTS

SERIOUS FUN FOR ALL!

DO-DO PRINTS EST CONSACRÉ À L'ÉDUCATION ET À
LA LUDO-DIDACTIQUE.
IL COMPREND UNE VASTE GAMME DE LIVRES
IMPRIMABLES ET ÉLECTRONIQUES POUR LES
ENFANTS, LES JEUNES ADULTES, LES ADULTES
ET LES AÎNÉS DANS LE BUT D'AMÉLIORER
LEURS COMPÉTENCES ET LES CONNAISSANCES
COGNITIVES D'UNE MANIÈRE AGRÉABLE.

LES PRODUITS DE DO-DO SONT CRÉÉS DANS
DIFFÉRENTES LANGUES AFIN D'ATTEINDRE LE PLUS
GRAND NOMBRE DE LECTEURS ET DE FOURNIR UNE
EXPÉRIENCE ÉDUCATIVE ET AMUSANTE COMPLÈTE.

DO-DO@BEMYSTUDIO.COM

www.ingramcontent.com/pod-product-compliance
Lightning Source LLC
Chambersburg PA
CBHW071816200526
45169CB00018B/342